naked divorce® for women

First published in 2011 by Ecademy Press
48 St Vincent Drive, St Albans, Herts, AL1 5SJ
info@ecademy-press.com
www.ecademy-press.com

Printed and bound by Lightning Source in the UK and USA

Designed by Simon K Williams

Printed on acid-free paper from managed forests. This book is printed on demand, so no copies will be remaindered or pulped.

ISBN 978-1-907722-78-3

I created this program because I have been there myself. I know what it feels like to want to make a change but not have the right tools or to be constantly offered solutions that take up a lot of time, energy and money and don't really solve anything.

I created the **naked divorce** because it was time for something better.

It was time for passivity to be given a kick and to unveil the courageous steps you can begin to take today to heal from your divorce.

So what have you got to lose?

Why not allow yourself to tumble down the rabbit hole and discover how many myths about healing from your divorce you have taken on board?

Why not allow yourself to discover the person you deserve to be?

I wrote this book knowing that although you may be experiencing all kinds of emotions right now, deep within, you have courage that you haven't yet begun to tap.

Deep within, there are probably things you have wanted to change about your life.

Your divorce can be the catalyst for this life change.

The only thing standing between you and this new version of yourself is taking some courageous daily steps with the right support in place.

This book is therefore an invitation into a world where life is not a struggle and healing doesn't take an indefinite period of time.

This might sound like a fantasy. But I promise: no matter what brought you here, or what your personal story is, success is possible.

It won't be easy, but I will walk alongside you every step of the way.

Adèle's story – why I created the 21-day program

> **❝** *If you don't know when enough is enough... then you're destined to contribute to your own suffering* **❞**

Bruce and I were sitting at the kitchen table when he blurted out that he had slept with two women while he'd been in California. He explained, "I made a conscious choice to experience great pleasure, to see if I was willing to miss out on this in our marriage. I am not."

He swallowed as he sat staring at me, looking slightly terrified.

"I am willing to work on transforming our marriage and have been reading books and working on it. But I feel stuck... I don't know if I can transform my desire for you."

I kept quiet. I wanted my marriage to be over.

I don't know where the words came from, but I spoke them.

"This is over and you should go."

He nodded his head. I walked out of the kitchen and finally allowed seven years of pent-up frustration to emerge. I sobbed. He came and hugged me.

"Have we just broken up?"

"Yes, Bruce. You should go. Go be free and live in the Caribbean. You never liked London anyway."

He nodded again.

I wasn't angry. Looking back on the years we'd shared together, this had been inevitable. I had dreaded this day for a long time. As much as I loved Bruce and our time together, I always knew deep down that it would end.

Bruce left soon after and went to stay with his father in South Africa. After a few days he called me. He felt it was time I knew the whole truth.

There were new revelations. Of the 18 women he had been with over three years, some of them were friends of ours.

I screamed down the phone in shock and then hung up and sat in silence. My head was spinning. I had known something was up but I'd ignored my feelings, stepped over them and accepted his years of explanations.

Now before you start - it's easy to want to judge Bruce. Don't. I am as much responsible for his affairs as he is. I had known very deep down from the very beginning that something was not quite right in our relationship. I knew I married a man who had no desire for me and I had ignored all the warning signs and my intuition.

I had done that. I am responsible for the failure of our marriage.

I had chosen to stay and by staying, I had contributed to the inevitable, to him seeking what his heart truly cried out for with someone else. Anger overwhelmed me and left me shaking, my fists clenched ready to strike.

I had been living in a fantasy world and had concocted a dream-like, fake relationship around me. The weeks that followed would turn out to be the most dramatic wake-up call of my life. I had settled for a seemingly contented and happy relationship but with very little passion or intimacy. My body was consumed with anger. I had one clear thought; to wreak havoc in my house.

I looked around my bedroom, at the familiar and treasured things. I got up with intent…

How it all started

I first met Bruce in 2002, when I was at a rock concert, I was 24. Bruce was different to the usual type of men that I went out with; there was something dangerous and edgy about him and that was alluring.

We went out a few times, but I had reservations about being in a relationship with him. Although I was in love, I don't think he really loved me and we seemed more like friends united by common aims in life, rather than a couple who had just started going out.

Although I resolved to end things, I also found myself caught up in the reverie of what it would be like to date a man like Bruce.

"I think I'm falling in love with you, but it's a different kind of love, a familiar and comfortable one. Maybe this is what real love is supposed to feel like."

Hearing those words from Bruce made me excited, and yet I felt weird. A voice was telling me to stop worrying and enjoy the moment. Here was an amazing man and he said he loved me! And yes, our love did feel familiar and comfortable, and that was wonderful. Yet, I know today that if I had any kind of self-respect that I would never have continued a relationship with a man who was not really in love with me. But, my denial willed me on and so Bruce and I fell into a relationship. We would tell ourselves and others that we'd chosen to be in the relationship but it was never a natural attraction - certainly not for him. I ignored the danger signs, so easily seen in hindsight. At the time I told myself that it could work, that it *had* to work.

After a year together I decided to fulfill a lifelong dream of living in London. Part of me longed for an adventure. I told myself that it would be a great opportunity to see if Bruce and I were really meant to be.

After living in London for several months, one day he called me, burdened. He had something to share. He'd been with another woman.

I went into shock, cutting my hand on a plate I dropped as I was washing dishes. As I listened to his profuse apology, the water turned pink. He was so sorry. I could hear the desperation in his voice, begging me not to break up with him.

I looked for excuses. I told myself that distance had made everything so hard. I blamed myself for not paying him attention, and for flirting with his friend, Gavin, who lived down the road from me.

I rallied to the challenge. We could overcome this. I told him I forgave him. I told myself that too.

Two weeks later Bruce proposed and I accepted. I felt something else was willing me on to keep the relationship alive. To be honest, I felt safer. He was my fiancé. It seemed like a guarantee that he would not stray. But it also felt like a noose around my neck. I felt numbed by the relationship. Being with someone who I knew didn't really love me as I loved him was a dishonor to myself. On so many levels I longed for him to love me the way I had experienced love before, and his lack of focused love was heartbreaking. I think in truth, I withdrew myself emotionally once I sensed his indifference to me. I know that if I was honoring myself would have ended it but I carried on because I told myself I was committed, that I loved him and that my suspicions about him not really loving me was all in my head.

In April 2004 we were married in a registry ceremony surrounded by friends and loved ones in London. It was not the day I had imagined. The night before the wedding, I went for a very long walk and almost didn't return. My gut was gnawing at me but I ignored it. We were hosts at a nice party and although there was love between us, I felt very sad. We moved into an apartment in Battersea and, despite my misgivings, the first years were really happy. We settled into a stable, loving relationship. It lacked passion and fire but because we had so much fun, getting up to thrilling things together, it seemed not to matter.

I learnt to motorcycle, windsurf, rollerblade, dive and do all the things Bruce was into. We travelled all over the world, visiting exotic and wonderful places. We attended many courses together, we grew together and I learnt so much from him. In a quest for personal development I learnt to be courageous, beyond all the barriers I had erected within myself.

He became my best friend and we were like peas in a pod. Many people said that we were the perfect couple and I believed we were. Being married made me feel safe and invincible. So what if we lacked passion, there were many other things that made our marriage work.

I made these excuses many times over.

Married life continued much the same, but in April 2006, Bruce started travelling more frequently for business purposes. I spent increasing amounts of time alone. I went to dinners on my own, visited friends on my own, and spent many New Year's Eves, christenings, weddings and birthdays unaccompanied by my husband. In 2007, we were apart for seven months.

I told my friends and family that we had a very cool, hip relationship. We were both extremely independent and very happy together. Inside I was not so sure. I was lonely and felt undesired, unloved and trapped. I often cried myself to sleep but never told anyone about it.

When Bruce did come home in-between business trips he behaved strangely and we argued. Once, I jokingly asked if he'd been with anyone else on his travels. He shouted at me, telling me I was insecure and had issues I needed to resolve.

I ignored my suspicions, blaming my insecurity. But something was wrong.

As much as people saw us as a real power couple who looked in love and happy, our relationship never felt quite right. A veneer camouflaged the sadness and deep pain I was hiding.

In 2007, I decided to go to Cuba on a girl's holiday. The tour guide on the trip was completely enamored by me. We danced till dawn every night and I was completely swept away by all the Cuban music, rum cocktails and attention I was receiving. I felt beautiful and sexy. One night he told me I was beautiful and the most amazing women he had ever met. I burst into tears. He was the first person I ever told about what things were really like in my marriage. I confided in him and he tried to kiss me many times during the trip but each time I pushed him away. He told me that I deserved to be loved and treasured and I felt amazing. Secretly I knew my boundaries were wearing away until the last night on the island, I cheated on Bruce. I allowed myself to let go and I enjoyed myself completely. At some point, my mind kicked in and I burst into tears. I pushed him away, ran to the bathroom and threw up. I felt horrible. I couldn't continue. I left his room and went back to my hotel.

Even though I backed out it was too late, I had betrayed my marriage vows completely and had behaved entirely inappropriately for a married woman. A part of me felt utterly disgusted with myself but a part of me felt alive and wanted. The conflict was overwhelming. My girlfriends confronted me the next day as they knew something was up but I lied to them and said I was hung-over. I was too much of a coward to share with them what had really happened.

I rationalized to myself that as I had never shared with my friends what my relationship with Bruce was really like, I didn't think they would truly understand why I did what I did. I was so busy portraying to the world that I had the perfect marriage and perfect life that any kind of honesty would bring my house of cards down. I justified my actions and told myself that lying was okay, "I didn't have sex, so it didn't really count."

Yeah right. I was just being a cowardly hypocritical liar. I was more concerned with looking good to my friends than having any integrity.

When I came home I told Bruce what had happened. He was absolutely amazing about it and was so understanding and compassionate. He said that he understood why it had happened, admitted that our lack of true intimacy was the source of the cheating and he forgave me. He apologized for not loving me as I deserved to be loved. I thought that perhaps we had had a breakthrough and believed everything was good between us but sadly, from that day onwards, we drifted further and further apart.

When Bruce and I discussed this moment years later, he said he regretted not coming clean with me on the day that I came clean with him.

In the final months of our marriage, we travelled to the Caribbean and Bruce didn't touch me once during the trip. I told myself that it was fine; I didn't need intimacy to have a great marriage. Perhaps intimacy wasn't a priority for either of us. I came home earlier but he stayed on and then left for California. He kept extending his trip and we spent New Year's Eve apart. He extended his trip again and January stretched to February and then March.

I knew deep within that we had come to the end of our road together. Needing to deal with that realization, I signed up for a 10-day silent meditation retreat, to confront things on my own and make the decisions I had to make. The rest of the story, you know.

> ❝ *The deeper sorrow carves into your being, the more joy you can later contain.* ❞
>
> *Kahlil Gibran from The Prophet*

Transformation

What would follow would be the most transformational weeks of my life. I could never have predicted that the deepest pain in my life would carve out wells to hold the deepest joy. I could never have predicted that all my years in change management would lead to me to creating something so healing for myself and for others. I felt like my whole life had lead to this journey.

Think about having a dislocated shoulder. You *could* walk around with your shoulder dislocated. It hurts, but after some time the pain will become normal. You will learn to live with it. Your movements will be inhibited but you accept this as part of the healing process. Now, you can walk around with your dislocated shoulder or you can dig deep and pop the shoulder back into the socket. It hurts like hell but once back in the socket, the shoulder heals properly. The **naked divorce** is similar – it's an intensive healing journey. Sometimes it will take courage to keep moving forward but once completed, you are on the road to successful future relationships.

Today Bruce and I have forgiven each other and have made peace with our marriage. His miraculous story of the power of coming clean is the subject of a very popular Tedx Talk on Secrets, which kill our aliveness in life which can be found on www.tedxsincity.com/. I am proud that he had the courage to share his story with the world. He is a good man and we both learnt a great deal from our journey together.

The real problem with divorce

Statistics across the USA, UK, Australia, South Africa, Canada and New Zealand over the past 12 years appear to show that people are not healing from divorce, leading to an increase in second, third and fourth marriage failures.

- On average, approximately 30% of marriages fail globally in first-world countries.
- The most common age of divorced women is between 37 and 42.
- Over the past 10 years, the USA has had the highest average divorce rate of 42%, followed closely by countries including the UK, South Africa and Russia.
- The average marriage lasts 11 years.
- In half of all divorces there are children involved.
- 62% of all divorced people say that they, "felt there were things they could have done to prevent their divorce and they wish they had done more."

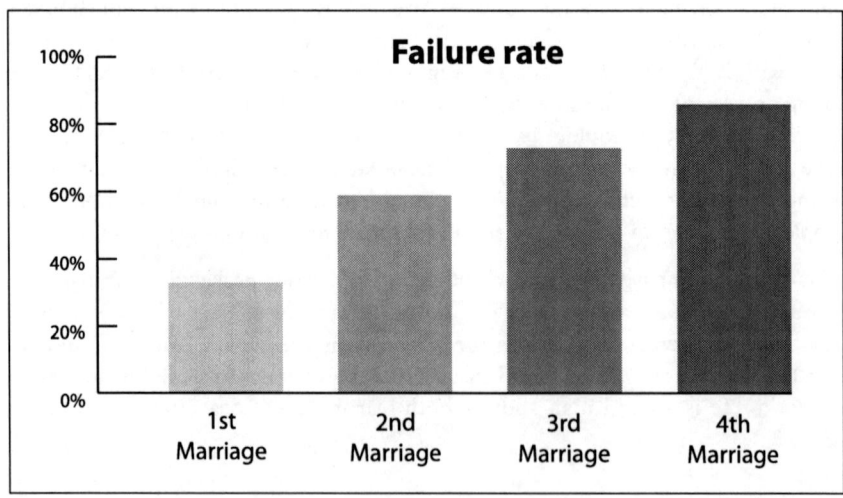

Fact-

65% of people divorced for a 3rd or 4th time said that they wished they had handled their divorces in a more ethical and graceful way, taking a more active role in their healing.

They also said that they wished they had gotten to the root cause of the break-up so that they didn't ruin their next relationship.

The very worst thing you can do is nothing

Healing doesn't simply happen over time. Healing is an active process, and processing all the feelings and emotions associated with your divorce is essential to getting over it. Divorce acts like a cut and if you don't dress the wound and work on healing it you will end up with a lot of scar tissue, which will leave a lasting imprint on your life. The real killer to healing is the complacency and resignation I have seen countless women sink into after their divorce. I have noticed that many people talk about their divorce and announce as quickly as they can ... that ... yes ... it was difficult, but they were, "absolutely fine and glad to be rid of their ex." They say things like, "I feel fine", "I feel perfectly happy with my life", "I am over that bastard", "I never think of him" or, "no, I am not dating and I am better off on my own."

All of these statements are a form of resignation. This is why most people have no idea how to heal. They handle the divorce as best they can, often intellectualizing and rationalizing that they are fine even when they are not. This often leads to a false sense of healing, which is on the surface and not really dealing with the healing at the source.

Before we discuss what recovery from divorce is all about, let's ascertain how you've dealt with loss in the past and how the 21-day experience may be different.

Exercise:

Take some time to think back on your life. How have you dealt with loss in the past? (Whether it was the loss of someone special or a beloved pet)

What steps did you take that were healthy and healing?

What steps did you take, or not take, that hampered your recovery?

Time does not heal wounds

During the very early days of my divorce I took some action and spoke to two therapists. This is what everyone said would be a good idea to do.

Both therapists told me that as I had been with my husband for seven years, that it would probably take me at least 18 months to two years to get over the relationship and that with weekly therapy sessions, I would heal.

The first therapist commenced the therapy session by taking me back to an incident from my childhood. I was two-years-old and was in hospital for many months due to a congenital hip birth defect. The doctors were spending months building me hip sockets and due to the strict rules of the hospital, my parents were not allowed to visit me very often. Consequently I developed some abandonment issues. Rather than focus on the divorce, my therapist was linking my feelings related to the divorce to the fear I'd felt in childhood.

We explored that incident for some time and after two hours of deconstruction (and a hefty bill later), I left feeling thoroughly disempowered and confused. Not only had my husband 'abandoned me', my parents, doctors and family had abandoned me, and in turn, not only was I now annoyed with my former husband, I was now annoyed with the world too.

The parallel relevance of exploring the moment of abandonment in childhood and my husband leaving, although fascinating, was not helping me get out of bed in the morning and deal with the issues right in front of me. I resolved that I did not want to spend months dissecting each aspect of my childhood, followed by my teenage years and then adult years in order to make sense of my divorce. I had very real issues to face in front of me right now. I had a career, had to get back to earning money and I wanted to talk about how I felt today and not about my life when I was two-years-old. This process went on for two weeks until I tried another therapist which was a similar tale.

Now, I know therapy works wonders for many people. I also know that it works very effectively in many situations and that millions of people all over the world choose therapy above any other process. Personally, it was very nice to have someone to talk to and I won't knock that for a second.

I do however think that certain people do not have the patience for therapy and I count myself within this category. I wanted to get on with my healing. I wanted to take active steps and get to a place of empowerment again. I did not want to indulge in self-pity or gaze longingly at my navel whilst I drifted back into my childhood. It felt like a distraction from the emotions I knew I needed to confront. I was seeking an alternative to traditional forms of healing and in most cases, the clients who choose to work with me, have similar feelings.

My specific issues with therapy were:

⇨ I had no understanding of what I was going through and going to therapy didn't give me any power in taking charge of my own healing. I felt dependent on my therapist.

⇨ It felt like we were going to do a great deal of analyzing during therapy and it was going to take an enormous amount of time. As human beings, we can tend to become fascinated by ourselves and our stories and I believe that taking great time to heal can be very destructive if we allow ourselves to become too self-indulgent. Renowned UK psychotherapist Nea Clark (http://www.balancedbusinessladies.com/) says, "There is no need to indulge your feelings over a long period of time. Time doesn't heal them. Better to do a program like the **naked divorce** and focus intensively on healing within a defined period of time. It's healthier for your mind but also for your body". Independent surveys conducted by the Stress Society of the United Kingdom have also shown that those who take a very proactive approach to healing lead happier lives.

⇨ The healing process didn't feel transparent, it felt like the therapists I saw either had no idea how I was going to heal or they had the secret to healing and the only way I was going to find out what the secret was, was to commit to seeing them on a weekly basis for 18 months.

⇨ I felt that there was no goal or focus to my healing. We would talk and I would say how I felt. This didn't work for me.

⇨ My therapists were not experts in divorce. They were expert therapists and knew techniques for healing from all kinds of ailments. What I didn't realize then and realize today is that divorce is a very specific set of circumstances and emotions and requires healing in a very specific way. Working with someone who didn't specialize in those emotions and circumstances was not particularly useful to me.

⇨ My healing did not fit into the, "let's meet once a week for one hour" structure. I required around-the-clock support with a phone call here, a text there, an email at one a.m., or a session with one day's notice. I wanted a friend to walk with me through the abyss, which was staring at me and not to interact in a conventional way. Everything in my life was moving so fast that by the time my weekly session arrived, everything had changed and I spent the session catching my therapist up on my life VS actually making any real progress.

Therapy, in my experience, is not very effective in dealing with trauma because true healing requires intensive focused action. Additionally, therapy and traditional healing practices have based their disciplines on the premise that you need time to heal. I often hear of counselors giving people advice similar to, "you just need some time to process everything."

The concept of needing time to heal is consequently so ingrained in our society, that challenging this notion is usually met with an extraordinary amount of resistance, and in some cases, even anger or dismissal. The thought of healing quickly feels fake, shallow or unbelievable and could be misconstrued as a trivialization of the healing process.

I really understand if you are thinking these thoughts.

In my experience in developing the **naked divorce** *Healing Formula*, time is actually a hindrance to healing, as over time the sense of urgency to take action dissipates.

Rosemary Kennedy (a renowned author and wife of Joseph Kennedy and the mother of President John F. Kennedy) shared her thoughts on time…

"It has been said, 'time heals all wounds.' I do not agree. The wounds remain. In time, the mind, protecting its sanity, covers them with scar tissue and the pain lessens. But the wounds remain."

What I tell my clients when they say 'time heals all wounds' is:

❝ Time doesn't heal anything, time simply passes. It is what we do with our lives while time is passing that either helps us, heals us, or locks us in the past ❞

Case study: Sally

Please note: *throughout the book, I make reference to case studies of my clients. Names have been changed to protect their confidentiality in all instances.*

A bright, highly educated young woman came to see me six years after her marriage had ended. She told me that although she had three relationships since her divorce, all of them ended in quick succession because she still felt hurt and angry feelings towards her ex-husband. To keep herself under control, she kept herself frantically busy. She threw herself into her work, taking on tasks others wouldn't do, answering emails and writing proposals until late at night, and traveling on most weekends. At home, she spent hours cleaning and straightening up her apartment so it looked like a picture out of a magazine. She was doing whatever she could to distract herself from acknowledging what she already knew – she was not over her ex. She was running from her grief and numbing her pain with her busyness.

She finally realized she had to do something and we began our work together. She later told me that she was embarrassed that when we started working together, that she was in the same place in her mourning as others who had only recently divorced a few months earlier. It was as if her mourning had gone no further from where it was five and a half years ago. She was stuck, and no more time would have eased or erased her grief. Time had done nothing for her; time had NOT been her friend.

After completing the **naked divorce** 21-day program she worked through what she had been running from for over five years and as an added bonus, found peace with her father's death. Her frantic behaviors have ceased and now she is a fully functioning young woman with plans for dating and a successful love life into the future.

Taking time to heal can lead to a false sense of healing

Scott M Peck coined the phrase, "Cheap Forgiveness" in his 1992 cassette series entitled 'Blame and Forgiveness'. He spoke of it being a cut-rate substitute, a quick and easy pardon with no processing of emotion and no coming to terms with the injury. What happens when people take their time to heal is they become resigned, complacent, and lazy; believing that the status quo is fine. *False Healing* to me, is synonymous with Cheap Forgiveness. It's the cut-rate substitute for true and real healing at a deep level. There is no processing of emotion and no coming to terms with the divorce.

There is also a real impact of *False Healing*…

1 *False Healing* can lead to illness

Case study: Sophie

Sophie is the mother of a good friend of mine. She was a very vivacious and charismatic woman. She loved her husband and young son deeply. One day her husband left her very unexpectedly. Three years and a very bitter divorce passed. Sadly, her son hated his father almost as much as she did and the pair never had a good thing to say about him.

The only things she lived for were her son and her dream to travel to Greece. Every month she saved for her trip to Greece but she never healed from her divorce and *soldiered on* whilst inside she was dying, hoping that time would heal her wound.

One day she started coughing uncontrollably. The cough was persistent and lasted a few weeks. Eventually she went to the doctor who suggested some tests. After a month the results confirmed that she had terminal cancer.

Within six months she had died. On her deathbed, she acknowledged her regret that she had never forgiven her former husband for leaving her.

As my friend tells the story, he knows that his mother's unwillingness to heal from the divorce was the source of her illness. He has subsequently chosen to reconcile with his father.

Dr Deepak Chopra, author, renowned endocrinologist, and leader in the field of quantum physics and mind-body healing, formulated his theory of cellular healing. It has been scientifically established that cells inside the body regenerate at different speeds – liver cells in six weeks, stomach-lining cells in three days, eye cells in less than forty-eight hours. Why is it then, you might ask, that a liver riddled with cancer in January would still be riddled with cancer in June? As the liver cells regenerate every six weeks they should already have regenerated several times.

Dr Chopra believes we all have phantom memories stored inside our cells. What he means is that inside each degenerative cell lies a traumatic memory. And before that degenerative cell dies, it passes on its memory to the next cell. So the new cell is born as a replica of the previous cell. Thus the cells keep replicating themselves, passing on the degenerative memory from one generation to the next, and so on. Although the cells replicated, what they were replicating was the degenerative cell pattern stored inside.

Dr Chopra compiled thousands of case studies of the process successful survivors had used to heal themselves from serious diseases. He discovered that they were able to access the cell memory and the associated negative emotion, which they worked towards resolving and then releasing. When they did this, the degenerative memory was not passed on to the next cell generation and thus the next cell was born as a new, healthy cell. This process is called cellular healing.

Pharmacologist Dr Candace Pert, whom has a PhD in cellular biology and biophysics from the United States, has backed up Dr Chopra's research through laboratory experiments. Dr Pert has unequivocally established that emotions and the body are neurologically linked and that there is a chemical expression for every emotion that we have.

When we repress an emotion the body releases a chemical into the bloodstream. This chemical travels to certain cell receptors and blocks them, leaving them incapable of communicating with the rest of the cells in the body. If those cell receptors remain blocked over a long period of time then there is a propensity for diseases to occur in the blocked areas.

Conversely, Dr Pert has also found that when you express emotions fully and in a healthy, non-repressive way, the cell receptors remain open.

When you bury your emotions over time, it can have a very lasting impact on your health, wellbeing and happiness. It can also lead to premature ageing and illness.

Some of the symptoms of buried emotions include:-

⇨ A feeling of extreme tiredness and general fatigue.

⇨ Losing hours in the day because you are preoccupied with daydreams.

⇨ Spending all day watching television or lying in bed sleeping.

⇨ Losing your lust for life and rarely wanting to talk about how you are feeling or doing.

⇨ Blowing up at the smallest of things – almost flying off the handle for no apparent cause.

⇨ Focusing on keeping busy rather than on feeling things. If you battle to sit still and have to keep busy all the time, consider that you might be repressing your emotions.

⇨ An inability to concentrate for any extended period of time.

⇨ Focusing on your ex and what he's doing rather than focusing on how you are feeling.

⇨ Tumultuous relationships with those close to you.

When you repress your emotions your behavior and reactions to events in the present are really reactions to past events, too. This has a negative effect on your relationships. You can't be fully present with those you love until you have released your emotions from the past. Not dealing with your emotions over an extended period of time can also lead to major illness in your body.

Dr Pert, Dr Chopra and other scientists like them have spent years researching the lasting impact of repressed emotion in the body. Some of this research appears to suggest that specific emotions can also lead to specific issues in the body such as:-

⇨ Repressing Anger (as it rests mostly in the shoulders and upper back) can lead to an unexpected outbreak of acne, issues with the jaw (as you have clenched your teeth), back and neck tension, and at its worst: cancer and chronic fatigue.

⇨ Repressing Fear (as fear rests mostly in the stomach) can lead to constipation, Crohn's disease, irritable bowel syndrome and other issues of the bowel and colon.

⇨ Repressing Sadness (as sadness lives mostly in the heart/lung region) can lead to heart/lung problems, throat and voice problems, and issues with your eyes.

2 *False Healing* can lead to premature ageing

Many people throw themselves straight back into work or their lives after divorce, regardless of the complexity of their emotions. As a career woman, you're particularly at risk of the *soldiering on* syndrome, which essentially means that you throw yourself into noble pursuits like working or taking care of children whilst inside you are crying out in pain and not acknowledging your right to those emotions. Pretending you are fine when you are not can lead to breakdown or harboring deep resentment and bitterness, which will not only impact your relationship potential in the future, but the quality of your life today.

Resentment and bitterness can literally affect your face as it carves a nasty pointed look. This is often referred to as the *divorce look*, when someone simply looks and behaves like they are divorced. Some women don't even know that people can sense their bitterness, but it is written all over them: the battle they did with marriage, and the resultant scars they carry with them. Whenever you mention their ex, a dark cloud covers their face which scrunches up with venom and anger whilst they sweetly say that they are, "fine" (whilst they wish he would burn in hell). These thoughts have an ageing effect too.

There is a character in Charles Dickens's 'Great Expectations' named Miss Haversham, who suffered this kind of deep resentment and bitterness from a failed relationship. Miss Haversham was jilted at the altar by the love of her life. Her bridegroom ran away and she had no idea why. Her life ended metaphorically on that day and she lived with crushing emotional pain that completely overwhelmed her. Paralyzed by the past, everything reflected her pain. Her home was left exactly as it was on the fateful wedding day; the wedding table covered in cobwebs, the guests' chairs empty. Almost 30 years later, she becomes guardian to a beautiful young child, Estella. In her bitterness, Miss Haversham sets about ruining Estella's young life, feeding her own sadness into the child who becomes an ice maiden. Miss Haversham's purpose is to exact revenge upon men as a whole. An old quote passed down from generation to generation goes something like this;

> **❝ *Holding onto resentment is much like taking poison and hoping someone else will die* ❞**

If you find yourself holding onto your anger and resentment, consider the impact on your life and your face.

Case study: Amy

Amy is an old friend from college who is amazingly successful in her job. Amy had been single for 15 years before she fell in love with Dave. For six months she was the happiest I had ever seen her. It was almost as if finding love had made her lighter on her feet and more at ease in people's company.

One day Dave left. No reasons were given. Amy was inconsolable. She became sick with grief and despair. She sought answers and when none were given, she became angry and bitter with resentment. If anyone mentioned Dave, her face contorted in anger and she would say, "I hope he rots in hell!"

Although it is some time later, she has concluded intellectually that he was simply the wrong man, but the resentment has remained. She has not dated successfully since. She keeps saying that she simply hasn't found the right man yet, but what she doesn't realize is that her persona has become tainted by bitterness. All of us who know Amy and love her, are desperately sad that she never moved on with her life, and that she never let go of her bitterness and resentment. What she doesn't see is that men are repelled by the anger they sense in her.

3 *False Healing* can lead to destructive behavior post-divorce

Sometimes pretending you are fine when you are not can have long-term damaging repercussions. Take the story of Sharon…

Case study: Sharon

Sharon married very young and although she loved Pete deeply, she felt trapped in the marriage. Pete had many affairs during their marriage and she thought that by falling pregnant, he'd change his ways. When she had her son, Oliver, she felt even more trapped and stuck in the marriage. Her anger at Pete for cheating on her worsened every day. She told herself it didn't bother her.

One day, she walked into the kitchen and told Pete she wanted a divorce. She packed her bags and left within an hour of telling him. She took Oliver to her mother's house for a few weeks and she decided to go out clubbing that night. She danced and drank until the early hours of the morning and went home with Rick, who she'd met at the club. She and Oliver moved in with Rick three weeks later. So began her journey into eight years of drug and alcohol abuse.

During this time, she called Pete many times to say she was absolutely fine and she totally forgave him for everything that had happened. But Sharon was not fine. Her substance abuse affected her and Oliver's lives. It was only when she lost custody of Oliver to Pete that it began to dawn on her that she had never processed her feelings from her divorce. She had spent eight years avoiding her emotions. She broke up with Rick and booked herself into rehab, committing to the journey of healing. She realized that there were no shortcuts and that she needed to get her life back. After two years of hard struggle she processed her feelings and lives with her son Oliver again.

Pete knew she was truly comfortable with the divorce when she called him one night to say how angry she had been for so many years. She admitted that finally she had found the courage to forgive him.

True forgiveness and true healing takes great courage and determination.

Today Sharon is free from the constraints of her past and is in a fulfilling and loving relationship with her new man. She chose to put an end to her days of hedonism and chose to heal from her divorce for real.

4 *False Healing* can have a severe impact on those closest to you

Many people overcome by anger or frustration as a result of their divorce, have no idea how their way of being is impacting their loved ones. I have heard countless stories of the brothers, sisters, mothers and fathers of those experiencing divorce who are exasperated because they don't know how to support their loved one. They are so tired of hearing their endless complaints, and so desperate for this person to seek help, but are not sure how to address the topic for fear of reproach. Every family occasion and get together is plagued by tales of divorce woe and complaints as the family has to suffer through the domination of their loved one's divorce.

If you are courageous enough to recognize that you may be burdening and dominating your family and friends with your divorce stories, then take a hold of the situation now. Stop the cycle of misery and begin the path of the *Healing Formula*.

5 *False Healing* can lead to relationship baggage

Relationship baggage damages relationships. So even though you may be hurting from your divorce, healing is critical in terms of securing your future happiness.

We all carry some emotional baggage but the question is – will you allow your troubles from the past to affect your current relationships? Not only will it impact your new relationship, but baggage is so unbelievably draining. If you are committed to your next relationship working out, you need to purge yourself of all your relationship baggage or make sure you manage it.

Day 17 of the **naked divorce** is about healing from relationship baggage.

6 *False Healing* greatly impacts your children

Dr. Sara Eleoff, MD (Pediatrician in Rochester, NY) published research in 2003 (and subsequently each year) on the impact of divorce on children. Her research concluded then as it does now that divorce is an intensely stressful experience for children, regardless of their age or developmental level.

Many children are inadequately prepared for the event and its ramifications. Her research study 'An Exploration of the Ramifications of Divorce on Children and Adolescents' found that less than 10% of children had emotional support during the acute phase of divorce, primarily because their parents were so wrapped up in dealing with their own pain that they were ill-equipped to support their children.

Before taking off in an aircraft, airlines brief passengers on the protocols to follow if there is a loss of cabin pressure and oxygen masks are required. The rule is that **masks should be fitted to the adults before they help their children**. The same thing applies to healing. If you are experiencing the trauma of divorce, it is imperative to prioritize your healing and support to ensure you are emotionally available to support your children. If you're struggling with the concept of getting over this divorce for your own good, consider your children. The pain experienced by children at the beginning of a divorce comes from several factors; a sense of vulnerability as the family disintegrates, a grief reaction to the loss of the intact family (many children do not realize their parents' marriage is troubled), loss of the non-custodial parent, a feeling of intense anger at the disruption of the family, and strong feelings of power-lessness.

Sara's research has shown that younger children may experience disturbances with sleep, nightmares and sometimes bed-wetting. Older children vary between fantasies about their parents reuniting or extreme anger towards one of the parents who become the source of blame. Adolescents are prone to depression, extreme anger, or suicidal thoughts but in some cases can come to understand the reason for the divorce and are capable of compassion. The issue is that the older the children are, the more their anger is tied into the shattering of their paradigm of relationships and the illusion that there is a happily-ever-after.

> **WARNING:**
>
> **It's important to guard against hiding behind your children's needs as an excuse for not healing from your divorce.**

The journey out of resignation

At some level, you may have some resignation about what healing could look like for you or some idea in your head that feeling different about your situation is not possible.

I am here to tell you that wherever you are within the divorce or break-up healing cycle, the *naked divorce* can work for you.

- You may find yourself in the middle of your divorce feeling the deep pain and sick feeling in your stomach. In this instance, you can achieve peace and completion EVEN IF the business-side of your divorce is incomplete. Those who have completed the *naked divorce* whilst they are still getting divorced, found that they became less emotional, and they were less triggered by events and circumstances whilst handling the legalities of their divorce.

OR

- It may be that you got divorced months or even years ago and are still feeling stuck or unresolved. Perhaps you just feel ready to process all those emotions now. The *naked divorce* works in bringing up anything incomplete so you may heal those parts of yourself and move on.

Ultimately, choosing to heal comes from a deep personal love for yourself and a commitment to life being better than it is right now.

Follow these simple steps to confront any resignation you might have and hit it on the head for good.

The journey out of resignation

STEP 1: Confront that you may be holding onto your suffering in some way.

STEP 2: Become aware of the real impact of not healing from your divorce.

STEP 3. Educate yourself on the *Healing Formula* and what it takes to heal.

STEP 4: Take focused action and concentrate on healing.

STEP 5: Take decisions on a daily basis to heal until you reach a momentum which leads to breakthroughs in your healing.

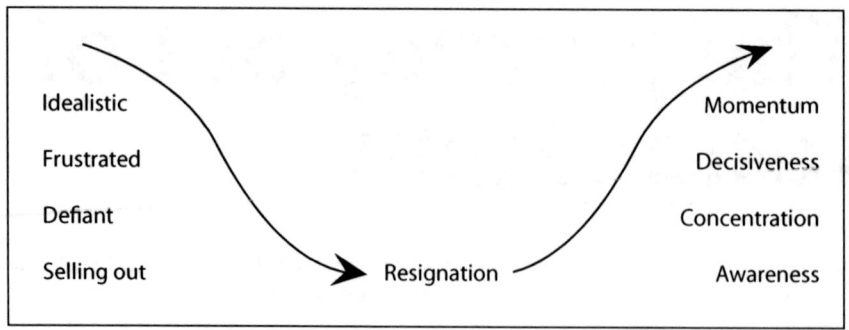

Idealistic		Momentum
Frustrated		Decisiveness
Defiant		Concentration
Selling out	Resignation	Awareness

If you are taking your time, then confront that you may be *choosing* to hold onto your suffering

You may not be sure about being ready to get over your divorce. Maybe you are not sure what to do or perhaps you picked up this book to see what will happen. Sometimes it's a question of commitment to the process, or being afraid of letting go. Perhaps you're still holding onto something.

Sometimes when we hold onto things, there is a certain payoff - some advantage or benefit that reinforces the cycle of behavior - to not letting go.

But this payoff has high costs, whether to our vitality, affinity, self-expression, or sense of fulfillment. So if you are suffering but can see no way out of the suffering, consider that simply the benefit you are receiving for suffering is so juicy that giving up the suffering is simply inconceivable.

If I take my example with my ex-husband; he cheated on me many times and if I am truly honest, I enjoyed being the victim for a little while. It was utterly delicious.

"Poor sad and lonely Adèle who was wronged by this bad man. I feel so sorry for you."

I got loads of attention and lots of hugs and sympathy. I felt righteous and justified and had a gang of followers. We had 'Team Adèle' VS 'Team Bruce'.

The problem was that inside I was still suffering. I was more interested in my agenda of getting attention, being the victim and feeling righteous instead of moving on, healing and living a happy successful life. So here is a little secret I will let you in on: **Your TRUE agenda always shines through.**

The problem for most of us is we have no idea what our true agenda is. We lie to ourselves and tell ourselves and others that we have good intentions, but if you are feeling disempowered in any way, shape or form, consider that your true agenda is revealed.

Your true agenda is in place so you can receive some hidden benefit in return.

Exercise:

Identify what the TRUE agenda has been in healing from your divorce. What do you think it might be?

What is the impact on your life of having this agenda?

What can you now see is possible?

What is a new agenda you are committed to having in your life?

If at this point you're not entirely convinced that healing from your divorce is a priority, then here's another point to consider...

Case study: Rose

Rose is a beautiful woman in her seventies. I know her well and love her dearly. Sadly, she never got over her marriage, which ended in divorce 17 years ago. Her ex-husband had an affair which lasted over 10 years and although he has moved on and married his lover, Rose is stuck.

Mention her ex-husband, or his new wife, and her face contorts with anger as she changes the topic, nervously fiddling with her wedding ring which she still wears on her wedding finger. For 17 years no other man has been able to get near her. As her heart turned to stone, she threw herself into other noble pursuits and interests such as taking care of an elderly woman, gardening, and her three cats.

Although many men asked Rose out on dates, she always declined. One evening I sat with Rose and asked her if she was happy. As she thought about the answer. I noticed tears rising. She said, "No, dear. I am sometimes so lonely I feel an ache in my stomach. I wish that I had chosen a different path, but so much time has passed now that I think perhaps it's too late."

Whenever I discussed her divorce with her, she was adamant that she was fine. After all those years she was in denial and would not consider even dipping her toe in the ocean of healing.

Sadly, there are many women like Rose, whose lives stop after divorce. It's almost as if someone snuffed out the candle in their lives.

Let's get something straight right away. There is nothing wrong with choosing to be single, or living with cats (which are just the cutest creatures), provided you're having fun and not limping under tons of baggage, hurt and anger.

Picture yourself in 10 or 20 years from now. What do you see?

Do you see a lonely old woman? Do you see yourself angry at the world? In essence, most people tend to repeat the same situations in their lives over and over (unless something else interrupts this flow).

I feel immense sadness at this story. What an extraordinary waste of 17 years. Rose became so conditioned by society to sit with her pain and suffering like it was normal, almost like the pain was her cross to bear.

Exercise:

Picture yourself in ten or twenty years from now. Do you see the future you wish or hope for?

Are you being idealistic or hopeful?

Be honest with yourself. Are you taking actions today that are consistent with the future you desire and hope for?

Awareness of the real impact of your divorce

This exercise will evaluate the impact of your divorce on your life. It's called the *Real Impact of My Divorce* exercise. I was inspired in participating in the work of Landmark Education and there was an exercise in the program called the Cost/Payoff exercise developed by Werner Erhard. This exercise on the next page was inspired by the work of Landmark and Werner.

Real Impact of My Divorce exercise

There are three cards with some options on them. Imagine there is an angel on your shoulder and in contrast, a little devil residing in your head.

Fulfillment
Vitality
Aliveness
Love
Abundance
Confidence
Relaxation
Joy
Happiness
Inspiration
Healing
Being a great parent
Health
Fun
Intimacy

I've been ignoring healing

I need to feel right because he wronged me

I get attention from people

I want to stay in my comfort zone

Avoid responsibility

Laziness

Enjoy getting time off eating ice cream

Enjoy people feeling sorry for me

Fulfillment
Vitality
Aliveness
Love
Abundance
Confidence
Relaxation
Joy
Happiness
Inspiration
Healing
Being a great parent
Health
Fun
Intimacy

I don't need to heal, I am fine

I need to feel right because he wronged me

I get attention from people

I want to stay in my comfort zone

Avoid responsibility

Laziness

I am a martyr and will suffer in silence

Enjoy people feeling sorry for me

Fulfillment
Vitality
Aliveness
Love
Abundance
Confidence
Relaxation
Joy
Happiness
Inspiration
Healing
Being a great parent
Health
Fun
Intimacy

I won't heal. It's important to suffer

I need to feel right because he wronged me

I get attention from people

I won't let him get away with it, he will pay

Avoid responsibility

Laziness

Enjoy people feeling sorry for me

The angel represents positive life-attributes which, include happiness, love in your life, health, vitality, self-expression, fulfillment, freedom, and sense of fun.

The little devil residing in your head represents your true agenda. You wouldn't be willing to give up all that you love in your life unless you were getting something back in return. If you feel you're resisting what I'm suggesting, this is good. It means we've hit a nerve.

There is always a true agenda running the show if you are experiencing a negative impact in your life. The true agenda may be hidden, but it's always there, ever present.

Instructions:

1 Take a moment to study these three cards.

2 Pick the card that feels the most like the space you are in now.

3 Circle the angel life-attributes which you feel have been sacrificed. The circled items are a representation of the negative impact that not healing from your divorce has had on your life.

4 Spend some time pondering what your true agenda has been in not healing from your divorce. In this process you might notice things about yourself that you haven't seen before. Use the true agenda on the card to prompt your own thinking. You might not like what you see. But I can assure you that facing up to these negative points could precipitate a significant turning point in your healing.

5 If you're struggling to find the true agenda, it's okay. This exercise can be confronting as most of the true agendas are wedged deep within our blind spot. One thing to try is to ask your family and friends (who are not afraid to tell you the truth) what they can see you get out of continuing your suffering. You may want to interview them.

6 Think of twenty points for each of these instances:

- What are you holding onto being right about?
- Why are you so angry?
- What are the reasons or justifications you are clinging to?
- What attention are you getting by holding onto this issue?
- Who are you dominating by holding onto this issue?
- Why are you refusing to let go?

7 Think of the negative impact this issue is having on your life. How much longer are you willing to sacrifice your life to hold onto your true agenda?

We have covered STEPS 1 and 2 and I hope you are now clear on the impact of holding onto suffering and not healing. Now let's look into STEPS 3 through to 5 which are covered within the remainder of the book.

the healing formula

As my background is in change management, I have a great amount of experience in what it takes to bring about lasting sustainable change with people. Once I had healed from my own divorce, I was so excited because I knew that the process I had created was amazing and transformational. In order to develop all of the facets of the program, I had to go through a lot of trial and error. I used myself as a test subject and then I gathered a whole host of women to put my theories to work.

My ultimate goal was to come up with a small, focused package. You don't try to figure out how to brush your teeth every day: you know how. There's a clear set of directions: brush for two minutes twice a day, floss and you're set. You've taken care of them and you don't have to worry that they will rot and fall out. It's the same with this program; I give you a clear *Healing Formula*. You follow the formula and you will heal.

Healing is not a linear process or something that simply happens over time. Healing is something that can happen in a flash whilst eating your Cornflakes in the morning or whilst walking the dog. Your thoughts suddenly become ordered and you realize something, the realizing of which suddenly frees you from the constraints of the past.

Those flashes of healing are unpredictable and many of us have no idea how to access them so we hope for those moments to find us over time. Scientists call those unexpected flashes breakthroughs. Complete healing is a sum of those flashes or breakthroughs and those who have healed successfully from their divorce sought out those breakthroughs in their lives.

When we have to look for a new job, search for the right house, study to get through school, and even if we want to win the lottery, we still have to buy the ticket. In life, we have to take the initiative to do something to cause something else to happen. Healing is no different. To heal, you need to throw yourself into a situation where healing is the outcome, where healing is inevitable, and where you focus completely on healing. When you throw yourself into your healing you create an environment where the unpredictable flashes are more likely to occur because you are asking the right questions, analyzing the situation in a different way, and taking actions to heal. By becoming intensively focused on your healing and taking daily actions, the breakthroughs which allow you to heal happen more predictably.

The *Healing Formula* is:

Healing Formula = Focused Intensity +

3 Key Breakthroughs + 7 Foundations of Transformation

Focused Intensity

Ever notice how when you focus on something with intention and full concentration, it gets done quicker? This is why classroom trainings over a few days are more effective than distance learning over six months. When you take your time, sometimes you focus on the subject and sometimes you don't, so ultimately getting the work done takes longer. The *naked divorce* works because you bring all your focus and intention towards healing AND you do this consistently over a 21-day period.

All it takes is dedicating approximately 90-120 minutes across each day of the 15 work-week days of the program, plus no more than 12 hours across each of the three weekends to focus intensively on your healing. Taking courageous steps daily makes a big difference to your healing but once done, you are done. We are also not saying, spend 21 days as a hermit - you can still dedicate your life to your work, your children, and other interests but your healing must take centre-stage for 21 days.

> ** If you take healing steps daily, your healing will be faster than if you took those steps weekly or monthly. Miraculous healing happens with courageous action **

The 3 Key Breakthroughs

Before discussing what the three key breakthroughs are, let's discuss where they come from...

I grew up in a town called Kimberley in South Africa.

Kimberley is known for its diamond mines. While growing up, I became fascinated with how diamonds are formed. It amazed me that something as dark and ugly as coal could be transformed into a brilliant diamond. My research uncovered that the journey from coal to diamond begins beneath the surface deep in the earth's crust. Coal can only transform into diamonds within an environment of extreme temperatures between 900°C and 1,300°C, combined with extreme atmospheric pressure.

- The extreme temperature and atmospheric pressure causes an explosion of magma which moves the coal at the speed of an uncorked champagne bottle, forming a 'Kimberlite pipe' through the path of least resistance to the surface. This resulting explosion is vastly more powerful than that of most volcanoes.

- The magma rises so quickly that the coal does not have time to convert to graphite, which is the more stable form of coal at the Earth's surface. But instead, the molecules are hugged together within the Kimberlite pipe and effectively skip some steps in the transformation, cooling down into brilliant and beautiful diamonds. This skipping of steps could not have happened without the Kimberlite pipe providing this strong container. The Kimberlite pipes are so strong that not only can they produce diamonds, they can handle the force of volcanic eruptions. The biggest deposits of diamonds worldwide are therefore found within these Kimberlite pipes.

- The diamonds that are formed are harder and more complex in structure than coal because they take on the properties of the heat and pressure they were exposed to. Due to the coal being held together, the molecules don't disintegrate, but transform into something stronger.

- This transformative alteration is known as **Perturbation**.

Ilya Prigogine, who won the Nobel Prize for chemistry in 1977, is widely regarded as the Isaac Newton of our time. In his work, Prigogine studied how biological organisms behave and transform when put under pressure, which gives us some insights into how human beings transform under pressure, too.

Prigogine's revolutionary research was adapted in the field of human behavior by Marilyn Ferguson. In her book, 'The Aquarian Conspiracy', Marilyn explored the concept of *Perturbation* in human behavior. She determined that how human beings handle those changes determine the journey of healing: either transformative healing or disintegration and chaos.

In the same way that coal is transformed into a diamond under pressure, a form of *Perturbation* is possible for humans who feel under pressure from a life change they are going through, provided they have something which supports them in being contained during the change.

The conditions for structural transformation are:

1   Intense environmental conditions need to be in place (heat, pressure, explosion or in the case of human beings – a strong, sudden, traumatic change – like the death of a loved one, losing your job, declaring bankruptcy, or experiencing divorce).

2   The organism is lucky enough to have a strong container or cocoon that holds it in place while it reconfigures itself into something more complex, to withstand the pressure being applied to it. Within this reconfiguration, the organism will actually *take on* the properties of the pressure being applied to it.

3   Conversely, if the organism is unfortunate so as to be left uncontained, then there is nothing to assist it in withstanding the pressure being applied, and it will move to a state of chaos or disintegrate. This is known as *entropy*.

When the conditions for structural transformation are met, *Perturbation* becomes inevitable. When there is *Perturbation*, then breakthroughs occur in abundance.

Perturbation in the **naked divorce** is created by applying a time deadline as well as ensuring you create a container for your transformation, which we call the *Divorce Cocoon*.

In creating the **naked divorce**, I have outlined exactly what the three key break-throughs need to be, such that there is no mystery as to what it will take to heal:

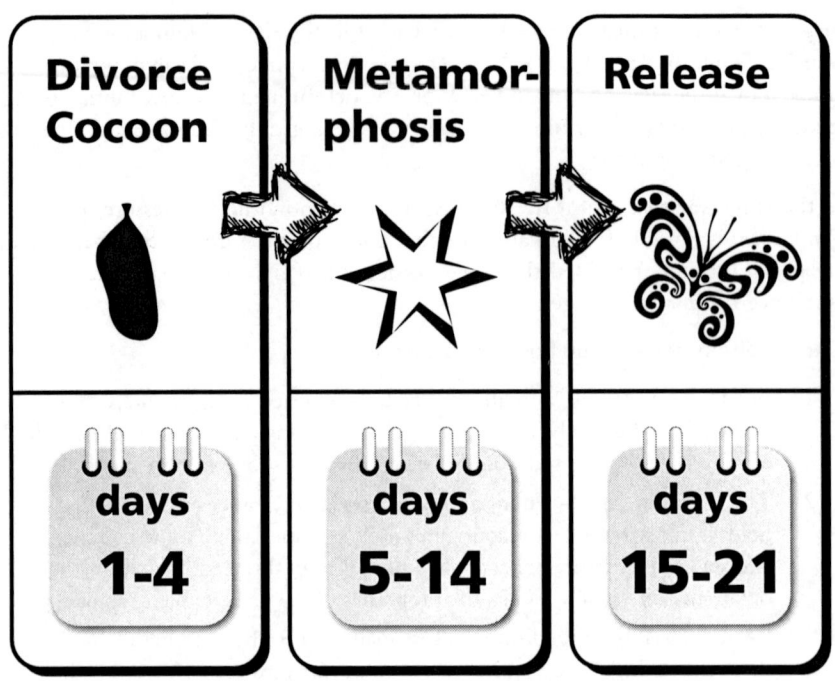

 BREAKTHROUGH 1: Divorce Cocoon (days 1-4)

When you have a powerful container around you, you can withstand and *use* the strong forces and pressure from your divorce as a catalyst to transform yourself into anything you want to be. Through the first breakthrough and the first few days of the **naked divorce** program, you will create a strong solid foundation so you have a supportive environment to contain your transformation.

As an analogy, the first stage of the transformation of a caterpillar into a butterfly, the caterpillar's skin grows into a strong protective cocoon, so within the **naked divorce,** this container is known as the *Divorce Cocoon.* Being cocooned leads to a sense of feeling invincible in life.

A person feels invincible when they:-

- Are able to stand tall in the face of tough change and not be thrown off course.
- Are confident and have a healthy sense of self-esteem.
- Are able to hold their position and withstand tough criticism, pressure and unfair judgment without being thrown off balance.

The first breakthrough is about creating this powerful invincible cocoon around you, and when it's in place you can withstand and *use* the strong forces from your divorce as a catalyst to transform yourself into anything you want to be. It also means you can heal faster. This transformation will make you stronger in the face of other challenges in your life.

 BREAKTHROUGH 2: Metamorphosis (days 5-14)

Once inside the *Divorce Cocoon*, the next phase called *Metamorphosis* begins. If we go back to our analogy, from the outside of the cocoon, it looks as if the caterpillar may just be resting, but the inside is where all of the action is taking place. Inside the cocoon, the caterpillar is rapidly changing. During *Metamorphosis*, it's important for the caterpillar to stay in the cocoon to experience the phases, just like it's important that once you commence the **naked divorce** 21-day program, to stay in the program until the transformation is complete.

To achieve the second breakthrough you will be doing intensive work to focus on your old relationship, what you learnt, what the source of your divorce was, getting over your ex-husband, healing your heart and repairing relationship wounds. Rapid changes happen within a fairly short period of time.

 BREAKTHROUGH 3: Release (days 15-21)

Back to the final part of our analogy; the transformation from caterpillar to butterfly is complete and the job is to exit the cocoon. The process of exiting the cocoon takes some time as the butterfly needs its wings to dry before it can use them. Once *Metamorphosis* has been completed, you are ready to begin the work on your future, your desires for your next relationship, your relationship with yourself, and getting back in touch with who you are as a person. Your metaphorical wings need time to dry and when you enter the final stages of *Release*, not only will you feel more alive but you will begin to be free from the constraints of the past and from making excuses to delay having the life you deserve and love.

The 7 Foundations of Transformation

The *naked divorce* program is designed to cover all aspects of mind, body and spirit so that the transformation is deep and lasting. Over the course of the program you will be working on mastering the **7 Foundations for Transformation**.

Like Stephen Covey developed the '7 habits of highly effective people', the **7 Foundations of Transformation** are key habits to adopt to ensure that your *naked divorce* program is a success.

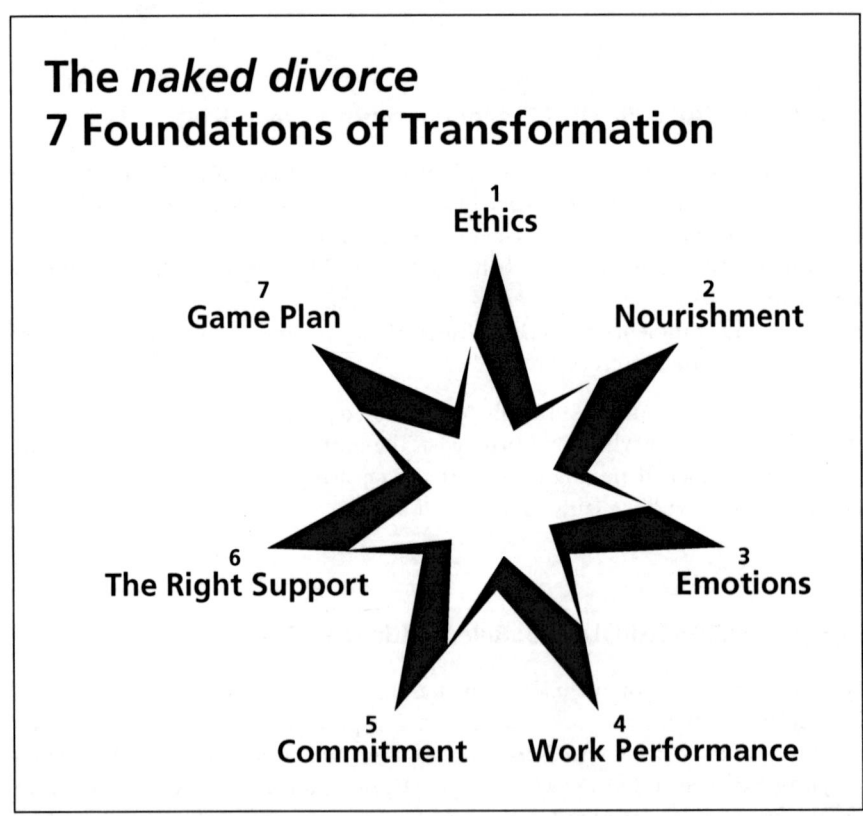

The *naked divorce*
7 Foundations of Transformation

1 Ethics
7 Game Plan
2 Nourishment
6 The Right Support
3 Emotions
5 Commitment
4 Work Performance

Foundation #1: ETHICS

There are some underlying ETHICS to adopt during the 21-day program. Every person who has completed the 21-day program successfully, had some basic ethics in place, so these will help you remain on track.

Foundation #2: NOURISHMENT

The 2nd **Foundation of Transformation** will support you in your healing work by ensuring you eliminate foods and drink that aggravate your hormones, interrupt your sleep patterns or interfere with your ability to concentrate. With the correct habits in place, your emotional highs and lows will normalize, your stress levels will decline and healing will be ethical and healthy for you.

Foundation #3: WORKING WITH YOUR EMOTIONS

People often avoid feeling their emotions by keeping busy numbing themselves with alcohol, or adopting *Short Term Emotion-Avoidance Tactics*. This is largely because human beings inherently fear emotions and are unsure of what to do with them. For most of us, we don't understand our emotions, how they work, how to tame them, or what we can learn from them. Additionally, with the dawning of 'Emotional Intelligence' concepts in the workplace, we are encouraged to keep our emotions under wraps, be calm, peaceful, and intellectualize them away.

Ignoring our emotions can lead to destructive and entropic disintegration, hence why it is curious to note that since the dawning of the 'Emotional Intelligence' age, the worldwide divorce rates have increased...

When there is healing to be done emotions are our greatest teachers and if harnessed, emotions can carve out powerful new ways of being. Within the *naked divorce*, there is a structured process for how to listen to your emotions, work with them as partners and harness their power as a catalyst for transformation.

The key is to keep your heart open whilst feeling your emotions and I will show you how to do that. Learning the techniques of working with your emotions can transform your life in many beneficial ways.

Foundation #4: PERFORMING AT WORK

It's key to remain focused on your work and keep your head in the game throughout the 21-day program. There are several techniques to follow to ensure that you have high energy and focus at work whilst at the same time you are being authentic in the processing of your emotions around your busy schedule.

Foundation #5: COMMITMENT

Commitment to the 21-day program includes ensuring that you set up your life in a particular way so you are not distracted during the program. Your commitment will be tested so to minimize these distractions, there may be certain things you need to handle before doing the program.

Foundation #6: THE RIGHT SUPPORT

Successful athletes have a coach who is rooting for them from the sidelines. It is very tempting to burden your friends with your divorce troubles but as you will see within this section, those closest to you are often a hindrance to your healing without even knowing it. Bless them, they try their damndest, but often because they love you, they will let you off the hook.

Healing does not happen linearly or once a week. Healing at pace requires around-the-clock support so that whenever you need to call or contact your support person, you have someone who can assist you.

What you really need is someone who will hold you accountable - someone who will hold your hand and kick your butt if required. Your *Divorce Angel* is a critical component to your success. You will have an opportunity to choose your *Divorce Angel* carefully from your own life but if you get stuck, the **naked divorce** team of *Divorce Angels* are available to support you 24/7.

In the **naked divorce** 21-day programs, we have a great deal of fun doing the program with groups of people like you, as the group-dynamic and sharing atmosphere is so supportive. That being said, you can do the program without us, provided you have a *Divorce Angel* on hand. If at any stage, you feel stuck, you can contact our team for support at www.nakeddivorce.com.

Foundation #7: A GAME PLAN THAT WORKS

There is an intended structure for following the **naked divorce** 21-day program and skipping steps is you simply doing the program your own way. There is nothing wrong with doing that, but then do not expect the breakthrough results within the defined time period. For a complete transformation of your life and breakthrough results, I request you follow the structure of the program.

For some of you, this will mean surrendering!

The 7 Foundations of Transformation ensure your success in healing from your divorce, so keep them in mind throughout the time you engage with the program.

In Summary

The *Healing Formula* is:

Healing Formula = Focused Intensity +

3 Key Breakthroughs + 7 Foundations of Transformation

the 7 foundations of transformation

Foundation #1 ETHICS

Like the spokes of a bicycle wheel, no spoke can be out of place or the integrity of the wheel will be compromised. The ETHICS of the *naked divorce* program are critical to the success of the program. They are:

1   Being self-expressed.
2   Avoid *Short Term Emotion Avoidance Tactics*.
3   Establish a *Grounded Routine*.
4   Sleep on any drastic changes you wish to make in your life.
5   Say no.
6   Cause VS effect.
7   Focus on you VS him.

Let's examine these ETHICS in greater detail:

1   Being self-expressed

Practice being radically honest with yourself about your divorce; how do you really feel about it? Many people act recovered. A false image or sense of recovery is the most common obstacle grievers must overcome if they expect to move on.

Putting on a brave face and pretending you're fine when you're not is exhausting. The cost in energy will be huge. Unresolved grief following divorce consumes tremendous amounts of energy.

Below are some things to avoid:

✗   Saying, "I'm fine" when you don't mean it.

✗   Putting on your happy face.

✗   Intellectualizing your feelings.

✗   Acting recovered.

✗   Ignoring your feelings.

✗   Focusing only on fond memories and building a pedestal for your ex.

✗   Focusing only on what was negative about the relationship and being unwilling to let go of disappointments and anger.

Here are some suggestions:

- ✔ Tell the truth.
- ✔ Be real.
- ✔ When your feelings come up, acknowledge and experience them.
- ✔ Be authentic to yourself and how you're doing.

It's important that you don't suppress your true feelings during the program. You may build walls around yourself to block input from others. This means living with secrecy, frustration, anger, and anxiety. If you have difficulty expressing yourself freely, it's possible you have been repressed a great deal, either in childhood or within your marriage.

When you're not fully self-expressed, you may feel as if you're not fully present, that you're a façade, a paper doll, rather than a whole person. Whenever you don't speak your truth (your feelings and thoughts), you shut down the joyful and creative spirit within. When you do eventually speak, you may feel extreme anger or seek revenge for feeling muted for so long.

To practice full self-expression, start by journaling all your thoughts and all the things you have wanted to tell others about how you feel. Start slowly by expressing yourself to those around you, one person at a time. Concentrate on it. Take note of all the times you remain silent when you know you have something to say.

Exercise:

Where are you not fully self-expressed in your life?

Do you have a habit of bottling up your feelings?

How effective are you in communicating your frustrations?

Do you blow up? Over what?

Knowing what you know now, what are you committing to for the duration of the *naked divorce* program?

----

2   Avoid *Short Term Emotion Avoidance Tactics* (S.T.E.A.T.s)

John James and Russell Friedman, who wrote 'The Grief Recovery Handbook' talk about confronting your emotions rather than filling your life with things that fill your time, but only provide a short-term relief. They tell the story of how a mother may deal with a child's crying by offering the child a cookie. The mother may say "Don't cry. Here, have a cookie and you will feel better." Later in life, that child could associate fixing their feelings with food. Eating the cookie in the moment, the child gets distracted and may forget about the incident that caused the upset, but the fact remains that there was no emotional completion of the pain caused by the event. The event and all the feelings associated with it, were buried.

Short Term Emotion Avoidance Tactics will help you feel better in each moment BUT the thing to be aware of is that you are not feeling better for real – it's a false sense of security - a false feeling of recovery. It fits into the *False Healing* category.

Short Term Emotion Avoidance Tactics are things you do to avoid feeling the pain, numb the pain, or to take the pain away in the short term. They are often escapism-type activities where you keep SO focused and busy that there is no time to think about how you are feeling or doing. If you fill your life up with lots of S.T.E.A.T.s, your healing will not progress.

The sad thing is that for most people who struggle to get over their divorce, they are engaging in a cycle of feeling the pain, applying a *Short Term Emotion Avoidance Tactic*, feeling the pain, applying another *Short Term Emotion Avoidance Tactic* etc. until over time they feel numb and they think this numbness is them healed from their divorce.

S.T.E.A.T.'s prolong the emotional rollercoaster of your divorce. So you never **fully grieve** for long enough or experience the loss critical to healing for real.

Your emotional rollercoaster will go up and down, up and down.

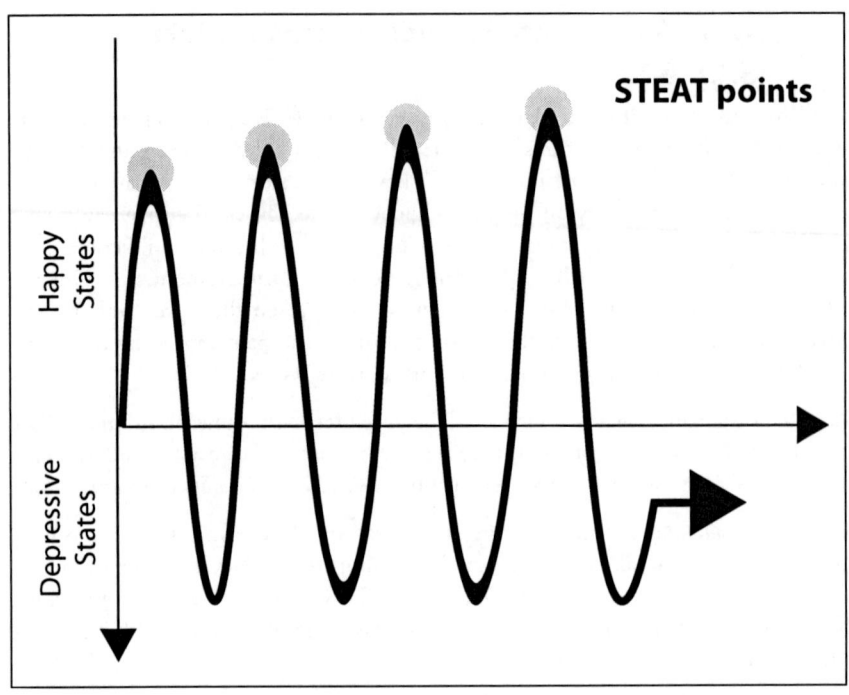

Short Term Emotion Avoidance Tactics include but are not limited to:

⇨ Excessive socializing.

⇨ Over-exercising.

⇨ Fantasy or escapism activities (books, TV, movies).

⇨ Shopping/retail therapy.

⇨ Work and becoming a workaholic.

⇨ Ignoring feelings.

⇨ Pretending something hasn't happened.

⇨ Overeating.

⇨ Eating foods loaded with sugar and fat ('comfort eating').

⇨ Excessive drinking of alcohol.

⇨ Excessive use of recreational drugs.

⇨ Using prescription drugs such as tranquilizers or antidepressants.

⮕ Exercising compulsively.

⮕ Behaving compulsively.

⮕ Excessive sex with or without a partner.

⮕ Excessive busyness.

⮕ Constantly intellectualizing and analyzing situations.

⮕ Excessive reading or TV viewing.

⮕ Spending hours watching romantic movies or fantasizing about the one.

⮕ Keeping conversations superficial.

⮕ Burying angry emotions under the mask of peace and love.

⮕ Spending countless hours with your children under the guise of being a good parent but with the actual agenda being to use your children in some way to help you feel better.

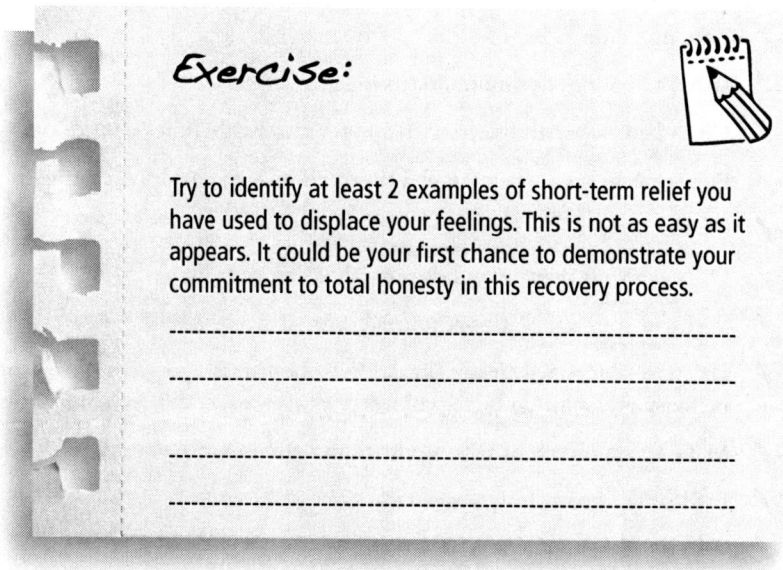

Exercise:

Try to identify at least 2 examples of short-term relief you have used to displace your feelings. This is not as easy as it appears. It could be your first chance to demonstrate your commitment to total honesty in this recovery process.

----

3   Establish a *Grounded Routine*

Often, the first thing that goes out the window during a divorce is your routine. Like me, many of my clients stopped eating, getting dressed, cleaning the house, etc.

On a practical level, when something as earth-shattering as a divorce hits you, your number one priority should be to go back to basics and establish a *Grounded Routine*.

A *Grounded Routine* has a very particular purpose; the more aware of and faithful you are to the rituals and routines that help you feel rooted, the more adaptable you will be when life throws you a curve ball. A *Grounded Routine* will prevent you from internalizing the chaos, so that no matter what goes on around you, you'll be able to maintain your balance and stay solidly grounded.

You can establish a *Grounded Routine* by soothing your skin, taking care of your feet, strengthening your legs, properly feeding your body, comforting and reassuring yourself, in body and soul. Creating order, gaining support from key people, and being honest and ethical in all your workings in your daily life, will strengthen your resilience during divorce.

Trite as it sounds, it is the simple things in life that make a difference.

- Take up pottery class or some creative activity.
- Listen to your body and honor its signals.
- Go to bed earlier and sleep with a hot-water bottle (if it's your thing).
- Prepare your own meals, eat at a table and stick to established eating times.
- Do the ironing.
- Organize your drawers and thoroughly clean your house.
- Write in your **naked divorce** journal every day.
- Listen to your **naked divorce** Break Up Reboot audio program (this complimentary program can be downloaded at www.nakeddivorce.com/book.)
- Make an appointment with a nutritionist and improve your diet.
- Eat loads of green, leafy vegetables.
- Take a daily multivitamin.
- Drink plenty of water; you need lot of water to re-establish balance in periods of emotional instability.
- Bake bread.
- Pay your bills on time.

- ✓ Buy a leafy plant to care for daily.
- ✓ Make jam.
- ✓ Get into the garden.
- ✓ Buy yourself flowers.
- ✓ Get to know your neighbors.
- ✓ Establish exercise times and adhere to them.
- ✓ Take a kickboxing or aerobic dance class.
- ✓ Have a picnic.
- ✓ Take more baths.
- ✓ Wear a comfy bathrobe.
- ✓ Set the breakfast table before you go to bed.

Whatever you choose to do in terms of establishing a *Grounded Routine*, the purpose is to create something to come home to. Even if your home is a physically chaotic place, find solace and comfort in your routine.

Video: I created a YouTube video on the topic of *Grounded Routine*. To watch me explaining the concept in more detail, go to **www.youtube.com/nakeddivorce**

4　Sleep on any drastic changes you wish to make in your life

I would highly recommend holding off on any drastic changes until at least three weeks after the program has been completed.

I know it feels empowering and exciting to put the past behind you but it's also important to make changes which are healthy and in tune with your life.

This program is challenging enough so limit any other drastic changes. It's all about timing and pacing the changes you want to make or you could find yourself in the same situation as one of my clients, Mary.

Case study: Whispers from the looney bin...

Mary was told by her former husband that she was boring. Their divorce was acrimonious and Mary was left feeling that no one would ever want her.

One night Mary decided to do something crazy to prove to the world that she was not boring. She decided that she would become GI Jane. Within a space of one hour, she had shaved all her hair off and signed up to a military fitness course (which started the next morning) that consisted of highly physical training, even though she hadn't seen the inside of a gym in years. She stayed up all night getting pumped up by drinking vodka shots and putting war paint on her face.

She arrived at the course at 05:50, and began training with everyone else. Everyone was looking at her very strangely and within 27 minutes, she had fractured her wrist in a crazy karate move and was sent to hospital. It was only when she was being wheeled into the operating theatre that it dawned on her that she had made some impulsive decisions which she would later regret...

If you are doing any of these activities, you are making drastic changes:

➪　You are obsessed with creating a new you and you want to change everything such as your hair, your clothes, your behavior.

➪　The change is SO extreme that even you have trouble to believing what you have done.

⇨ Bills are drastically increasing or decreasing.

⇨ You are keen to quit your job tomorrow.

⇨ People are questioning these drastic changes and possibly talking about you behind your back.

Exercise:

Are there any drastic changes you are considering?

What is driving you to make these drastic changes ?

----

5   Say no

Loving yourself is not simply about treating yourself well, taking care of yourself or having an inflated opinion of yourself. Love for yourself includes establishing healthy boundaries when it comes to other people, including your ex. It may feel hard to set limits with your ex or with other people in your life. You may feel ashamed or guilty. Doing things against your will, will leave you feeling used and resentful. It's really important in the next few weeks to *say no* to things you don't feel comfortable doing and *say no* whenever you feel intruded upon.

A simple and direct, "NO, I am not able to help you with that" is the best solution. If you want to give an explanation you should keep it simple, "NO, I have already made another appointment for that time" or, "NO, sorry. I am afraid I have to decline because I have no spare time" or, "NO, it's not okay for you to pop in whenever you feel like it."

Other ways of saying NO:

⇨   I can´t do this right now.

⇨ NO, thanks. Not this time. Thank you for asking.

⇨ Sorry, but NO.

⇨ Please accept that I cannot come.

⇨ I'd rather not.

On Day 19 of the **naked divorce** program, you will spend more time focusing on setting healthy and ethical boundaries, but begin this work now.

Exercise:

List 3 ways in which you allow yourself to be intruded on:

1 ....

2 ....

3 ....

List 3 ways in which you can choose to establish your boundaries and respect yourself in the next few weeks:

1 ....

2 ....

3 ....

6   Cause VS effect

Many of us confuse responsibility with blame. So you may feel that if you take responsibility for your divorce, you are stating that you are to blame. I want to be clear that **taking responsibility has nothing to do with blame.**

Responsibility is purely a way to regain power over a situation and stating, "yes, I had something to do with this happening." The ultimate purpose is to regain control over your life.

It may not always feel like you have a choice, but you do. I remember thinking, "I don't have a choice – this situation was forced upon me." That may have felt very real and true for me at the time, but I could control how I responded to what life threw at me. Becoming disempowered would have been my choice.

In life, we have a choice of either feeling at the *effect of life* or feeling in charge and at the *cause of life.*

Tad James, the founder of Timeline Therapy™ discusses the concept of cause VS effect' in the study I did to become a certified Timeline Therapy™ professional. Here is a summary of his principles:-

Feeling like you are at the effect of life

Do you believe that other people or events are responsible for your feelings? It might be at this particular time you are feeling this more than normal. This is totally understandable whilst you are dealing with your divorce. If you are feeling like, "he made me angry" or, "he ruined my life by leaving me", it does have an impact on you in a negative way.

This is what might be happening at this time:

⇨ You may be in a position where you are giving your power away to other people and you may believe that the answers, solutions to issues and power in life lie outside of yourself.

⇨ It may feel like the divorce has all the power in your life and that you have lost control.

⇨ You may be feeling worried about what others think.

⇨ You might even be seeking someone or something to rescue you from your situation.

Eleanor Roosevelt said, "*No one can make you feel bad about yourself without your permission.*" When we make other people or events responsible for our feelings, then we also give them control of our lives.

This way of living life is called *living at the effect* of life.

In a relationship, what is powerful is for both people to be fully responsible for themselves and their emotions. If you think it's your partner's responsibility to make you happy or it's their fault when you are sad, you are not living responsibly or *at the cause of life.* Consider that your partner's only job in life is to top-up an already happy version of you. Your job is to make yourself happy.

Feeling like you cause your life

When you are living at the cause of life, you acknowledge that you may have something to do with how your life runs, how your divorce will be, your emotional state and what actions you take. One of the biggest steps in healing is actually adopting the mindset that you are in charge and you have the power. Power statements include:

- I take the action.
- I have the power.

- They are my emotions and are not caused by anyone else other than me.
- I am responsible for my life and how it runs.
- If bad things happen in my life, I don't allow those things to crush me, I rise up and find an empowering meaning from what happened, take responsibility for what I can be responsible for and learn the lessons that propel me forward.
- I don't make excuses or argue my limitations.
- I am learning from this situation and this is what I have learnt…

This will not always be easy to do when you are feeling low, however, it's all about practice. Just one simple thought like this every single day will make all the difference in the world. This way of living life is called *living at the cause of life*. Healing from your divorce now is all about taking ownership, being responsible and choosing to move on with your life. Practice *living at the cause of your life* every day. In the beginning it may be challenging but after 21 days of practice, it will come more naturally to you.

Exercise:

What part of your divorce can you take responsibility for?

Think of people you know who spend more time living at the cause of life (heroes, powerful women, billionaires):

What can you learn from these people?

What steps can you take today to demonstrate that you are practicing *living at the cause of your life*?

CHANNEL YOUR HERO FOR A DAY:

Spend one day walking around as if you are your hero. For example, if you choose Oprah, practice BEING her for a day. Think about how she would approach the situation you are in, what she would say, what she would do. This exercise is SO MUCH FUN and you will learn magical things in that day. Whenever you feel disempowered, try and channel your hero for a day.

7   Focus on you VS him

Let me tell you a bit about one of my clients. I shall call her Molly.

Case study: Molly

Molly came to see me towards the end of 2009. She had been divorced for six years and in that time had not stopped obsessing about what her ex-husband was up to. In the beginning, she would talk about only one thing…

"You know, he is seeing Suzy now and I think they have been dating for a few months (not that I have noticed) and I don't think she is right for him. He's also got an earring now and changed his car – why do you think he did that? Well, actually I don't care but it is strange isn't it? A lot of our friends say that he's changed for the worse and just isn't the same guy now. I would agree. He has even taken up sky-diving! He is clearly having a midlife crisis! Suzy isn't even that pretty, she looks strange with her little skinny legs and fake tan. My friend Sally says that she gives them another six months and they will split up, too."

What Molly wasn't aware of, was that she was fixating on her ex-husband and how HE was doing, what HE was thinking, feeling and who HE was seeing. This focus on him was actually her way of escaping and avoiding dealing with her own emotions. Although a great deal of time had passed, she was no further along in her healing.

Working with her, the key component which shifted her into healing from her divorce, was supporting her in shifting her focus from him onto herself. It was painful but once her grieving was complete, she found peace, harmony and a new life once she stopped fixating on him.

The last time I saw Molly, I asked her how her ex-husband was doing and she said, "You know, I don't have a clue. Let me show you some pictures of the hot air balloon ride I did two weeks ago. I have always wanted to do it and now I have!"

One thing which I see time and time again with my clients, is this concept of *Target Fixation*.

Target Fixation is a process by which the brain is focused so intently on an observed object that awareness of everything else diminishes.

With *Target Fixation*, the observer can become so fixated on the target that they will forget to take the necessary action to avoid it, thus colliding with it. This is a common issue for motorcyclists and mountain bikers as statistically most collisions are due to *Target Fixation*. A motorcycle or bicycle will tend to go where the rider is looking; if the rider is overly focused on something in the path ahead of him, the cycle can collide with that object simply because of the rider's focus on it, even though the rider is ostensibly trying to avoid it.

As a keen motorcyclist, I am well aware of the hazards of *Target Fixation*. In fact, on one motorcycle trip in the Himalayas, I collided with the back of a motorcycle I was fixated on in front of me. This almost led me to fly off a cliff so it was a pretty frightening moment!

Focusing on your ex and what they are up to leads to no good. You are in essence, fixated on them and end up having daily collisions with unnecessary pain and suffering over and over again.

When I observed this type of fixation on the ex with most of the people I worked with, I realized that tackling FOCUS inside of the **naked divorce** was very important.

For some of you who have been divorced for years, it may easy to not think about your ex however, do notice if you are constantly thinking of your job or your children as a distraction from your healing. The lesson is to think of yourself during this program. It's time to be selfish and be fascinated in how YOU are doing and to grow your awareness and analysis of yourself, rather than something else.

Examples include:

➡ Whenever you want to think about what your ex had for breakfast or if his new girlfriend has remembered to launder his socks – think instead about yourself, your own eating and laundry habits.

➡ Whenever you find yourself drifting off and wondering what your ex meant when he said he loved your new hairstyle, think about the new bath towels you are purchasing on the weekend.

➡ Whenever you find yourself wondering why your ex said what he said, focus instead on painting your nails.

Training your mind to stop being preoccupied with thoughts of your ex and what he is thinking or what he is up to, OR to stop pointless thoughts of your neighbor or friend, or job, it is a little like training a new puppy:

1) **Start by gently ignoring the yelps for attention.** If you notice your mind flashing to your ex or another unhelpful distraction, relax. Imagine that the thought is a soft, fluffy white cloud. Imagine this cloud drifting across your mind like a cloud floats across the sky. Just notice the thought and gently let it go. Tell yourself that this unhelpful thought is just floating across your mind. Engaging with this thought is like engaging with a puppy's yelps for attention and this is not constructive.

2) **If the yelps continue, keep a short leash.** If you find yourself constantly drifting into an amazing fantasy story or if you find yourself stuck in a cycle of analysis paralysis, sometimes it's good to reign in that thought with one swift action. Immediately say to yourself, "NO, enough is enough." Make a swift sudden action and stand up, saying out loud that this line of thinking is not constructive. Become immediately fixated on doing something else like journaling about your feelings or going for a focused power walk. The key is swift, intentional action to jerk yourself out of the lethargy of daydreaming. If your leash is too long and you indulge negative thinking for too long, it takes longer to come back into the present.

3) **Reward with healthy treats if well behaved.** If you notice that it's been a few hours or days since you last engaged in unhelpful thinking, then reward yourself with a healthy treat. Something like taking yourself out on an outing.

In summary

Each day of the *naked divorce* includes an exercise that reminds you of the ETHICS of the program. Each day you have an opportunity to rate yourself and then devise actions you can take to move up a level (a rating of one is low on the scale and a rating of 10 is high on the scale).

The example below is one a client completed while doing her *naked divorce* homework:

Ethics	Rate yourself on a scale of 1-10	Actions I will take to move this ETHIC to a level 10 in my life
Full self-expression	8	• I commit to stop hiding out and telling Sally that Bill and I are getting divorced. • I will call Angie to tell her the truth about her dress I borrowed and that I did lose it.
Avoid STEATs	10	• Am SO proud of myself for being so healthy and focused at the moment. I even caught myself almost hiding behind the kids and it didn't happen. WOW!
Establish a Grounded Routine	6	• I commit to having a hot bath before bed so I don't stay awake all night worrying. • I will go home at a reasonable hour and make time to cook dinner. • I just called Myra to help me with the washing and ironing, which was piling up – feel SO much better!
Sleep on any drastic changes you wish to make in your life	2	• Hmm. I sucked at this today as I decided to dye my hair blond. It came out orange and now I have to go to the hairdresser tomorrow to fix it. Argh!
Say no	5	• I will tell Paul tomorrow that he cannot come over before 3p.m. because that time doesn't work for me
Cause VS effect	10	• Feel pretty good just completing this list and proud that I haven't been a victim once today!
Focus on you VS him	9	• Have not thought about him once today, so to reward myself have just booked a massage for tomorrow after fixing my hair disaster.

Tip-

Whenever you feel lost during your divorce, come back to the ETHICS of the program. Each day, take a look at actions you can take to put them back in place.

Foundation #2
NOURISHMENT

Whilst experiencing a trauma like divorce, a range of different responses are triggered; you may feel loss and pain, your balance is upset and your feelings dip and soar. One moment you long for your ex, desperate to see him, and the next you want to rip his head off. This volatility and confusion add to the general sense of craziness.

Managing your health and diet

It is really key to take care of yourself when your life is disrupted by a trauma. To heal ethically and healthily, the first thing you need to focus on is re-establishing routines and taking care of yourself.

Getting divorced is a great opportunity to review your eating habits, your diet and your general health.

My story:

I used my divorce as an opportunity to really overhaul my state of health and general fitness. For two years prior to the end of my marriage, I was very unhappy with my weight and general health.

I decided that part of my healing program would include an overhaul of my health and general fitness regime. I looked back to when I was nineteen and what I envisaged for my life and I realized that one of my dreams was to complete a triathlon.

It was a great goal because it gave me a lot of focus. I hired a trainer, reviewed my diet completely, and chose to become a Pescatarian as a result. I trained every day and the weight fell off me, my skin glowed and my confidence soared.

I found the regular running, cycling, and swimming cathartic because I spent time thinking about my life and future and what I wanted to achieve in the next phase of my life. I also rested a great deal and balanced out the cardio exercise with Pilates and Yoga. Completing my first triathlon was an incredible experience. I could not believe I did it. I inspired myself do more and be more in my life, and used my routines as a way to learn discipline and focus.

My friends and family didn't recognize me after my divorce because I became incredibly disciplined. I also noticed that a few times whilst entering a venue,

I was asked for my ID. I loved seeing the face of the bouncer when he noticed that I was born in the seventies.

This was not possible for me without learning about the value of focusing on my health and well being.

Regardless of whether or not you want to take on a personal physical challenge, it may be a great idea to consider treating yourself like an athlete during the *naked divorce* program.

The 21-day program is a marathon of sorts, with highs and lows. Giving yourself the vitality and energy to complete the journey will stand you in good stead.

Consider these principles of treating yourself like an athlete:

- A dedicated athlete never misses their workouts or practices.

- An athlete is aware that success is underpinned by regular exercise, disciplined training, healthy eating, sleeping well, and taking care of their body.

- An athlete will pace themselves, ensuring that they pay attention to their body at each exercise session. They don't want to overdo it or injure themselves during training.

- Athletes understand that to build strength and stamina they must practice regularly and plan their training and meals.

- An athlete participates fully in the process and in competitive situations. An athlete doesn't sit on the sidelines or shrink back from the game.

Thinking of yourself as an athlete and taking care of yourself in that way will produce extraordinary results in your life.

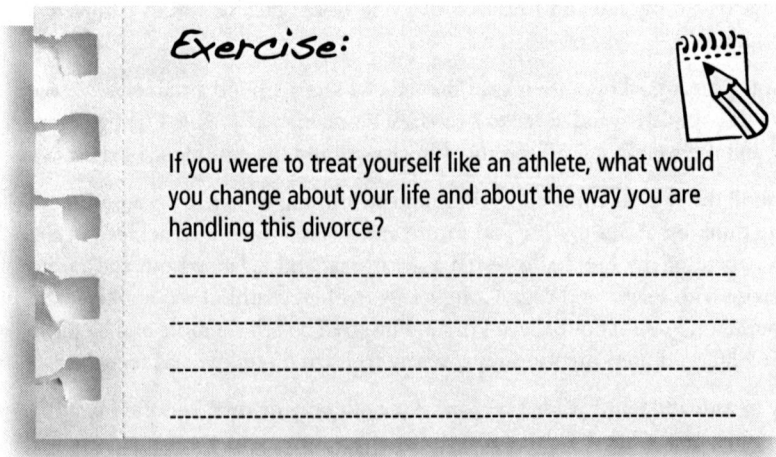

Exercise:

If you were to treat yourself like an athlete, what would you change about your life and about the way you are handling this divorce?

Nourishment Lesson #1: our hormones and neurotransmitters do go haywire during a trauma like divorce

The thoughts and feelings that make up our consciousness are linked to biochemical activities in our brain. These biochemical activities play a vital part in our behavior.

Hormones: Cortisol and Adrenalin

Cortisol, also known as Hydrocortisone, is a hormone produced by the Adrenal Cortex. It is released in response to stress or shock, such as induced by divorce. Together with Adrenalin, the primary function of Cortisol is to increase blood sugar. It helps us store sugar in the liver as Glycogen, aids in fat, protein and carbohydrate metabolism and suppresses the immune system. Mother nature equipped us with this hormone to assist us in fight-or-flight situations, such as running from a lion. Its job is to quickly convert stored energy sources in the body into usable energy.

Although there isn't a lion coming at you, divorce is a major shock and your body believes that your life is in danger. So it pumps out Cortisol to prepare you to run away.

Cortisol also stimulates gastric acid secretion. This is why you sometimes feel nausea or light-headedness - almost as if you've sustained a blow to the stomach. This is also why many people don't eat much when dealing with heartbreak; they literally lose their appetite.

Cortisol is also associated with a weakened immune system. As it can also cause memory loss. Chronic elevations in Cortisol are detrimental to your health in the long term. Cortisol has been linked to Adrenal fatigue, hormonal imbalances, heart disease, excessive blood sugar levels, elevated cholesterol, and pretty much anything else that stress precipitates within the body. Getting your Cortisol under control is key to rapid healing. This is covered later on in this section.

Neurotransmitters

Neurotransmitters create and reflect your feelings, moods, thoughts, and behaviors. This powerful group of chemicals in the brain is responsible for physiological and psychological changes in how you experience your life. All behavior has a corresponding chemical pattern in the brain.

There are more than a dozen neurotransmitters but two of these, Serotonin and Dopamine, play a crucial role in orchestrating your behavior, thoughts, emotions, and experiences during divorce.

When we're stressed, our body releases Cortisol and Adrenalin that decrease our Serotonin and increase our Dopamine levels.

These neurotransmitters affect our feelings.

1)   Dopamine

A great deal of Dopamine is released under stress and whenever levels of Cortisol and Adrenalin are heightened. Dopamine is responsible for us being more alert and attentive during the fight or flight response. However, when we're not releasing the Dopamine by fleeing or fighting, the elevation of this neurotransmitter causes that aching feeling in your chest. The feeling of heartbreak – like your heart is being torn in two, is caused by elevated levels of Dopamine.

When your Dopamine levels are too high, you may be caught in distorted perceptions of reality, leading to risk taking and increased aggression. But there are things you can do to regulate your Dopamine levels. These are covered at the end of this section.

The feelings below are all linked to increased Dopamine levels:

⇨   Feeling jittery and restless.

⇨   Urges to drive past our ex's house, to check his Facebook account, call him up and talk to his friends.

⇨   You throw yourself into your job and become obsessed with work, to the point of becoming a workaholic.

⇨   You feel trapped and crazy, like a caged animal, and you want to break things.

⇨   You feel like you might drive your car into a wall. You feel you're not alive unless you're taking dangerous risks.

⇨   You fear being alone and having nothing to do. You cannot tolerate relaxation or calm.

⇨   You have a tendency toward compulsive behavior, perfectionism and withdrawal. You worry a lot and may see things in a negative way. You may be hyper-vigilant and overly controlling.

⇨   You are impulsive, have a short attention span, feel blocked and scattered, and easily fly off the handle.

⇨   You are compelled to clean and organize things around you. Once you start cleaning you may get sucked into the activity and find it hard to stop.

⇨   You are prone to violence and aggression. You may deliberately create conflict.

⇨   You feel a lack of intimacy and you do not want to make deep connections with others or feel your emotions.

⇨   You feel insecure and paranoid and try to control your environment in overt and destructive ways.

⇨ You are chronically stressed, frustrated, and anxious.

⇨ You are overly competitive and determined to win at all costs. You are demanding and lack the trust of those around you.

⇨ You are not able to concentrate, lack focus and feel almost manic.

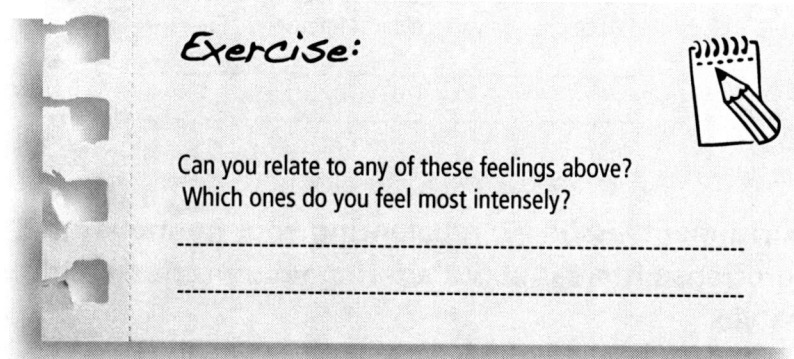

Exercise:

Can you relate to any of these feelings above?
Which ones do you feel most intensely?

----

2) Serotonin

Serotonin is the neurotransmitter associated with feeling good, inner peace and well-being. Optimal Serotonin levels are required for all positive affective states and all balanced emotional conditions. When Cortisol and Adrenalin are released during divorce, Serotonin levels immediately drop as your body prepares for fight or flight. This depletion of Serotonin is why we become so incredibly weepy.

When your Serotonin levels are extremely low, you may lapse into a cycle of struggle and hopelessness.

The feelings below are all linked to lowered Serotonin levels:

⇨ You become reclusive and avoid situations that make you anxious.

⇨ You feel driven to avoid all conflict and want to hide away.

⇨ You feel overwhelmed, resentful, and victimized by your circumstances.

⇨ You crave sweets and carbohydrates and tend to overeat (especially comfort foods). You tend to eat more in the afternoon or evening.

⇨ You are prone to heat intolerance and may feel panicky.

⇨ You are a night owl, experience insomnia, and have trouble getting to sleep.

⇨ You feel depressed and hopeless and without any personal power. You may feel sad and cry a lot.

Can you relate to any of these feelings above?
Which ones do you feel most intensely?

Nourishment lesson #2: rebalancing your hormones and neurotransmitters is about altering your nutrition and lifestyle

Your behavior and experiences affect your biochemical profile and your biochemical profile affects your behavior and experiences. By being alert to the red flags that tell you when your brain chemistry is out of balance you can take steps to restore your equilibrium and be in charge again.

It's really important to note that what society teaches us in order to cope with divorce often makes us feel worse!

Now the sad thing is that for most of us, when we experience heartbreak, we go and bury our heads in a tub of Ben and Jerry's ice cream or indulge in crisps or drink alcohol or coffee. Those foods and drinks actually INCREASE the Dopamine levels within our body and will lead you to feeling even more crazy and insecure. If you want to stop feeling the heartache, eating healthily is critical to stabilizing your Dopamine levels and stimulating the release of Serotonin and Oxytocin that will help you feel better.

Under the section, **Foundation of Transformation # 7: A GAME PLAN THAT WORKS**, you will begin preparing effectively for the program. There is a range of supplements to take which combat or reverse the effects of Cortisol, boost Serotonin and decrease Dopamine. There are also dietary tips as all these chemicals can be affected by your diet.

➡ Use Cortisol-reduction supplements (shopping list section under **Foundation of Transformation # 7: A GAME PLAN THAT WORKS**

➡ Serotonin levels can be controlled through diet and supplements. In particular, focus on getting more Vitamin C and omega-3 fatty acids, and eating more complex carbohydrates instead of eating sugary foods. Divorce healing vitamins can be purchased on the **naked divorce** website: www.nakeddivorce.com.

⇨ There are specific tissue salts to use, which are effective for restoring the salts in your cells. These can be depleted through the hormonal imbalance precipitated by stressful events such as divorce. They can be found in most health food shops. Within the **naked divorce** 21-day Survival Kit, all the supplements, vitamins and tissue salts required are provided as part of the program. You can find out more on the **naked divorce** website.

⇨ Eat at regular intervals throughout the day. Don't skip meals as your body will release Cortisol.

⇨ Avoid too many carbohydrates as they trigger a Cortisol release in response to constantly elevated insulin levels.

⇨ Get to bed earlier.

⇨ Avoid all stimulants or restrict yourself to only one-two per day: nicotine, energy drinks that contain ephedra-like compounds, and caffeine. Stimulants shift the body into sympathetic dominance, in other words, that fight or flight reaction. Stimulants can also disrupt your sleeping patterns. If you must have your daily coffee, try decaffeinated, or ensure you don't drink coffee after midday.

⇨ Keep your workouts under one hour. At the one-hour mark, your testosterone levels begin to decline and Cortisol levels rise. 45-minute workouts are even better.

⇨ Maca Root Powder is also known to reduce Cortisol levels and restore the adrenal glands to health.

⇨ Use stress reduction techniques. To calm yourself and restore your hormonal balance, listen to the **naked divorce** Break Up Reboot. It's a relaxing audio program designed to refocus your mind on your HEALING GOAL (discussed on Day 0) and realign the neurotransmitters in your brain. Listening to it every day for 21 days will dramatically increase your healing process and reboot those feel-good emotions. You can download your complimentary **naked divorce** Break Up Reboot today at: www.nakeddivorce.com/book.

⇨ Massage therapy can reduce Cortisol as well as stabilize Dopamine levels.

⇨ A study by a Japanese cosmetics company in 2006 showed that applying make-up reduces Cortisol levels in a mentally stressful situation. So it's important to keep getting up in the morning, getting dressed and putting on your make-up, even if you don't feel like it!

Optimizing you brain chemistry and neurotransmitter profile not only supports you in healing faster after divorce, but the spin offs include improved well-being, the achievement of your goals and dreams, and the attainment of the successful, healthy and integrated life you aspire to.

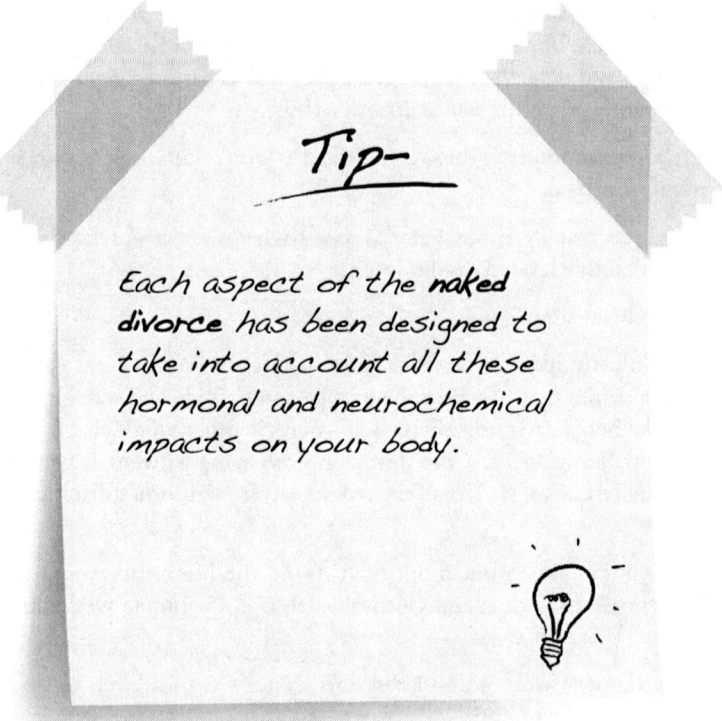

Tip–

*Each aspect of the **naked divorce** has been designed to take into account all these hormonal and neurochemical impacts on your body.*

Nourishment Lesson #3: watch out for antidepressants

I completely agree that in many circumstances antidepressants are lifesavers and make an important difference in people's lives, but I am very concerned about the increase of antidepressant use in today's society.

A report written by Dr. Mark Olfson, a professor of clinical psychiatry at Columbia University/New York State Psychiatric Institute in New York City in 2009 showed that antidepressant use among US and UK residents almost doubled between 1996 and 2009, along with a concurrent rise in the use of other psychotropic medications.

"Over 10 percent of people over the age of six were receiving anti-depression medication" said study author Dr. Mark Olfson. According to background information in the study, antidepressants are now the most widely prescribed class of drugs in the

United States. The expansion in use dates back to the 1980s, with the introduction of the antidepressant Prozac (Fluoxetine).

Although I will concede that there must be times when antidepressants are considered useful, many doctors are prescribing them left, right and center – particularly if patients look vulnerable or display signs of stress.

The long-term effects of antidepressants are unknown. I know from my own personal experience of taking antidepressants in my first few years at university that it took me months, even years to fully get the drugs out of my system once I started coming off them.

I would caution you to be wary of your doctor subscribing antidepressants when you're feeling low during your divorce.

Although antidepressants offer temporary relief while you get back on your feet again, studies have shown that they are not good in the long run. Charly Groenendijk who conducted his research into antidepressants in 2003, showed that in some instances antidepressants can actually increase Cortisol and suppress Dopamine completely so that you don't feel like doing anything. Antidepressant medications artificially increase Serotonin levels at the synapse by blocking the re-uptake of Serotonin into the presynaptic cell.

Moving off antidepressants can also be very difficult in the future as your body has to get used to producing its own Serotonin once again.

If you can, try to get through your divorce naturally and following the methods prescribed in the **naked divorce**. It has been designed to help you get through the pain of divorce quickly, healthily and naturally.

If you feel you need support, please go to www.nakeddivorce.com or consult with your medical practitioner for more information.

Foundation #3 WORKING WITH YOUR EMOTIONS

> **❝** *I feel like a piece of fabric fraying at the edges, one piece of thread at a time. I can only really handle what is right in front of me. Almost like I have tunnel vision* **❞**
>
> *Debbie, 42*

My story:

It was within the first four days of my divorce. At 02:30 am I was on my third glass of wine and hadn't eaten in three days. I had been in my pajamas for 36 hours straight and had chain-smoked 40 cigarettes (and I'm not even a smoker!).

There was a pile of laundry on the couch waiting to be ironed and used tissues everywhere. The house was in absolute chaos and I didn't feel like doing anything. I wasn't answering my phone or talking to my family or anyone else. I had a vision of being found dead of a broken heart at the age of 65, still wearing my pajamas, with no love or man in my life.

The only time I left the house, I was so distracted, I almost drove into a wall. I thought that if I could convert my emotional pain into physical pain, I could take a pill for it. How bizarre my thoughts were!

The reality is that I was in despair. I felt completely out of control. For someone who is usually organized and structured, this was a very new feeling.

Nothing helped and I remember thinking, "Why the hell is this happening to me?"

I had read 27 books on breaking up in two weeks. I had spoken to two therapists. I had spoken to a counselor. I listened to music. I listened to a personal development CD. I spoke to friends. Nothing helped. I was going crazy. I was so uncomfortable in my own skin. The pain felt unbearable, I just wanted to feel normal again.

If this sounds familiar to you or you can relate in any way, welcome to the club. You are completely normal and you will be okay. Here are some completely normal responses to divorce:

⇨ Numbness – numbness can be physical, emotional, or both. The numbness lasts for different periods of time for different people.

⇨ Disrupted sleep patterns – not being able to sleep or sleeping too much is completely normal.

⇨ Changing eating habits – it's normal to have almost no appetite or a need to eat nonstop, or both, alternately.

⇨ Rollercoaster of emotional energy – extreme ups and downs. As a direct result of these emotional highs and lows, you may feel emotionally and physically drained.

⇨ Depression – feeling low and depressed is normal.

⇨ Despair, desolation and desperation.

⇨ Reduced concentration.

⇨ Feeling hopeless.

⇨ Feeling helpless.

⇨ Feeling strong anger or rage.

⇨ Experiencing dramatic mood changes.

⇨ Exhibiting a change in personality.

⇨ Losing interest in most activities.

⇨ Experiencing a change in sleeping or eating habits.

⇨ Performing poorly at work.

You will feel low for the first few weeks, even months. That's normal. After that, you'll start to feel more like your old self. You'll start to rationalize things and you'll begin to work out what to do next. This is a turning point, and it means you're thinking about your future. The pain will still be there, but it will become easier to bear and in the **naked divorce** program you'll find many things you can do to work through the pain and speed up your recovery.

You may feel it tempting to keep busy and avoid being alone. However, if you want to heal, the KEY is to FACE your emotions and process them. I know this may sound like a frightening idea. I remember thinking that my own sadness and grief would swallow me whole. What I did realize after a few days was that every single emotion had another emotion underneath it, almost like there were layers of emotions which needed to be peeled off.

My job was to simply move through each emotion, find the boundary or ending of the layer and move onto the next emotional layer. There was actually a natural ending to each emotion but only when I truly experienced and acknowledged the preceding emotion. When you resist your emotions and avoid being with them by indulging in *Short Term Emotion Avoidance Tactics*, you prolong the healing cycle unconsciously. You will consequently have no say about how much time your healing will take or what will happen.

Lucy's emotional journey: This graph below tracks the healing experience of one of my clients prior to meeting her. It illustrates the first year of the past five years of her life as drawn by her.

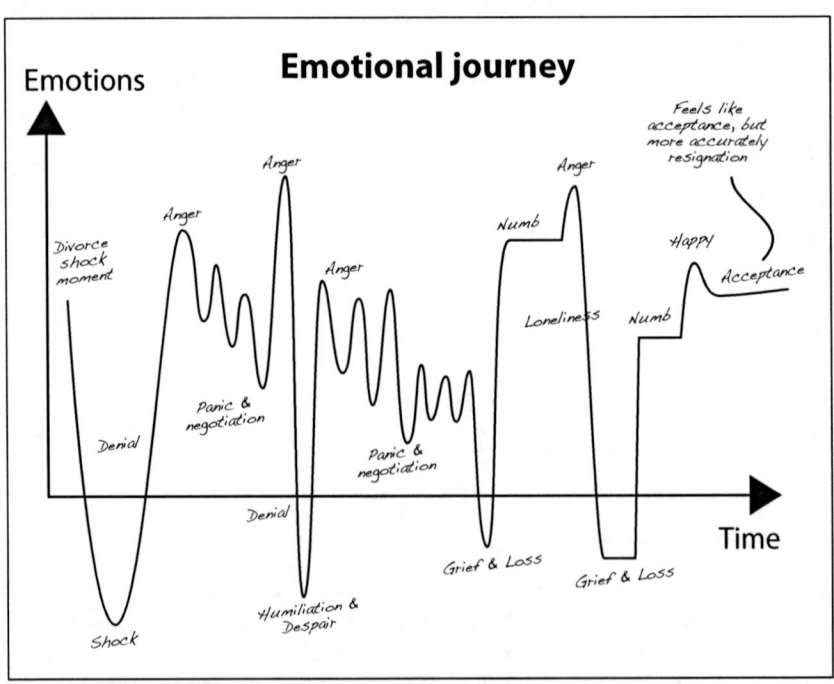

Lucy's rollercoaster started off with a big shock stage, an initial paralysis at hearing the bad news of her husband leaving her. She described it as a big kick in her stomach and an indescribable ache.

This was followed by a denial stage where she spent days trying to avoid the inevitable, telling herself it was not happening. This was followed by an anger and betrayal stage where Lucy was very angry with her husband. Unsure of how to process the emotions she simply ignored them, and began panicking that she had lost him. She spent weeks pleading for him to return, promising to be a better wife to him. When she realized that he wasn't coming back, she again felt anger. She shouted and screamed at him. When he didn't retaliate she felt humiliation and disgust with herself. This disgust soon turned into despair, closely followed by more anger, which she didn't process and more pleading with her husband to take her back.

She momentarily felt grief and loss then went out and slept with a colleague from work. Afterwards she felt numb, briefly angry, then numb again. When the colleague didn't call her back, she was overcome by loneliness and more grief and loss. She then started drinking more alcohol and soon returned to numbness. As the divorce came through, she felt momentary happiness. Her life continued along this path for several years. In the second and third and forth years, she continued the cycle of up and down. The numbness lasted days, then weeks, then months. She said for years, she simply went through the motions in her life. Almost feeling like she was dead inside.

When we started working together five years later, she was feeling very numb and resigned. She told me that life since her divorce was a series of ups and downs and that over time she just felt quite numb and had understood the numbness to be a form of acceptance. Upon examination, we actually found that deep sadness, resentment and anger were still very much present in her life. The numbness was masking the deep grief and upset over her husband leaving her. She has fallen victim to being passive over time and thought that simply the passage of time would cause her healing. We also discovered that she made use of *Short Term Emotion Avoidance Tactics* (S.T.E.A.T.s) like alcohol, food, sex with random strangers, and spending hours and hours at work to avoid feeling the pain of her heartbreak.

She realized then that although she had learnt a great deal during the past five years, she had not healed from her divorce and did not know what to do to heal. She commenced the **naked divorce** journey and achieved the inner peace she had been seeking all those years.

Lucy's emotional rollercoaster is not too dissimilar to any of my client's emotional rollercoaster's after divorce. The problem for Lucy was that there was no knowledge of which emotion was coming next or how long the emotional ride would take.

> **❝** *Go towards the pain. It will hurt but not for long. Be brave, you can do it!* **❞**

Lucy's healing cycle also didn't stop, it kept going for five years and just when she thought she was had healed after an extended period of numbness or false acceptance, she would get knocked back by something that happened in her life and the emotional rollercoaster would speed up again, revealing another emotional dip or bend or loop. To avoid feeling the feelings at each point, she sought out *Short Term Emotion Avoidance Tactics* (S.T.E.A.T.s) to bring her instant relief, and what she didn't know at the time was that those *Short Term Emotion Avoidance Tactics* just prolonged the cycle of the rollercoaster ride. She felt extremely stuck in her life and that there was no way for her to get off the emotional rollercoaster, or exercise any control over decreasing the time on the ride. She was simply strapped into her seat and needed to hold on for the duration of her journey.

I could tell you hundreds of similar stories and to me this is the saddest part about divorce healing – the years of your life that are spent in purgatory. Because there is no clear process to follow to overcome the emotional grief, no grief cycle which maps out what emotion might come next, and no structured support along the way; so everyone deals with divorce as best they can. This can often lead to long-term depression and a lack of contentedness with life.

Lucy was very brave when she proactively confronted and dealt with her emotions so they didn't hang around polluting her life.

The *naked divorce* grieving cycle

The *naked divorce grieving cycle* is something I created based somewhat on the work of Elizabeth Kübler-Ross, my experience as a change management consultant, the invaluable lessons I learnt from my divorce and from studying numerous cases as a *Divorce Angel*.

If you can learn to truly FEEL each emotion and stand strong within it, each layer of emotion will pass and a new emotion will arise.

The emotional highs and lows experienced after a divorce can feel very extreme as they alternate between activity and passivity in our very human and desperate efforts to avoid the change.

The difference between Lucy's emotional journey and the **naked divorce grieving cycle** is that by taking the right courageous steps throughout your healing journey, you are in the driver's seat of your divorce and are not allowing your life to be buffeted around by your emotions.

The initial state before the cycle begins is often quite stable, at least in terms of the subsequent reaction to hearing the bad news (compared with the ups and downs to come, even if there is some variation, this is indeed a fairly stable state).

And then, in the calm of this relative paradise, a bombshell bursts...

The **naked divorce grieving cycle**

1   **Denial stage:** trying to avoid the inevitable.
2   **Anger and betrayal stage:** frustrated outpouring of bottled-up emotion.
3   **Panic and negotiation stage:** seeking a way out. Making deals with your ex.
4   **Humiliation, fear of failure or looking bad stage:** gradually sinking into a spiral, feeling embarrassed and avoiding seeing people.
5   **Despair stage:** realization that something awful is coming your way and you're strapped into the rollercoaster and helpless.
6   **Loss, grief and depression stage:** a final realization of the inevitable, surrendering to the grief.
7   **Space and nothingness stage:** once you have grieved and grieved, experiencing loss and pain, you're left with a feeling of nothingness. It's different to numbness because you feel very present and can notice things around you. Your senses are heightened. You may also find that you cannot cry anymore. You experience an emotional vacuum.
8   **Acceptance stage:** seeking realistic solutions and finally finding the way forward, it's not a feeling of resignation. It's a feeling of profound understanding of the way things are and the way things are not.
9   **Responsibility and forgiveness stage:** taking responsibility for where you may have caused cracks in the relationship and contributed to its subsequent breakdown and divorce. Forgiving your ex and yourself for any failings during the relationship is a critical part of true and real healing.
10 **Gratitude stage:** transformational experience. Learning from your divorce and seeing positives and negatives from the experience. This stage completes the healing.

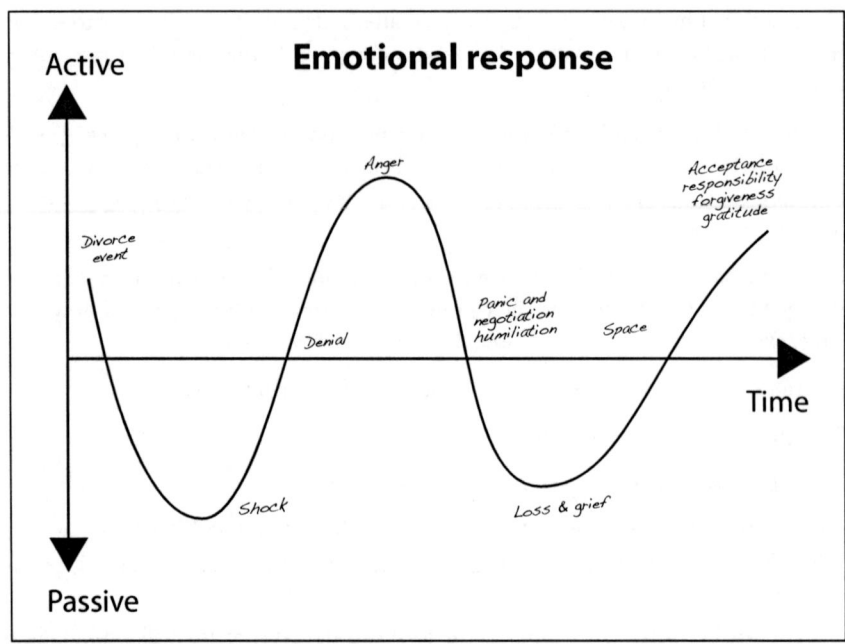

Often, just understanding where you are in the process and accepting that it is a process that you will get through, really helps. It's important to keep in mind that although the graph looks linear, you will bounce between the first six stages many times.

One minute you may be feeling angry and the next minute you're back in despair. But by feeling the emotion deeply and profoundly, it will pass and reveal the next emotional layer. If you avoid *Short Term Emotion Avoidance Tactics* whilst processing your emotions, the emotional rollercoaster will end sooner. It's only when you're finished grieving authentically, to the point of being aware of only space and nothingness around you that will you be truly ready to move through to the advanced stages of the cycle.

By the time you complete the 21-day program you'll achieve those most advanced stages of the **naked divorce** *grieving cycle*.

Tip-

If you would like some idea of where you are within the divorce grieving cycle, you can take the **How Hung Up Are You quiz** *here: http://www.nakeddivorce.com/products/find-out-how-hung-up-you-are/*

Acknowledging and truly feeling your emotions is the key to your healing

In describing the importance of acknowledging our emotional states, American psychologist Dr Maurice Elias says, "emotions are human beings, i.e. warning systems as to what is really going on around them. Emotions are our most reliable indicators of how things are going in our lives. Emotions help keep us on the right track by making sure that we are led by more than the mental/intellectual faculties of thought, perception, reason, and memory."

In her article titled 'How to Understand, Express and Release your Emotions', author Mary Kurus, a renowned psychologist based in New York, writes that emotions control our thinking, behavior and actions. If you ignore, dismiss or repress your feelings, you're setting yourself up for physical illness.

> **" The unconscious mind is the domain of your emotions. To truly heal on an unconscious level, you need to pay attention to your emotions and sensations. ""**

You cannot control your emotions BUT truly acknowledging them and feeling them, allows them to move on

You cannot control your emotions. You can try invalidate them but you cannot actually avoid them. Think of the people who trundle along day after day, seeming to function normally. And then one day they'll suddenly explode over something seemingly trivial or harmless. This behavior is a result of a pressure-cooker syndrome; apply a little heat in the form of a tense situation and repressed emotions boil over. The more you try to control your emotions the more your emotions resist. Eventually you lose emotional control.

It's not popular in today's society to express negative emotions in public. Seeming out of control is interpreted as a sign of weakness. We're often uncomfortable around people who express strong emotions. As a society we're taught to hide our emotions, to be ashamed of them and to be afraid of them, so we talk about our emotions instead of simply feeling them.

It's easy to want to judge our emotions and make some emotions bad or some good. The interesting thing that I have observed in working with so many people is that you cannot turn down the dial of one emotion and simply turn up the dial on another. You can try, but it will feel fake and can kill your true aliveness.

Suppression of anger means your ability to express deep love or peace is also suppressed. Suppression on any level impacts your ability to be truly vulnerable or truly connected with someone else.

To feel MORE in life, you need to turn up the dial to ALL of your emotions - even the undesirable and not-so-nice emotions. Allow yourself to heal THROUGH truly experiencing all of your emotions. All of my clients who experience Day 9 of the *naked divorce* later say that they are no longer afraid or confronted by their emotions and feel a sense of freedom and ease in being with their emotions.

My story:

I was staring into my coffee mug when it dawned on me. I had been experiencing a very deep and anxious depression for over a week. I realized that the depression stemmed from trying to run away from how I was feeling and that it was the running away that was delaying my healing. I was trying to avoid feeling sad, crazy and depressed. The avoidance was debilitating me. After this realization, I began letting go of avoiding all the emotions I was feeling and began to truly feel them. Don't get me wrong – it hurt like hell - but it's still the most profound experience of my life: knowing that my emotions didn't kill me, they made me stronger.

We are emotional creations and we must learn how to know our emotions, be with them, and release them. The journey to becoming a powerful woman includes having the capacity to BE with strong emotions around you. The only way to achieve this state of being is by having the compassion to BE with your own strong emotions. Women used to heal through their emotions for centuries, and it was part of the journey from girl to woman. You will find if you truly feel your emotions, they will carve new powerful womanly characteristics within your psyche.

> **❝** *Healing from divorce is about surrendering to the feelings surrounding the event. Let go and feel each emotion. You will note that each emotion, once truly experienced, does not last much longer than 30 minutes* **❞**

The steps to releasing your emotions

I developed these steps to releasing emotions over many months of trial and error, using a myriad of techniques I'd learnt over the years. They've not only worked for me but they've been effective for my friends and clients.

 Video: I created a YouTube video on the topic of Releasing Emotions. To watch me explaining the concept in more detail, go to **www.youtube.com/nakeddivorce**

STEP 1: Articulate what the emotion is that you're feeling

You start by labeling your emotion. You've heard the expression, "I just don't know how I'm feeling anymore." The *naked divorce* provides a daily exercise to articulate your emotions by selecting the emotion label that mirrors how you're feeling from the table below.

Begin by identifying the emotion as best you can.

For example, feeling fidgety and bored can be an indication of anxiety and panic and at the heart of those emotions is unexpressed despair.

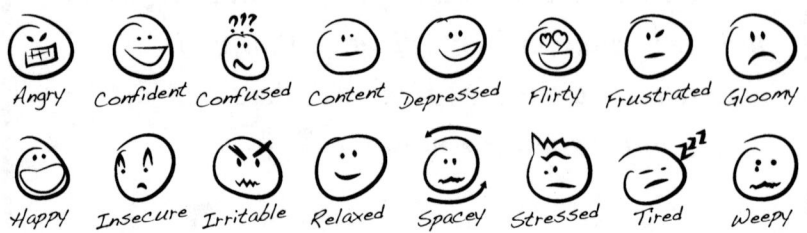

Angry Confident Confused Content Depressed Flirty Frustrated Gloomy

Happy Insecure Irritable Relaxed Spacey Stressed Tired Weepy

I have drawn up an emotional chart for you to assist you in articulating your emotional state. It's not a definitive list as each of us are different, but the list can be used as a prompt to help you think about your feelings and work out which emotion your physical sensations represent. Understanding your emotions is key to really getting to know yourself better.

Possible Physical sensations	What you may be telling yourself	Possible Emotions
Pain in the chest, nausea, numbness against the skin, an inability to concentrate or stomach anything.	• This is not really happening. • This cannot be happening.	Denial, shock, heartbreak.
Fiery feeling in the chest, heartburn, feeling fidgety accompanied by a need to shout or scream, like you cannot sit still, fists want to clench, tightness in throat.	• How could you? • Why is this happening to me? • Why does this always happen to me? • Why me? • This is not fair! • I feel so much rage!	Irritability, Anger, sense of betrayal.

Feeling fidgety and restless accompanied by an ache. Cannot sleep, pain in your chest, feeling that you will hyperventilate, panic sensations across your skin, fluttering in your throat, heart palpitations, stomach ache, feeling crazy.	• I can fix this. • If I just do X and Y, he will come back to me. • Explanations for what happened and making excuses for him. • Bargaining with him to get him back. • The feeling that the ex is like a drug accompanied by wondering how I will get over my addiction to this person. • Strapped into the rollercoaster, helpless. Total panic and feel like melting down. • Feel completely out of control. • Want to run away/numb the pain with alcohol/drugs/seeing people/food. • Restless/not at peace. • House/routine descends into chaos. • Feel like going crazy and driving car into a wall.	Anxiety, desperation, craziness and despair accompanied by a sense of needing to bargain and negotiate.
Cannot get out of bed, don't like bright lights, want to run away and hide.	• Withdrawal/hiding. • Beating yourself up. • Can't talk to anyone about this. • Pretending everything is fine when it's not. • Doing things out of character to prove you are fine.	Denial, humiliation, shame and a fear of failure.
Pain in chest, can't stop crying, can't sleep/eat/function normally. The feeling that you are dying inside.	• Oh no, this is really happening! • My heart feels ripped out. • I think I may do something to myself. • Moping around the house. • Feel like a zombie. • Feeling desperate and lonely. • Morose thoughts. Will I ever recover? • Emotions are overwhelming. • Can't function. • It's all my fault, I failed.	Loss, grief and depression.
Feel quiet and empty, but not grieving any more. Feel alert and present. Can't cry any more. Feel nothingness. Noticing things around you: cars, birds, trees, washing not done.	• No thoughts. Your mind is quiet. You are present and feel at peace with everything. • Getting into action again.	Space and nothingness.
No more pain in your chest or body, a feeling that life goes on and everything will be ok.	• I am OK. Went through hell and I am still here. • I can cope and haven't died of a broken heart. • Realizing that the relationship was actually not that good for me. I am able to see both sides. • The fairy tale is gone and I am actually OK with that.	Understanding everything accompanied by feeling victorious, proud and accepting of the situation.
Head up, shoulders back, standing tall.	• I failed in the following areas... • I can acknowledge and take ownership of my part in the divorce. • I can see how I contributed to the divorce without beating myself up.	Taking responsibility. Being courageous, strong, peaceful and clear.
Relaxed body posture, a sensation of gliding rather than walking.	• This has happened and I am so grateful it did. I have learnt so much. I am in a better place.	Grateful, happy and at peace.

STEP 2: Ensure you're in a safe place before expressing your emotions

Ensure you're in a safe space before expressing your emotions. You shouldn't be at work or in a public place. You need a private space where you're free to let go and express yourself. So find a room or a quiet location to let go. I alternated between driving my car to a remote location, using a back room in my house or a hotel room. It is incredible how soundproof hotel rooms are (well at least I hope so!).

STEP 3: Fully feel your emotions whilst keeping your heart open

There's no need to fear your emotions. Don't fight them, run away from them or block them. Regardless of what they represent, welcome them in, hug them towards yourself and be with them. Emotions dissipate and slowly disappear if you feel them and allow yourself to be present with them. Close your eyes and feel them as deeply as you can. You know that sensation when you have sat in the bath for too long and your skin becomes 'pruney'? In the same way, feel your emotions until you get pruney and are naturally ready to let them go. Whilst feeling your emotions, keep your heart open. What this means is FEEL the emotions deeply but allow each emotion to wash over you and not become stuck anywhere in your body or in anger within your heart. Keep feeling the one emotion till it moves onto the next emotion, allowing a natural movement.

There are several ways you can begin to release your emotions, especially those related to anger and hurt.

1. Go into an empty room, put a pillow over your mouth and scream. Or go for a drive alone, pull over at the side of the road and shout it all out. Do it as loudly as you can. Scream the words, "I hate being hurt!", or whatever it is you're feeling. So many people have never screamed out their hurt or their rage. Continue to do this as long as it feels right inside. And allow yourself to cry your feelings out.

2. If you don't have the space to scream aloud, imagine you are screaming out your rage, hurt, and pain. Imagine it completely. See it, and hear it and feel it as deeply as you can.

My story:

> I remember screaming for 20 minutes. I kept shouting, "Rage! Rage! Rage!"
> I fully felt every part of that rage in every part of my body. I did not stop until it felt like the emotion was gone. By doing this, I released the emotion to ensure no blockages occurred within my body. It was exhausting but felt fantastic.

3. If you're a physical person, take a pillow, take a stick and hit something, feeling your hurt every time you lash out. Each time you hit out, say the words, "I hate being hurt!" or, "I'm so f*&^%^ upset!" or whatever it is that you are feeling.

4. If you like to write, write about your anger, your hate, sadness, upset, frustration or disappointment.

Tip-

One of the most important things about releasing an emotion is to concentrate on the emotion rather than what caused the emotion. Forget who did what to you. Concentrate on the "I hate xxx" or "I'm SO angry" or "I'm SO hurt". It's the emotion you need to release.

STEP 4 – Acknowledge yourself and drink water

Expressing emotions is thirsty work. You may even lose your voice a little. When you're done expressing your emotions, stop, breathe, and then drink a big glass of water. Sit quietly and notice what you're present to. When you've fully expressed your emotions, you will probably be feeling a sense of what I call space, or nothingness, which is step seven in the **naked divorce grieving cycle**.

Foundation #4 PERFORMING AT WORK

Your career VS your divorce

Keeping your career on track while coping with a divorce is like juggling eggs: you have to remain focused to continue performing, and falling apart is not an option.

The *naked divorce* program has been designed to provide a structure for your healing while you work and, if you have children, manage your family. In the *naked divorce* you will proactively tackle your healing every day, in the mornings, in the evenings and over weekends, so that your emotions do not sneak up on you. The office is no place to vent your repressed feelings, but if that's where you find yourself when a rage attack threatens, there's an exercise at the end of this section that will help you remain calm and at peace.

The *naked divorce* etiquette for dealing with your divorce at work

The general rule of thumb when facing divorce is that you should take leave from work to gather yourself and even three or four days will do. Not only will you need this time to be alone to think, but you'll need privacy to do so.

Some people find they need a routine to carry them through a crisis and the comfort of routine is one thing, but be wary of throwing yourself into work as a distraction too soon. When you do go back to work, there are some tips that are helpful.

General tips:

 It's very common to feel foggy and unclear during the first few weeks of a divorce, as your mind is preoccupied with feelings. It's therefore a good idea to write down all action points and notes from meetings so that you have a reference. Pay special attention to requests being made of you. Write everything down.

 Ensure you communicate clearly about what you are willing to take on and what time frame you can commit to for those outputs. Add on a buffer of 30% to all deadlines as you won't be your usual, productive self.

 Make a point of taking a lunch break each day for a few weeks. Leave the office and take a walk. It's important to take time out when you're under severe stress.

 To remain calm at work drink a great deal of chamomile tea and use Rescue Remedy drops on a regular basis.

 A great way to remain calm and focused at work or to relax when heartbreak threatens to overwhelm you is to listen to the **naked divorce** Break Up Reboot. Download your complimentary program today at: www.nakeddivorce.com/book.

Video: Listen to more tips about handling your career during divorce by watching the videos at: **www.youtube.com/nakeddivorce**

> ❝ *Take eye drops and good, soft tissues to work. If you find you need a good crying session in the bathroom, use the eye drops so that your emotional state is not overly obvious to everyone.* ❞

 If possible, don't discuss the details of your divorce with your colleagues. Even if they're good friends, discuss details outside of work and only with those you know will not make your divorce the office gossip of the day. Avoid crying sessions with your colleagues at a bar. I know that it can be delicious to win the sympathy vote, but this strategy is not easy to come back from. Having the details of your divorce batted about the office will only add to your stress and

this could therefore count against you if you are looking to climb the corporate ladder later on.

The *naked divorce* etiquette for handling your boss at work

⇨ Firstly, tell your boss what you're dealing with. Do this in a brief and matter-of-fact way. Ask for a few days off. Deal with any urgent matters that won't wait until your return to the office. If you think you might get overly emotional, write a formal email or letter.

⇨ No matter how evolved your workplace may be, most working environments are not equipped to handle an employee's personal issues. Unfortunately divorce is a personal issue. HR departments are often unsympathetic and do not offer adequate support (certainly in the cases I have seen and experienced).

⇨ Keep in mind, although it's hard to hear, you are hired to do a job. All your firm cares about is whether or not you can do the job you are hired to do. Your firm does not owe you anything as most companies expect their employees to leave their personal issues at home. Therefore, try to remain professional and as unemotional as possible. If you feel yourself getting emotional, excuse yourself and leave the building for 10 minutes. A personal tip from me is don't let others see you being overly emotional if possible, they might judge your competency based on your ability to handle strong emotional stress.

 Newsletter: In my weekly newsletter, you will find lots of tips, techniques and letter templates for dealing with your boss. Sign up at: **www.nakeddivorce.com**

⇨ Communicate very clearly with your boss about what he or she can and can't count on from you. Give deadlines and try your best to stick to them. However, if it looks like you are struggling to meet a deadline, communicate with your boss immediately and recommit to what is possible.

⇨ Your colleagues and boss will be looking to see if you are working less hours. Therefore, unless you have permission to work less, work the full-allotted time you are hired to work. If you arrive late, communicate immediately that you are going to be late AND ensure you work later to make up the time.

⇨ If you have the option to work from home, do so. It's easier to maintain professional etiquette via email than to be around the colleagues and people you work with everyday when you're dealing with raw emotions.

⇨ Inform the accounts department as soon as possible about your pending divorce as your tax code may change. If you feel nervous about calling and aren't feeling organized, prepare a list of things to communicate and email this through. Ensure that you include your current tax code in the email.

The *naked divorce* etiquette for handling your divorce at work if you are the boss

⇨ If you are the boss going through a divorce, the key thing is appoint someone you trust to delegate responsibilities to. Explain to this person that you are dealing with some personal issues at home (don't get into specifics) and that you will require some extra support in the coming weeks.

Tip-

Delegating during your divorce is not only a stress reliever for you, it's a great opportunity for others to shine and take leadership in your team. Empower them with new responsibilities.

⇨ When you delegate, be very specific about what outcomes need to be achieved. Have a discussion with this person or people about what you envisage and what the end game is and ask them to build plans for how those outcomes are to be achieved. Ask them to break the tasks down as much as possible.

⇨ Once everything is handled and you have a structure in place to achieve the outcomes laid out, take some time off to handle your personal situation.

➡️ If you have a very close-knit team share with them what is going on, but keep it brief. This is not the time to get the sympathy vote or try to get everyone to feel sorry for you. It's important to remain powerful and grounded in their eyes. This will win their respect and regard in more ways than one.

➡️ Even if you have close relationships with clients, I wouldn't recommend telling them about your divorce. Simply mention you are taking some time off and who their contact person is whilst you are away.

➡️ If necessary: check in with your team whilst you are away to ensure that the delegation has worked successfully. This will give you peace of mind.

The *naked divorce* etiquette for handling your divorce if you have your own business

➡️ This is the tough one and I can tell you from personal experience, that driving ways to earn money whilst feeling raw emotions is not an easy thing to do.

➡️ I recommend getting the healing over with as soon as possible so you can get back to earning money. If you delay your healing, you may begin attracting all kinds of negativity to your business. Prioritize getting over your divorce as soon as possible so you can get back to work.

This is what I recommend:

1) Focus on the **Foundation of Transformation #1: ETHICS**. In particular, establish a Grounded Routine and avoid Short Term Emotion Avoidance Tactics so you can prioritize your healing.

2) Focus on **Foundation of Transformation #2: NOURISHMENT** as soon as possible.

3) Prioritize starting the *naked divorce* program as soon as possible so you establish the *Divorce Cocoon* and manage it being in place. Personal performance is a function of stability and routine. Not having this in place will make your mind scatty and keep you unproductive.

➡️ For entrepreneurs, the *naked divorce* really comes into its own as we are the people who cannot afford to lose pace with our businesses. Keeping your mind in the game is essential to success so following the steps in the program will assist you with this.

➡️ It really depends on how big your business is. If you have a team (even if it's small), try to delegate wherever possible but check in with your team as often as you can to ensure objectives are still being met. Follow the tips above for managing your divorce if you are the boss.

If you don't have a team and you are self-employed, what I recommend is to:

⇨ Take some time-out if possible, to ensure your living arrangements and personal situation is stabilized again.

⇨ Communicate with your clients that you have a personal emergency to deal with and when you will be back at work. Let them know how your account-abilities will be handled in your absence.

⇨ If you cannot take time-out, get clear on all your revenue and expenses and work out exactly what your financial requirements are and by when.

⇨ If you don't think you can keep to your financial commitments, then get into immediate communication with your creditors and work out a plan, ensuring you lower your expenses as much as possible to ride the storm.

⇨ Follow the general tips covered earlier.

⇨ Ensure you sleep more, eat healthily and take care of yourself.

The *naked divorce* exercise for handling your emotions whilst you are at work

When you feel you need to put your emotions aside to focus on your work, practice the following exercise. Cycle through the four 'A' words:

Be **A**ware of the emotion.

Accept the emotion.

Acknowledge your right to your emotion.

Act normal.

This is how it works:

1. When feeling overly emotional, stop.
    1. Stop doing anything.
    2. Just sit.
    3. Be still.
2. Breathe.
    1. Breathe long and deeply, right into your belly.
    2. Let the breath fill your lungs like the ocean surging up the shore.
    3. Breathe like this for 20 breaths. And if you cry, you cry.
3. Become **aware** of what is happening. It's simply the increase of Cortisol and Dopamine combined with the depletion of Serotonin which are contributing

to feelings of depression or craziness. It's an uncomfortable feeling, but it will pass if you let yourself be with it and keep taking your **naked divorce Daily Divorce Healing** vitamins.

4. Visualize. Liken the erratic emotions to a puppy that has run off without a leash. Understand that your emotions cannot be controlled, whilst at the same time you do not need to engage with them. Allow the emotions to simply be. Just notice them. Watch them and remain calm whilst breathing deeply. Try to describe the emotional form. What is the emotion's color, texture and shape? Give that part of yourself that feels crazy a label, or a name like Red Dragon, or Mad Dog. Ask the emotion, "What am I to learn from you? What will set me free from you?"

5. **Accept** and acknowledge the craziness and anxiety. If you allow yourself to see the emotions as visitors, they will eventually pass.

6. No matter how you're feeling at that moment, behave normally. **Act completely normally**. Even if it feels fake, it doesn't matter. You will have time to process these emotions later in the day when it's appropriate. You know that the craziness will pass. (Acting normal whilst feeling crazy emotions is a great Cognitive Behavioral Therapy technique and works very effectively.)

7. Make yourself a hot water drink. Chamomile or peppermint tea is very soothing. Alternatively, add some lemon and two teaspoons of honey to a cup of boiling water. Drink it slowly. With each sip, sense the craziness retreating, like a tide. Calm down.

8. Take a walk outside if you can. Walk slowly and gracefully, as if you're gliding. While walking, cycle through your five senses and ask yourself, "what do I see, hear, touch, taste and smell?" Keep the focus outside your mind and on what's around you. Be vigilant about looking at your surroundings rather than listening to the voice in your head.

9. Remind yourself that there will be an opportunity to feel your emotions when you're in a safe space later.

10. Remind yourself that everything will be okay. Think of all the things that people have overcome in their lives. Think of someone who has overcome immense obstacles to achieve greatness and beauty in their lives. This can be you.

Foundation #5: COMMITMENT

Commitment = Results

When you make a choice to heal and let nothing else stand in the way of your success, something fundamentally changes and your choice begins to shape your future and ultimately, your destiny.

> *Until one is committed, there is hesitancy, the chance to draw back, always ineffectiveness. Concerning all acts of initiative (and creation), there is one elementary truth the ignorance of which kills countless ideas and splendid plans. The moment one definitely commits oneself, then providence moves, too. All sorts of things occur to help one that would never otherwise have occurred. A whole stream of events issue from the decision, raising in one's favor all manner of unforeseen incidents and meetings and material assistance, which no man could have dreamed would have come his way. Whatever you can do, or dream you can, begin it. Boldness has genius, power and magic in it. Begin it now.*
>
> *Johann Wolfgang Von Goethe*

What humans tend to do in life is check things out before committing. We try something out for a while, and if we like it and it sits comfortably with us we will commit to it. I want you to consider that to truly get over this divorce and move on with your life, free from the bounds of the past, requires great commitment. You need to commit first and then work out all the logistics, issues and factors inside your powerful commitment.

In life there are many logical reasons why you should delay healing from your divorce, "I have to get the kids to school", "I have an important board meeting coming up, and deadlines" or, "I don't have time to do this program, I am far too busy." What is powerful is not letting these circumstances rule your life. If you CHOOSE to heal, then you will be willing to do whatever it takes to achieve your goal. If you focus on how hard your life is and how you cannot fit the program in, then you will give up the moment it gets tough. HOWEVER, if you make a powerful choice, you will be propelled towards the inevitable: healing completely from your divorce within 21 days.

Commitment assumes the courage to make declarations you don't know how to fulfill and then working out how to make those declarations come true.

My story:

I think it was the day I found I'd broken every glass in my kitchen that I realized I didn't want to feel like a basket case any longer. I wanted to get over my divorce. I'd run out of reasons and excuses. I wanted to take action. I'd reached a place of recognition; I knew I was going to move on, come hell or high water. You will arrive at this place of recognition when you know you're willing to do whatever it takes to move on.

So, my question to you is this:

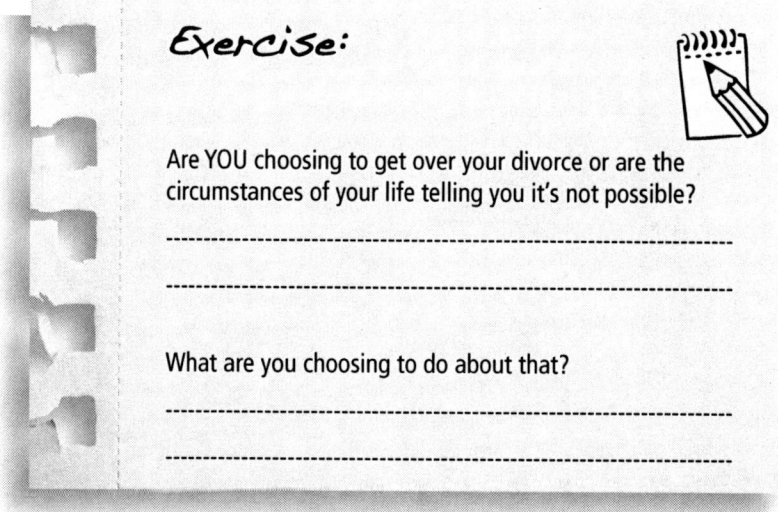

Exercise:

Are YOU choosing to get over your divorce or are the circumstances of your life telling you it's not possible?

What are you choosing to do about that?

Set yourself up for success

Minimize contact with your ex

If you are just getting divorced and still feeling raw from your break up, minimize contact with your ex, particularly during the first 15 days. Continued contact with your ex during the *naked divorce* could lead to confusion and may lead you off the track, feeding your needy side.

Help yourself first

To ensure that you're ready and able to support your children through the trauma of divorce, or get back to managing your team at work or leading a project again, help yourself first. Without helping yourself first, you'll be in no position to help anyone who relies on you.

Foundation #6: THE RIGHT SUPPORT

Why your friends and family are sometimes the worst support during your divorce

Although your friends and family are an important part of your life, you may find that they're ill equipped to support you through your loss. I found that even though my friends and family were well meaning, they didn't know what to say to me and I often didn't feel better around them.

Before you chuck up this well-meaning lot, remember that although they're trying hard, they're just not equipped or trained to help you. Society has conditioned them to deal with loss in a particular way. It's not their fault. They love you very much and they hate to see you suffering. They'll try to take the pain away and will do whatever they can in the moment to achieve this.

Whenever I hung out my friends they would try to distract me from the pain I was feeling or unknowingly invalidate my emotions and my right to feel lousy. I'd leave feeling superficially better but also feeling as if I'd moved two steps backwards. I soon realized that I'd have to get divorce support elsewhere.

Bear these in mind about some of your friends and family (you'll probably recognize some of the points below.)

They may say weird or inappropriate things

We've all been there; the awkward moment where you say something you wish you didn't say. Family and friends often succumb to some old clichés in their struggle to try and make things better. They are all attempts to move you out of your emotional state but these statements are often damaging to your overall healing.

Common phrases my clients have heard include:

- "Thank goodness this happened before you had children."
- "God will never give you more than you can handle."
- "You'll find someone else."

- "There's someone special out there for you."
- "It's better to have loved and lost than not to have loved at all."
- "Be grateful you were once married and knew love."
- "Now you are free to relive your teenage dreams of being single."

These are awful platitudes designed to make you feel better. But they don't!

You cannot fix matters of the heart with intellectualizations of the mind. These statements do not encourage your healing.

They have no idea what to say, so sometimes they change the subject

When I was young I attended my best friend's mum's funeral. I felt so awkward. I was standing next to my friend and her face was a picture of despair and grief. We'd been playing dolls a week earlier and now I had no idea what to say. I stared at my shoes. I couldn't wait to get out of the church and away from the coffin and her pain. I looked at her and cracked a joke, trying to lighten the atmosphere. She didn't look up. She simply turned and walked away.

You've probably experienced this with one or two of your friends. When you talk about your divorce, they change the subject, pretend not to hear you, or crack a joke. They do this because they love you, they want to make things better for you, but they have no idea what to do. Understand their ineptitude.

Some want to revel in the drama

Some family and friends love the drama of your situation. They will ask to know everything about it so that they can revel in the excitement and intrigue of your divorce as a distraction from their own lives. Be wary of these people because getting into the drama of your divorce will not help you.

They don't want to talk about divorce

After a while you'll realize that some of your friends and family simply don't want to talk about your divorce and will encourage you to do things to get over it so that hanging out with you is fun again. The bottom line is - you need to talk. You need to be heard. You do not need fixing. There is nothing wrong with you or the fact that you're emotional or struggling.

They are afraid of catching this disease called divorce

I remember coming home after a night out with a girlfriend, feeling awful and deflated, like an insect that had been squashed and scraped across a pavement.

I had just recounted my divorce story (okay, it was the second time) but halfway through, she looked out the window, absorbed in her own world. I was shocked. Had I said something wrong? Was I boring her? Was she disinterested?

She then changed the subject.

While I sat listening to her rattling on about some issue at work, the conversation in my head went something like this:

- "It's okay for everyone that I feel the pain, but I cannot appear to be floundering."
- "I am expected to discuss the divorce with my friends only once (don't overdo it as no one wants to hang around with a basket case)."
- "I mustn't mope around because it's not healthy. It also makes people feel awkward."
- "But while falling apart I can't seem too happy either. That would brand me as insensitive or immature."

I realized that I was alone in my divorce. I had caught the disease called divorce and this made me persona-non-grata. When I mentioned my ex husband's indiscretions, I knew she was wondering about her own husband. I could see that all she wanted to do was go home to check that they were okay. (Months later she admitted this was the case.) I excused myself and gave her the opportunity to do that. I know my friend felt awkward. She wanted to help but didn't know what to say. I remember the same feelings of inadequacy at my friend's mother's funeral.

Myths about getting over your divorce

Friends are fantastic, but they all have their own lives and issues. I was the only one that could help me.

In the table on the next page are some common phrases that my clients have told themselves in the past or have heard others say.

Myths about getting over your divorce	The deeper 'meaning' you may have taken on board about loss...
Don't cry	Don't feel bad
There are many fish in the sea	Replace the loss with something else quick
Be by yourself	Grieve alone
Time heals all wounds	Just give it time and the numbness I feel is actually acceptance
Be strong for my children/mother/brother	Be strong for others and don't show my emotions
I must stay active	Keep busy and distract myself from my emotions
I mustn't fall apart	Don't drown in my emotions
Don't mope around	I must bounce back quickly or I will have no friends left
Don't bring my emotional baggage into the office	It's not OK to express my emotions
Don't fall in love with anyone else too soon	Rebound relationships are bad

WARNING:

Be wary of buying into any kind of intellectual theorizing. Ban all these phrases from your head.

Give your family and friends a *Weirdness Pass*

Give the people in your life a *Weirdness Pass* which is a ticket allowing your loved ones to say weird or inappropriate things while you're dealing with your divorce.

They don't know any better and no one trained them on how to deal with the situation.

Remember not to take on board anything that they say. Remain aware of what they are saying, and of the myths and possible generalizations in their comments, to guard against becoming embroiled in their intellectualizations.

Weirdness Pass

This card gives the bearer a Pass for Weirdness

Simply hand over this card to anyone, to
give them the right to be weird around you

Exercise:

Are any of these myths, intellectualizations or thoughts
shared above, familiar to you? What myths about divorce
have you found yourself buying into?

Which friends or family members have you noticed are
being a bit unsupportive?

Can you find it within yourself to give them a *Weirdness
Pass* so you can forgive their ineptitude?

Divorce Angel

Appoint a *Divorce Angel*. This should be someone in your life who is preferably not a close friend or family member but someone you can discuss your **naked divorce** experience with.

Your *Divorce Angel* is your champion who will walk alongside you in the darkness of your divorce, back into the light.

Be careful whom you choose. If you select someone who dislikes your former husband or has any kind of agenda for you or your life, each discussion could turn into a rant session. Also, someone you know too well could feel too much empathy for you. This could impede your progress.

When choosing your *Divorce Angel*, avoid a person that:

✘ has tumultuous personal relationships.

✘ likes to talk about themselves a great deal.

✘ is opinionated or bossy.

✘ likes to tell you what to do.

✘ will feel sorry for you or see you as a victim in a bad situation.

✘ dislikes or hates your ex.

✘ is so involved with their own life that they will abandon you.

✘ has a hidden agenda where you are concerned.

Your *Divorce Angel* should be someone that:

✔ you don't necessarily know that well, someone who won't buy into any of your drama.

✔ is wise and has it together.

✔ has successful and healthy personal relationships.

✔ is not afraid to tell you the truth.

✔ cares about you and is willing to commit to you being empowered.

✔ will stick with you through this program.

It's important to understand that your *Divorce Angel's* job isn't to be your therapist or a shoulder to cry on. They're there to help you stay on track and to ensure you're taking care of yourself.

Make a list of five potential *Divorce Angels*. Pick the first one and make a time to talk. Be honest with them. Show this book to them and ask if they will be available for discussions and some of the homework exercises.

Ask if it's okay for you to check in with them once a day, for no more than 15 minutes, during the 21-day program.

If they agree (well done!), ask them to read through the guidelines for the *Divorce Angel* and ask them to sign the declarations and commitments at the end of this section.

If they don't agree, don't take it personally. It is a commitment and a responsibility that some might not have the time for. Move on to the next person on your list until you find your *Divorce Angel*.

WARNING:

I don't recommend doing the *naked divorce* without a *Divorce Angel*. The program was designed to be done with a *Divorce Angel* at your side.

If you wish to have an impartial super-trained *naked divorce* coach to be your personal *Divorce Angel*, feel you require any additional support, or just want to do the program with people like you (so much more fun) you can join the many *naked divorce* support programs by checking **www.nakeddivorce.com** for more information.

The Divorce Angel guidelines

So your friend asked you to be their *Divorce Angel*. That's a fantastic honor and says a great deal about you. If you're thinking it's a big responsibility and you are accountable for her healing, relax. This is not therapy and you are not her therapist. All you need is a pair of listening ears, some patience and a commitment to follow the guidelines below during your 21 days of support. The most important thing is to check in with her daily and watch out for the warning signs.

I, _____

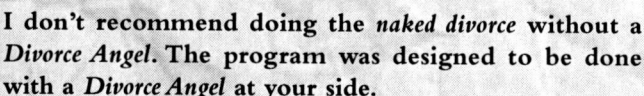

☐ understand that it is NOT MY JOB to get her over her divorce. She has to do the *naked divorce* on her own.

☐ know that my job is to listen to her and not to offer any advice.

☐ commit to be vigilant and watch out for any warning signs (covered at the end of this chapter) and am aware of the Notice of Important Information and Health Warnings (at the end of the chapter called

Time to Choose). If I notice anything out of the ordinary, I will notify her doctor, family or the *naked divorce* team immediately. I have their contact information.

☐ understand that it's okay to set limits. I have a life, too, and I don't want to be taken advantage of. If 15 minutes on the phone is all I can do, then that's cool. I will let her know when I am available and what to do in case of emergency meltdowns.

☐ will put aside any personal feelings I have about her ex. I will focus on how she can heal from her divorce and how she can bounce back within 21 days.

☐ will take a stand and be honest with her. I will not allow her to sink into bitterness, resentment or victim-type behavior. My job is not to be nice. My job is to challenge any negative thoughts and instead of giving her solutions I will ask her open questions about the impact of her behavior on her life.

☐ promise to keep everything she shares absolutely confidential. Absolute confidentiality means that I carry any personal information she shared to the grave with me.

☐ understand that the 21-day program is designed to be the duration it is designed to be. I will support her to push herself through the eye of the needle but if she needs to slow down, I will support her wishes.

☐ will not compare my healing to hers. I understand that she is an individual and it's essential for her to heal from her divorce in her own way. I will endeavor to respect her individuality.

☐ will be vigilant about using disempowering language. I have read this entire chapter and will guard against offering general, intellectualized encouragements for healing.

☐ understand that people struggle to stay committed to something big in life. I will endeavor to support her in completing the *naked divorce*.

----
naked divorce participant

Date

Divorce Angel

Date

The *naked divorce* warning signs

It is completely normal and appropriate to feel extreme sadness and a complete loss of control as the result of a divorce. It is normal to feel hopeless and helpless. It is normal to feel you want to withdraw from life to grieve and get over your lost relationship. It is also normal to feel numb and to wonder about dying, but only if this is a passing thought.

If you're dwelling on morbid thoughts, you need to address them. Below are the warning signs to watch out for. Contact your doctor, family or the *naked divorce* team if you suspect you're moving into dangerous territory.

My story:

I lived very recklessly for a few days after my divorce. I was driving my car, feeling very numb to everyone and everything around me. I wanted to feel alive again so I hit the accelerator. The car went faster and faster. I didn't care. Suddenly the road curved to the left. I was seconds from colliding with a wall and even though I saw it, for a moment I wondered how it would feel to crash. I pulled over and sobbed, knowing that, I had hit a metaphorical wall. I vowed at that moment to take better care of myself and stop being reckless with my life. I also chose to forgive myself for the rash behavior, understanding that the numbness I was feeling was part of the healing cycle.

www.suicide.org advises a full list of warning signs that you can review. I have re-written this list as I believe the behaviors described should be red-flagged only if they are above and beyond what is reasonable for someone dealing with divorce.

Please review the warning signs below with your *Divorce Angel* and ensure that when you check in with them, that your *Divorce Angel* keeps these warning signs in mind.

Normal feelings that should be monitored if they continue longer than seven weeks:

⇨ Feeling hopeless and helpless.

⇨ Experiencing dramatic mood changes.

⇨ Exhibiting an extreme change in personality.

⇨ Losing interest in most activities.

⇨ Experiencing an extreme change in sleeping habits.

⇨ Experiencing an extreme change in eating habits.

⇨ Performing poorly at work.

If you experience these symptoms, please seek help from your doctor immediately:

⇨ Appearing depressed most of the time.

⇨ Talking or writing about death or suicide OR planning your death.

⇨ Withdrawing completely from family and friends for an extended period.

⇨ Feeling trapped; feeling there is no way out of the situation.

⇨ Abusing drugs or alcohol.

⇨ Exhibiting a change in personality – above what is reasonable for your divorce.

⇨ Giving away prized possessions.

⇨ Feeling excessive guilt or shame.

⇨ Acting recklessly. Emotional loss will already have impaired your concentration levels. As a result, impulsive behavior could place you in danger.

Be responsible for your well-being during the *naked divorce* 21-day program and keep a vigilant watch over the above warning signs.

Foundation #7: A GAME PLAN THAT WORKS

It's important to have a game plan for the program so you are ready for it and have scheduled it in.

This is what you need to know

People are creatures of habit. Research shows that those who participate in a daily routine are three times more likely to stay on course than those who participate in that routine six days a week. They also fare five times better than those who participate three, four or five days a week. Therefore, for best results, work daily for all of the 21 days. If you miss a day, simply start again the following day.

Be kind to yourself. The mind does not like change and your divorce, as well as tackling the *naked divorce*, represents change. Your mind may tell you that it doesn't like the program, that it won't do any good, or that you don't have the time. Don't listen! Simply tell your mind, "Thank you for sharing that" and do the program!

The *naked divorce* will take approximately 90-120 minutes each day during the week and a bit longer over the weekends, supporting your healing process after the break up. Each exercise will take as long as it takes. The program has been designed to run over 21 days. You may take longer than 21 calendar days, just ensure you follow the order of the days and don't skip over any exercises.

If you need a day off, that's okay too. Provided you complete all the exercises in whatever timeframe works for you, you will find yourself bouncing back quicker and feeling better about yourself and your past relationship. Your ability to move on will be accelerated.

The best way to use the *naked divorce* is to read through each of the days carefully. Do this a couple of times so you're quite clear about each step. Then work through it methodically, putting 100% of your concentration and commitment to work for you. Remain open and watch for miracles. If you find yourself feeling lucky at any time during this program, make sure you acknowledge your good fortune and yourself for all the good work you've done.

What you must do PRIOR to commencing the program:

STEP 1: Go to the end of the book and print out the Daily Checklist 21 times and paste into a book. Alternatively, go to www.nakeddivorce.com/book and download the workbook which has the Daily Checklist printed out 21 times as well as other important components to keep in mind during your program

STEP 2: Go to www.nakeddivorce.com/book to download the Break Up Reboot which is a healing journey that will end the hurt, speed up your recovery process, and open your heart to love again. Listen to this recording daily for 21 days during the *naked divorce* to help you heal faster.

STEP 3: Go to the end of the book and print out the Daily Declarations and laminate them. Buy all the items in the Shopping list and handle all the elements within the *Things to Handle* list

STEP 4: Ensure you have a *Divorce Angel*.

STEP 5: Overhaul your eating habits and diet as per the book. Ensure you use supplements to help you

Please note: Make it easy for yourself and purchase one of the *naked divorce* packages that include all the shopping list items, 21-day workbook, Break Up Reboot, Daily Declarations Divorce healing vitamins and much much more!

WARNING: Do not proceed with the program without the Daily Checklist. It is critical to do the exercises, the reading, listen to the Break Up Reboot and follow the Daily Checklist daily. The *naked divorce* is designed in a very particular way to achieve certain objectives.

Tip-

SHARE ANY MIRACLES

Either at
www.nakeddivorce.com

Or by emailing
mystory@nakeddivorce.com

We would love to hear what you
are creating!

What you will be doing daily

Daily Instructions

1. Begin each day by taking your supplements and drinking a hot cup of water and lemon. This will rejuvenate you.

2. Open up this guide or your download workbook and fill in the date.

3. Read the lesson for the day and read the exercise to be done. Allow your mind to think about the answers for the exercise during the day.

4. Complete the Daily Conditioning Processes for that day.

5. Take your **naked divorce** Journal with you wherever you go so you can work on your homework during the day.

6. In the evening after dinner, avoid television and spend time working on your homework for the day.

Daily conditioning processes

The 'I feel' process

You can become numb to your emotions while healing from your divorce. As a woman, it is vital that you remain present to your feelings. Give yourself permission to feel and be deserving of your feelings, whatever these are. This exercise is designed to make you aware of how you are feeling and what those emotions are. The exercise works especially well in the mornings and gives you an opportunity to take time every day to keep track of how you are feeling.

Daily Declarations

This exercise also works well in the mornings. I recommend getting the Daily Declarations (printed at the end of the book or available for download) laminated and sticking them up in your shower. Complete the Daily Declarations in front of the mirror or while you shower each morning. Put your hand over your chest to feel the vibrational energy of your statements. Read the declarations out loud and with conviction. After some time you'll notice a shift in how you feel about yourself. Almost all of my clients are completely addicted to their Daily Declarations now. One of my clients, Sue, actually said that although a year has passed since she completed the *naked divorce*, she still does the Daily Declarations because they make her feel so good.

The 'acknowledge your successes' process

This exercise works well in the evening before bed. Like-attracts-like and success-breeds-success. The more you feel that you are wonderfully made, and awesome partner material, the more amazing things will come your way. You cannot feel fantastic about yourself if you do not look for and acknowledge your successes. The successes can be major or minor. It doesn't matter. What matters is that you acknowledge yourself for whatever you've done. Look specifically for the progress you made in any arena, be it financial, business, health, fitness, relationship, loving yourself, hobbies, etc.

Checking in with your ETHICS

ETHICS	Rate yourself on a scale of 1 - 10	Actions I will take to move this ETHIC to a level 10 in my life
Full self-expression	8	• I commit to stop hiding out and telling Sally that Bill and I are getting divorced. • I will call Angie to tell her the truth about her dress I borrowed and that I did lose it.
Avoid S.T.E.A.T.s	10	• I am SO proud of myself for being so healthy and focused at the moment. I even caught myself almost hiding behind the kids and it didn't happen. WOW!

Establish a Grounded Routine	2		• I commit to having a hot bath before bed so I don't stay awake all night worrying. • I will go home at a reasonable hour and make time to cook dinner. • I just called Myra to help me with the washing and ironing, which was piling up – feel SO much better!
Sleep on any drastic changes you wish to make in your life	2		• Hmm. I sucked at this today as I decided to dye my hair blond. It came out orange and now I have to go to the hairdresser tomorrow to fix it. Argh!
Say no	5		• I will tell Paul tomorrow that he cannot come over before 3p.m. because that time doesn't work for me
Cause VS effect	10		• Feel pretty good just completing this list actually
Focus on you VS him	9		• Have not thought about him once today, so to reward myself have just booked a massage for tomorrow after fixing my hair disaster.

What to do when you are feeling overly emotional at inappropriate times

When you're feeling overly emotional at work and you feel you need to put your emotions aside to focus on your day, practice the *Exercise for handling your emotions while you are at work*, featured earlier in the book.

Daily exercises

If you follow the **naked divorce** to the letter, you will not only heal from your divorce more gracefully and meaningfully, you will be happier and more fulfilled. Remember, be kind to yourself. If you fall off the wagon, simply begin again, get back on track and focus on completing the program.

Although the exercises and techniques can bring about immediate, radical change in your life, they will not let you run away from or obscure whatever life is trying to teach you.

These techniques allow you to leave the pain of heartbreak behind. But life may give it back to you if you don't learn from what it is showing you.

The purpose of the pain is to teach you so you learn and you are protected in the future.

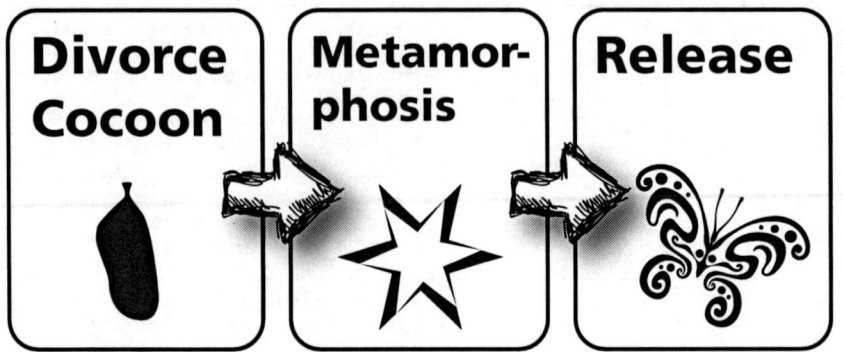

Exercises to establish the Divorce Cocoon (days 1-4)

The first four days are all about establishing the *Divorce Cocoon* that is the cornerstone of becoming invincible during the program.

In this time you will:

- Get grounded in the ETHICS of the program.
- Get grounded in the STRUCTURE and *Grounded Routine* of the program.
- Find ways to handle your emotions and find out where you are within the *naked divorce grieving cycle*.

Exercises during Metamorphosis (days 5-14)

Metamorphosis begins by surrendering and truly feeling your emotions. You will start to work through how you feel about your ex and your divorce.

There will be a TEST that you need to pass checking that your *Divorce Cocoon* is in place before you commence with *Metamorphosis*. Do not move into *Metamorphosis* until the *Divorce Cocoon* is established.

In this time you will:

- Write your relationship story.
- Get clear about everything you learnt from your old relationship and list what you will do better in the future.
- Find out what generalizations you have made about your ex.
- Restore a balanced view of your ex (whether that means falling out of love with him or putting an end to hating him).
- The anger exercise.
- Find out all your past patterns from past relationships so you can be aware of them.
- Hear the sorry you have always wanted to hear from your ex.
- Diagnose old patterns which existed within your relationship.

- Find the true source of your divorce.
- Forgive your ex.
- Do a Vow Break.

Handling your ex gracefully is a core component of the ex-factor etiquette covered at the end of the book. In the long run, the friends you have in common will admire you for your grace and for not lowering yourself to revenge levels.

Exercises during Release (days 15-21)

The final seven days are all about you rebuilding yourself emotionally. In this time you will:

- Dehypnotize yourself from false beliefs and rid yourself of the ex-hexes of relationship baggage.
- Work on your values and who you are now that you're no longer married.
- Work on setting boundaries.
- Develop a personal manifesto for your life.
- Get back in touch with the dreams you had for your life and put plans into action to live some of those dreams, starting today.
- Acknowledge yourself and celebrate your achievements.

This is the home stretch. For me it was the most exciting and personally moving part of my journey. This is also the part I enjoy the most when working with clients. It's so wonderful to see a woman regain her sense of personal power again.

Schedule your life around the program

"Failing to plan is planning to fail." – Alan Lakein, author on personal time management. To get through your divorce you have to dedicate daily time to your healing. This requires planning and preparation.

Planning is an up-front investment in success so that you can:

- Avoid wasting effort.
- Consider and include all factors, focusing on the critical ones.
- Identify all the changes that will need to be made. If you know what these are then you can assess in advance the likelihood of being able to make those changes, and take action to ensure that you will.
- Gather the resources you need in advance.

Tip-

Do not try to fit the **naked divorce** 21-day program into your life – this has no power.

Fit your life around the 21-day program and have it be the centre of your life for 21 days.

This way, you know you will succeed with the program.

For the duration of the program…

☐ Plan the start date for your 21-day **naked divorce** program. The program has been designed to start on a Friday. Give yourself at least a week to handle some of the things on the **naked divorce** *Things to Handle* list and the **naked divorce** shopping list within this chapter before commencing the program.

☐ If at all possible, try not to arrange nights out during the week so you can focus on your healing work for the day. (It's only for 21 days - it's worth it!)

☐ If at all possible, try not to arrange any social engagements during the three weekends of the **naked divorce**. This will enable you to focus on the healing work.

☐ Schedule at least one massage within the 21 days.

☐ Schedule your days so you get to bed earlier than normal (aim for no later than 22:30).

☐ **DURING WEEK DAYS:** Set aside at least 90-120 minutes daily to work through the **naked divorce** exercises and daily checklist. Schedule a morning healing routine of approximately 20-30 minutes and then schedule 60-120 minutes later in the day (either at lunch time or in the evening before you go to bed). Fit your work and home routines around the homework tasks wherever possible. The most important thing is to establish a routine and stick to it.

☐ **DURING WEEKENDS:** Set aside enough time on weekends to do your intensive healing work. (Arrange a babysitter for your children if you need to.)

• **Weekend number 1:** Schedule in six hours on Saturday and six hours on Sunday - Schedule to spend the first weekend of the *naked divorce* arranging your living arrangements or spring-cleaning and tidying your existing home AND sorting out your finances and foundational integrity (for more details on what this will entail, you can look at Days 2 and 3 of the program). It may be a good idea to invite a few people to assist you in sorting out your finances or spring cleaning your home.

• **Weekend number 2:** Schedule in 4-6 hours on Saturday and 3-5 hours on Sunday

• **Weekend number 3:** Schedule in 2-3 hours on Saturday and 3-4 hours on Sunday

☐ Schedule in exercise, time to cook meals, and administrative tasks, too. Because there will be a lot to handle, it may be a good idea to take a step back from administrative tasks for a few days to give yourself space to do the program.

☐ Schedule time to take baths. Water is very soothing when you're awash with strong emotions.

☐ OPTIONAL: Weigh up whether it works for you to take the book and your workbook with you wherever you go. It's up to you but I recommend working on it whenever you get a moment, particularly when you're feeling vulnerable or sad. Working on your exercises is something you can do to help yourself feel better.

Exercise:

Take the time right now to add these activities to your diary or schedule.

Now, schedule in handling the following activities in the week prior to commencing the program…

The *Things to Handle* list

Ensure you limit or remove these items from your home during the program:

☐ Alcohol, drugs and stimulants. (Alcohol, drugs and stimulants remain in your body for five days and keep you numb to your emotions, so eliminate them at least five days prior to commencing the program.)

☐ Chocolates, sweets, cakes, candy, crisps and sugary products.

☐ Junk food.

☐ Coffee and carbonated sodas.

☐ Television, going out and fantasy/escapism.

Ensure the following items are available for your use and are arranged:

☐ A baseball bat or beating stick. (I am serious about this one. But don't worry, you won't be harming anyone!)

☐ A CD/mp3 player.

☐ Print the **7 Foundations for Transformation** to be found at the end of the book. Put them up in your home in a place where you will be reminded of them daily.

☐ Print out the *naked divorce* Daily Declarations to be found at the end of the book and if possible, laminate them to put up in your shower cubicle.

☐ Create a place in your home to do your daily homework. Place a bowl of flowers there, or some special objects that represent happiness to you.

☐ Appoint a *Divorce Angel*. Find someone in your life that is not necessarily a close friend or family member but someone you can discuss your *naked divorce* with.

☐ Your ex. If your ex is used to hearing from you regularly, let him know that you are doing the *naked divorce* program to heal from your divorce. Request his support and let him know you won't be seeing much of him while you do the program as you need to focus on your healing.

☐ Friends and family. Tell them that you're doing the *naked divorce*. Request their support and let them know you won't be seeing much of them either as you'll be focusing on your healing.

The *naked divorce* shopping list

It's important to assist your body in its healing too, so I describe this as healthy and restorative retail therapy. Instead of purchasing these items individually, you could go online and order the 21-day Survival Kit from www.nakeddivorce.com.

You should have available:

☐ A journal to write in every day.

☐ Colored pens.

☐ Fragrant bath products and candles.

☐ 5 bags of ice to keep in the freezer for Day 9's exercise.

☐ Green Tea and a bag of lemons.

☐ Yogi Calming Tea (if not available, purchase peppermint or chamomile Tea).

☐ A 5-litre bottle of water.

☐ Nutritious (and preferably organic) food. Focus on foods that are rich in color, for example: green leafy vegetables, red tomatoes, strawberries and grapes, yellow pumpkin, peppers, fresh oranges, fruits in season, and fresh fish.

Cortisol reduction supplements:

Purchase the **naked divorce** *Daily Divorce Healing Vitamins* and tissue salts at www.nakeddivorce.com or purchase these vitamins separately:

☐ A good complete multiple vitamin and mineral supplement.

☐ Magnesium-C, one capsule three times a day.

☐ Advanced essential minerals, two capsules three times a day. (Mineral absorption and assimilation can be impaired by stressed adrenal glands. Minerals are essential for energy metabolism.)

☐ B5, one capsule a day.

☐ B6, one capsule a day.

☐ Vitamin C and Omega-3 fatty acid-rich foods with more complex carbohydrates (Serotonin levels can be controlled through diet and supplements and these foods will help).

☐ Tissue salts, which are wonderful for restoring the salts that live in your cells but which can become depleted because of the hormonal imbalance precipitated by the stress of divorce. They can be found in most health food shops. Tissue salts are available in homeopathic tablets that dissolve on the tongue. They are available individually as described on the next page.

☐ Tissue salt # 12: SILICIA: This tissue salt will sooth irritation and frayed nerves or excessive anger.

☐ Tissue salt # 6: KALI PHOSPHATE: This will help if you are feeling mentally and physically exhausted, sleep-deprived, anxious and stressed.

☐ Tissue salt # 4: FERRUM PHOSPHATE: This will boost your immune system, which takes quite a beating during divorce.

☐ Tissue salt # 2: CALCIUM PHOSPHATE: To alleviate that pale and gaunt look, palpitations, sadness and poor healing and recuperation.

Time to choose

This is it. Your moment of choice. The **naked divorce** program will take commitment. You need to be honest if you want it to work. I can try to motivate you, and I can give you the tools – but you're the one who will have to be ready to get rid of the excuses and commit to doing the whole program without skipping any of the steps.

You know how it goes right?

You can take the path most travelled, allowing your divorce, with all its attendant pain, suffering and loss of time, to overtake your life. You can deal with it as best you can and hope to feel better in a few months from now. You can soldier on and hope for the best.

> **WARNING:**
>
> **Focusing on avoiding your pain will simply give you more of what you have right now because resisting your emotions doesn't make them go away.**

OR

You can take the path less travelled and commit to do everything it takes to get you over your divorce in a focused and healthy way. It's not an easy path. It will require something of you. Sometimes it will be painful, and we don't like pain. We will do anything to feel good, even hiding behind denial. HOWEVER, the beauty of this program is once it's done, it's done. You can go on and have a wonderful life, free from relationship baggage and grief.

I'm asking you to walk this path with me.

You can withstand the pressure of the pain if you have the *Divorce Cocoon* in place and you will have adequate time and support to put this in place at the start of the 21-day program.

Life is short and precious. I don't want you to waste one minute on suffering. I don't want to see you trapped in a cycle of anger, anxiety, suffering or misery. Let's think back to the earlier analogy of the dislocated shoulder; consider that perhaps popping it back into its socket in one go can have its benefits, rather than ignoring it over time.

There is a test on the next page that will establish how ready you are to commit to healing from your divorce.

The *naked divorce* Readiness Test

Complete the following questions. The best way to honor yourself right now is by being brutally honest.

#	Question	Yes	Not ready	I am not sure	Not applicable to me	Not yet	No
1	Am I ready to begin healing from my divorce?						
2	Am I willing to do whatever it takes to heal and set aside 90 minutes each day during the week and 3 weekends to complete this program?						
3	Do I have the courage and determination to be open to forgiveness and letting go?						
4	Am I ready to stop focusing so much on what my ex is up to and focus on what my life could be about in the future?						
5	Am I ready to stop the divorce topic dominating my conversation with my friends and family?						
6	Am I ready to stop having the divorce affect my children negatively?						
7	Am I willing to stop telling myself I am fine when I am not? Am I ready to be honest about how I am doing?						

☐ If you answered *Not ready, I am not sure, Not yet or No* to three or more of these questions, you're probably not ready to get over your divorce and you're probably holding onto your suffering. If this is the case, complete the ***Real Impact of My Divorce*** exercise earlier on in this book so that you have a clear picture of the actual toll this divorce is taking on your life. If you find you are still not ready, then put the book aside. Come back to it when you feel you are ready.

Whatever you do, do not start the program in a half-baked way. It will not lead to any breakthrough results.

☐ If you answered *Yes or Not applicable to me* to all of the questions above, then you are ready to tackle your healing wholeheartedly. If this is the case, read on.

What you will learn in the 21-day program

By walking this path with me through the *naked divorce*, this is what you will learn:

- You will learn to build a strong foundation in your life to contain your emotions and contain the pressure you will experience as you heal from your divorce.
- You will learn about the science of healing. I researched healing from divorce and will share everything I have learnt.
- You will learn how to deal with the emotions and the processes you will encounter.
- You will learn to how to feel calm and to re-establish emotional equilibrium.
- You will find out why your marriage didn't work and how to get over your ex.
- You will learn to change bad habits and eliminate destructive psychological patterns.
- You will learn to build a great relationship with yourself, your children, friends, family and community.
- You will learn to regain self-confidence and open the door to new love.

I will be your coach. I will hold your hand all through the process, but I will also kick your butt when necessary.

So, if you're ready to accept that, let's go!

Notice of important information and health warnings

Some people experience some heightened levels of stress during the 21-day program. Although stress is a part of life, for some people, this stress is abnormal if they have a history of mental illness or emotional problems. If you have a history of emotional problems or mental illness, you may find yourself more vulnerable during the program. If at any stage, this heightened level of stress is a cause for concern, seek medical attention immediately. If you have a history of mental illness or emotional problems either personally or within your family OR if you have concerns about your ability to complete the program or handle the daily commitment of the program or handle the stress of examining your relationship, whether temporary, occasional or intermittent, and whether treated or not, do not participate in the **naked divorce** 21-day program. If you are not sure about your ability to participate in the program then discuss your participation with a mental health professional. It is ultimately your choice but I have been advised that you do not participate in the 21-day program if you:

(a) are uncertain about your ability (either mentally, emotionally or physically) to participate in the 21-day program or are currently in therapy and your therapist has advised you to not participate in the 21-day program;

(b) have a history of manic-depressive disorder which is also known as bi-polar disorder either personally or within your family, are taking, have taken or been prescribed to take within the previous 18 months any medication to treat bi-polar disorders; any drugs or medicines, whether prescription or non-prescription, intended to treat or affect mental processes or mood or to treat a chemical imbalance (such as Lithium, Gabapentin or Depakote); or anabolic steroids;

(c) have considered suicide, self-harm or harm to yourself or another or have a history of depression (acute or chronic), whether or not this has ever been treated or diagnosed; are taking, have taken or been prescribed to take within the previous 18 months anti-depressants (such as Celexa, Cipram, Prothiaden, Elavil, Prozac, Zoloft, or others);

(d) have a history of any psychotic disorder (an example would be schizophrenia), (either yourself or within your family) whether or not you or your family are being or have ever been treated or hospitalized; are taking, have taken or been prescribed to take within the previous 18 months anti-anxiety drugs (such as Klonapin, Xanax, Dormicum, Librium, Ativan, or others); anti-psychotics (such as Stelazine, Risperdal, Zyprexa, Dogmatil or others);

(e) have a history of drug abuse (including steroids and canabis) which has not been treated or have used any drugs or steroids in the past 12 months.

My declarations and commitments to myself

I, _____

☐ have carefully read the **notice of important information and health warnings** and I understand the recommendations and instructions.

☐ I acknowledge and understand that the 21-day program was designed for people who clearly understand they are responsible for their own health and well being before, during and after the 21-day program.

☐ I represent that I am not participating in the 21-day program to handle any emotional problems better handled by a medical professional and I fully understand that no portion of the 21-day program is delivered or supervised by medical or health professionals.

☐ I understand that I alone am responsible for my choice to participate in the 21-day program

☐ I warrant that I am responsible for my own health at all times prior to, during and after my participation in the 21-day program.

☐ I promise to do the program EXACTLY as it is designed and not to do it my own way.

☐ I promise to commit to apply the *Healing Formula* of the **naked divorce** wholeheartedly.

☐ I promise to keep **The 7 Foundations of Transformation** in my mind throughout the program. I will go back to restoring them whenever I feel a loss of power.

☐ I promise to work diligently at my healing every day.

☐ I promise to put both feet into the program. Even when there are days I don't want to do the work, I will do the work because I am committed to myself and my healing.

☐ I promise that if I do skip a day, I will get back on track as soon as possible. I won't allow it to mean anything where my healing is concerned.

☐ I promise I will complete all steps of the **naked divorce** and will not take any shortcuts.

☐ I have read through the warnings earlier in the book and I validate that it's safe for me to do this program.

☐ I promise to love myself and to be kind to myself throughout the program. I am wonderfully created.

☐ My *Divorce Angel's* name is _____. My *Divorce Angel* has signed the guideline sheet.

☐ I promise to check in with my *Divorce Angel* daily.

☐ I promise to take care of my health and nourishment during the **naked divorce**.

☐ I promise to guard against becoming a workaholic, having meaningless sex, indulging in retail therapy, and excessive socializing or partying as I understand that during this intensive healing process I need to take good care of myself.

---------------------------------   ---------------------------------
Signed   Date

part four

21-day
program

day

0

HEALING GOAL

Write your HEALING GOAL

When you have your journal, on page 1, write a paragraph about where you see yourself at the end of the program.

We shall call this your HEALING GOAL. This HEALING GOAL is used in conjunction with the *naked divorce* Break Up Reboot.

This concept of having a big HEALING GOAL is based on a program developed by my ex-husband called the Relaxation for Manifestation which can be found on www.AttractionCD.com. In his program, Bruce talks about how to bring about a goal by creating an inspired outcome using all of your five senses.

1. Choose a very specific HEALING GOAL that you will work with on a daily basis. Make sure that this goal is something that is really important and meaningful to you. It should make you feel good imagining yourself having achieved that goal.

2. Create a picture in your mind's eye that would indicate to you that your goal has already been accomplished. For example, if your goal is to heal from your past relationship and be even better off than you were before, your inspiring outcome might be that you are walking down the street, your head held high, looking gorgeous and feeling empowered, amazing, light and free. Your ex walks past you and calls your name. You wave and feel grateful and inspired. There is no worry or angst remaining as you go over to say hello. Your inspiring outcome is the end result. (You don't have to have your ex in your goal, this is just an example).

3. To find your inspiring outcome, ask yourself the following three questions:

    a. "How would I know that my goal had been accomplished?"

    b. "Where would I be and what would I be doing when my goal has been accomplished?"

    c. "What will I see, hear, and feel when my goal has been accomplished that will indicate to me that my goal is realized?"

4. Write out your HEALING GOAL describing in exact detail what you will see, hear, feel (emotionally and physically), taste and smell when your goal is complete.

5. Listen to your complimentary *naked divorce* Break Up Reboot program as often as you like, imagining the same goal for at least 21 days consecutively. Make sure you will not be disturbed while you listen to the program.

The *naked divorce* Break Up Reboot contains powerful suggestions specifically designed to gently suggest powerful affirmations to your subconscious mind. As you listen you'll hear dual voice commands at one particular point in the recording (two very different voices, one in each ear), a powerful tool, which distracts the conscious mind whilst your unconscious mind is supported in making positive changes.

 Note: You can hear each suggestion and can RELAX in the knowledge that YOU are making POSITIVE changes to your subconscious mind.

Express your goal in all five senses:

- V - Visual (sight)
- A - Auditory (sound)
- K - Kinesthetic (feeling, both touch and emotion)
- G - Gustatory (taste)
- O - Olfactory (smell)

As your mind experiences reality, it filters reality through your five senses i.e. it receives input from what you are seeing, hearing, feeling, tasting and smelling.

The purpose of listening to the **naked divorce** Break Up Reboot, is to help you imagine your HEALING GOAL using the five senses.

Research shows that when you use your imagination like this, you can create an imagined experience so real that your mind cannot tell the difference between your imagined experience and reality. When this happens and your mind believes that your imagined experience is actually real, chemical reactions take place in your brain, effectively storing your imagined experience into your memory banks as if it were a real memory.

As you repeat this process of imagining using the **naked divorce** Break Up Reboot over time, you can program new false memories into your mind. Your mind can then use these false memories as the basis for creating your reality. The end result of all this is that you can begin to think, feel and behave in new, more productive ways that will lead you closer to your goals. New ways of thinking, feeling and behaving have you attract new opportunities and resources into your life to help bring your dreams and goals into reality.

Note: Before you program your mind, it is important to get specific about what you want to program your mind with. Fill in your HEALING GOAL using single words or short phrases. An example of what a completed HEALING GOAL looks like can be found on the next page.

Example HEALING GOAL

Imagine that your inspired outcome for realizing your perfect HEALING GOAL is to see yourself dancing and looking incredible and being adored by all the men around you. You feel amazing! Here is an example of what you might write down describing your HEALING GOAL.

Visual: (sight)

Flashing lights, bodies moving to the music, smiling people, arms up in the air, catch reflection of myself in the mirror looking amazing, gorgeous guys smiling at me and making motions towards me, champagne in tall glass…

Auditory: (hearing)

Hearing the music, glasses clanking together, murmuring of voices, laughing, guy asking me to dance etc…

Kinesthetic: (touch)

Cold champagne in hand, feel warmth of a body next to mine, the touch of the fabric against my skin etc…

Kinesthetic: (emotions)

Happy, contented, empowered, at peace, warm heart, excited, peaceful, grateful, appreciative, joy, mind quiet etc…

Gustatory: (taste)

Salty as I lick my lips, champagne etc…

Olfactory: (smell)

Champagne, after-shave etc…

VAKGO sensory elements

To help you extract the VAKGO information from your HEALING GOAL, I have included a list of some sensory elements that make up each of your five senses.

If you find yourself having difficulty creating some of the sensory information in your HEALING GOAL, go through the list below for the particular sense that you are working on, and see if it jogs your imagination.

Visual elements:

Objects

People

Shape

Size – big / small

Color

Brightness

Contrast - light / shade

Texture

Auditory elements:

Volume – loud / soft

Distance – near / far

Quality – clear / distorted

Background sounds

Kinesthetic (touch) elements:

Temperature – hot / cold

Wind / water / rain against skin?

Texture and pressure

Clothing – how your clothes feel against your skin.

Are you holding anything in your hands? / Are you touching anything?

Are you sitting or lying down – if so, what does that feel like?

Movement and posture

Kinesthetic (emotional) elements:

Emotional quality – e.g. joy, excitement, pride, gratitude etc…

Intensity – strong / weak

Location in your body – e.g. heart area, solar plexus area, head area.

Gustatory elements:

Texture

Intensity of taste

Hot / cold

Sweet / sour / salty

Olfactory elements:

Pungency / intensity of smell

Smells good / bad

Distance – close / far

MY HEALING GOAL

Date: ....

My HEALING GOAL is (no more than a simple paragraph):

....
....
....

My inspired outcome is...
(write one or two sentences summarizing your outcome):

....
....
....

Visual (sight)

....
....

Auditory (hearing)

....
....

Kinesthetic (touch)

....
....

Kinesthetic (emotions)

....
....

Gustatory (taste)

....
....

Olfactory (smell)

....
....

The Divorce Cocoon

The next four days are about establishing a supportive and grounding *Divorce Cocoon*.

TIP FOR THE DAY: If your best friend was going through the pain of divorce, think about what you would do for him or her and then look at how you can be your own best friend during this time.

Rule #1: Be gentle with yourself.

Theme: Be gentle with yourself

Date: Friday, _____

🕑 **Estimated time to complete the exercise: 90 minutes**

Remember to go through the daily checklist

Tick when done

Read through the thought for the day: ☐

Today is about you. Decide to focus on yourself and how you do today. If you are going through a divorce right now, then ensure you follow the principle of no contact with your ex. Let's not concern ourselves with what he is or isn't doing. Understand that any feelings of angst are just your Cortisol and Dopamine levels playing up again. When you are at work, practice the four A's from the **naked divorce exercise for handling your emotions whilst at work.** But if you get a break and you feel like crying, do so. When you get home tonight and need to scream, find a pillow and scream into it. Indulge your emotions. Experience them fully, and then gently let them go.

If you went through your divorce some time ago then the next few days are about looking after yourself and setting up the foundational structure of the *Divorce Cocoon*.

Your brain may tell you things in the first few days about it all feeling a bit fast: this is your natural human resistance to transformation. Your psyche may feel under threat so if it feels too fast, try to push through the discomfort as the program was designed to be done within 21 days for a specific reason. If however, it's all too overwhelming, there is no pressure: you control the speed of your transformation.

Read through the exercise you'll be doing later today.
Allow yourself to think about it during the day.

Exercise:

Go to http://www.nakeddivorce.com/ products/find-out-how-hung-up-you-are/ and complete the questionnaire. Make a note in your journal about where you are in the grieving process and how you feel about where you are.

Think about what you will tackle this weekend, whether it be your finances or your home to lay a solid foundation for your *Divorce Cocoon*.

day

02

COCOON

*TIP FOR THE DAY: Divorce is extremely unsettling so establishing a **Grounded Routine** and solid foundation is key to your healing. Focus on your home and finances for the next two days and work hard at clearing out junk and restoring order. The order, structure and routine will be grounding for you.*

Theme: Home clean-up

Date: Saturday, _____

🕐 **Estimated time to complete the exercise: 6 hours**

Remember to go through the daily checklist

Tick when done

Read through the thought for the day:

☐

The next two days are all about establishing order around your home and in your finances. You want to get stuck in and sort out any key matters concerning your foundation and base. As women, we tend to find that a sense of disorder and clutter in our homes and finances easily invades our minds and states of being. Here are some overall considerations for the next few weeks. This weekend is all about tackling a few basic things to give you stability to complete the **naked divorce**.

If you are going through a divorce right now, then read the three sections below. If you went through a divorce some time ago, it might be more appropriate to skip to the exercise.

If your living situation is still unresolved

When you're splitting up, your home is a refuge in a sea of uncertainty. Your children are comfortable there, so you may yearn to hang on to your house after the divorce. But does it make financial sense?

Weigh up the expenses involved in keeping the house against your desire for emotional stability for you and the children. What will you gain if you move? In some areas, rentals and housing prices are so high that even a smaller house or condo may be out of your price range. Also, it may not be possible to find an affordable house in the same or another high-quality school district.

Property division is one of the most important decisions during a split-up. "The property division in a divorce is final and you can't undo it even if you realize later that you made a mistake," says Carol Ann Wilson, a certified divorce planner and author of 'The Financial Guide to Divorce Settlement.' "Other areas of a divorce decree can be changed, such as child support or visitation, but not the property settlement."

While the property settlement is final, there is flexibility in crafting it. One option is co-ownership between you and your ex for a set number of years. Taking sole possession and refinancing to keep mortgage payments reasonable is another possibility. If you do choose to stay, consider contacting all the companies you have bills with and ask for your or your ex's name to be removed from the bills. Ensure you get the keys back from your ex.

In some cases, it makes sense to downsize immediately to a smaller house, especially if the expenses involved in keeping the house are more than you can afford. Some people associate the house with their failed marriage and are anxious to start fresh somewhere else.

Make an effort to sort out your living situation this weekend so that you have a place you can call home. You'll probably not be able to take all your belongings at once, so pack the most important things.

Other than the obvious things to pack, see the list below for some ideas:

⇨ Bills, medical and legal documents

⇨ Useful telephone numbers

⇨ You may need to arrange putting your stuff into storage if needs be.

⇨ Redirect your mail. Contact your local post office and ask them to redirect your mail for a month or two.

⇨ Notify your doctor, dentist and school of your new address or change in circumstances. Your doctor may be able to refer you to other organizations for help. It's also a good idea to have a general health check.

⇨ Contact everyone you have bills with and ask for final bills to be sent to your new address.

If your living situation is resolved

⇨ Make a list of all items in your home that need repairing. Work out a budget for the small things you can do to make you feel you're claiming the home as your own. How much of the work can you do yourself? Make a list of family, friends or DIY specialists who can help you with other jobs.

➡ If you feel it's appropriate, redecorate your bedroom. Move the furniture around, change your bedding or paint the walls a different color so you feel new in your bedroom.

➡ If you don't have the money to repair or redecorate, then spring clean. Use today to clean out junk and sort out cupboards and spaces you have left untouched for years.

➡ Catch up on your cleaning, dusting and ironing.

➡ Get clear on the real maintenance costs of your home.

➡ In addition to the regular bills, budget for unexpected repairs and regular maintenance. You don't want to be caught short if you need a new water heater.

➡ Consider household insurance that covers unforeseen problems with the heating or plumbing.

➡ Hire a building inspector to evaluate the house and list any major repairs that may be on the horizon.

➡ Identify potential trouble spots. If, for example, the house is more than twenty-years-old and still has the original roof, a new roof may be necessary. Discuss these issues and how they will be tackled with your ex.

Tip-

CLEANING PARTY

Organize a cleaning/redecorating party and ask your friends to help you redecorate your bedroom. You buy the (low-fat!) pizzas, paint and paintbrushes and they provide the manual labor!

Exercise:

1. From the reading above, spend today making a list of all the things you need to do to sort out your home or your living situation over the next 6 months.

2. Whether it's a spring clean, redecoration, moving furniture around, plan to do a chunk of this work today.

3. Then schedule to complete the rest of the work over the coming weeks and months. The goal for the end of the day is to feel physically exhausted but to feel clearer in your mind and more on top things.

day
03
COCOON

TIP FOR THE DAY: Besides the immediate decisions around your home and finances, defer any major decisions about your life for at least six weeks. Sleep on it. Your emotional state could cloud your decision-making abilities.

Theme: Financial clean-up

Date: Sunday, _____

🕐 **Estimated time to complete the exercise: 6 hours**

Remember to go through the daily checklist

Tick when done

Read through the thought for the day: ☐

If you are going through a divorce right now, you may be feeling physically sore today. That's okay. Press on and if you feel like crying, do so. If you feel like screaming, scream into a pillow. If you feel like calling him, don't. Avoid contact. Focus only on the next bill that needs to be filed. Just think how amazing it will feel tonight when you review the progress you've made with building your foundation.

Whether you are going through a divorce right now or some time ago, read through this entire section.

Complete your daily homework – start this in the morning.

Dealing with your finances

"I find that when both partners feel they are fairly treated, they will have a good relationship in the future," says Sally Coullahan, a certified divorce financial analyst in London. "These issues carry over into parenting, so if the wife made bad decisions in the divorce and didn't get enough financially, it affects the kids, too."

Video: I have done several interviews on the topic of handling your finances during and after divorce. Watch these here:
www.youtube.com/nakeddivorce

Here are some considerations for handling your finances during and after a divorce:

⮕ Look through all your bank accounts and bills. Make notes on what has to be handled each month.

⮕ Avoid living off your credit card or getting into debt.

⮕ Draw up a budget, working out what you can spend and how much money you have coming in. Work out an action plan to correct anything you wish to correct.

⮕ If you feel things are out of control, make an appointment with an accountant, financial advisor or trusted family friend to advise you on your financial situation. There are also free resources you can look into at www.nakeddivorce.com/resources/ where you will find help across 11 categories for each country (UK, USA, Canada, Australia, New Zealand and South Africa.)

⮕ Start a savings account and work out a savings plan (even if it's a few extra pounds or dollars a month).

⮕ If you need help with bills, ask friends or family for short-term loans rather than to get into consumer debt.

⮕ Be proactive and advise all your creditors of your financial position.

⮕ Write down a list of things to discuss with your partner and agree on a time to talk. You'll need to think about the house, car, children, debts, finances, any pets and your shared possessions.

⮕ Get advice on your mortgage if you have one. Be absolutely clear on any additional charges on the property or any attached investments you need to arrange.

⮕ Contact your local council or state to enquire about any benefits you qualify for.

⮕ While arranging your divorce, consider drawing up all the correct documentation to resolve your matrimonial finances.

⮕ Notify your bank of changes. If you have a joint account, can you withdraw your share of the money and cancel the account? If your ex also has access to other accounts you may need to change his access.

⮕ Get a copy of your credit report. Refer to this website for the local credit agency in your country:
http://www.creditguru.com/worldagencies.htm#nam.
The primary agencies are: Experian (www.experian.co.uk) or Equifax (www.equifax.co.uk) or Transunion USA (http://www.transunion.com/) so you can see if there are any debts in your name.

➡️ If you feel daunted by finances, take a class on accounting or basic book-keeping at your local college. Be proactive and draw up a filing system for your bills.

➡️ If you are based in the United Kingdom, visit: www.moneysavingexpert.com/, which is a great resource for how to save money on all your bills, credit cards and insurances.

➡️ Schedule time just after completing the *naked divorce* to draw up your last will and testament. There is a great blog on how to do this to be found at www.nakeddivorce.com.

➡️ Pension. Meet with a financial advisor to discuss your pension plan.

Exercise:

1. From the reading above, spend today making a list of all the things you need to do to clean up your finances over the next six months.

2. Whether it's some filing or sorting or budgeting, plan to do a chunk of this work today.

3. Then schedule to complete the rest of the work over the coming weeks and months. The goal for the end of the day is to feel physically exhausted but to feel clearer in your mind (because things are noted down) and more on top things.

day

04

COCOON

*TIP FOR THE DAY: If you're tempted to contact your ex, don't. It is better that you put some distance between yourself and the situation. If you feel a burning neediness to call him for answers about how this all happened, etc, note that you're probably in the Panic/negotiation stage of the **naked divorce** grieving cycle and still have a lot of Dopamine kicking around in your system. Stay off the caffeine, alcohol and stimulants, eat lots of green, leafy vegetables and stick to your supplements. The panicky feeling will pass.*

Theme: Get grounded inside the Divorce Cocoon

Date: Monday, _____

🕐 **Estimated time to complete the exercise: 90 minutes**

Remember to go through the daily checklist

Tick when done

Read through the thought for the day:

☐

It may seem extremely basic but establishing a solid foundation is critical to ensuring the success of the program and ensuring you have a *Divorce Cocoon* in place so when you start with *Metamorphosis*, then you are ready to handle whatever comes your way.

Spend time today re-reading Foundation #1: ETHICS and ensuring you score at least a six on the rating scale, then check in to ensure that you are aware of all **7 Foundations for Transformation** and have them in place.

Pay particular attention to the *Grounded Routine* and ensure you have daily routines which ground you in place.

Read through the exercise you'll be doing later today. Allow yourself to think about it during the day.

Work through each of **The 7 Foundations of Transformation** and ensure that each element is in place and you are clear on how to work with each foundation.

- **1 ETHICS** - Spend some time today ensuring that the ETHICS of the program are intact and that you score at least eight on each item in the table on the next page.

#	ETHICS	Rate yourself on a scale of 1 - 10	Actions I will take to move this ETHIC to a level 10 in my life
1	Being self-expressed		
2	Avoid S.T.E.A.T.'s		
3	Establish a Grounded Routine		
4	Sleep on any drastic changes		
5	Say no		
6	Cause VS effect		
7	Focus on you vs. him		

Work through each of **The 7 Foundations of Transformation** and ensure that each element is in place and you are clear on how to work with each foundation.

Examine each foundation and check the following. If anything is missing, put it in place:

- **2 NOURISHMENT -** are you in the pattern of taking your healing supplements? Have you changed your diet to ensure you are eating healthier (an increase in green and red foods)? Have you decreased your intake of sugar and stimulants?
- **3 WORKING WITH YOUR EMOTIONS -** are you clear on how to release your emotions in a healthy and ethical way?
- **4 PERFORMING AT WORK -** have you had key conversations with your boss and/ or staff at work? Do you feel able to work and process your emotions at another time? Have you practiced the exercise for handling your emotions whilst you are at work?
- **5 COMMITMENT -** can you categorically say that you commit to completing the program and that you will do whatever it takes to complete it?
- **6 THE RIGHT SUPPORT -** have you been having check-in sessions with your *Divorce Angel* and do you feel you have the support you need to complete the 21-day program?

- **7 A GAME PLAN THAT WORKS** - have you purchased everything required, handled everything there is to handle and scheduled in the time you need to complete the 21-day program?

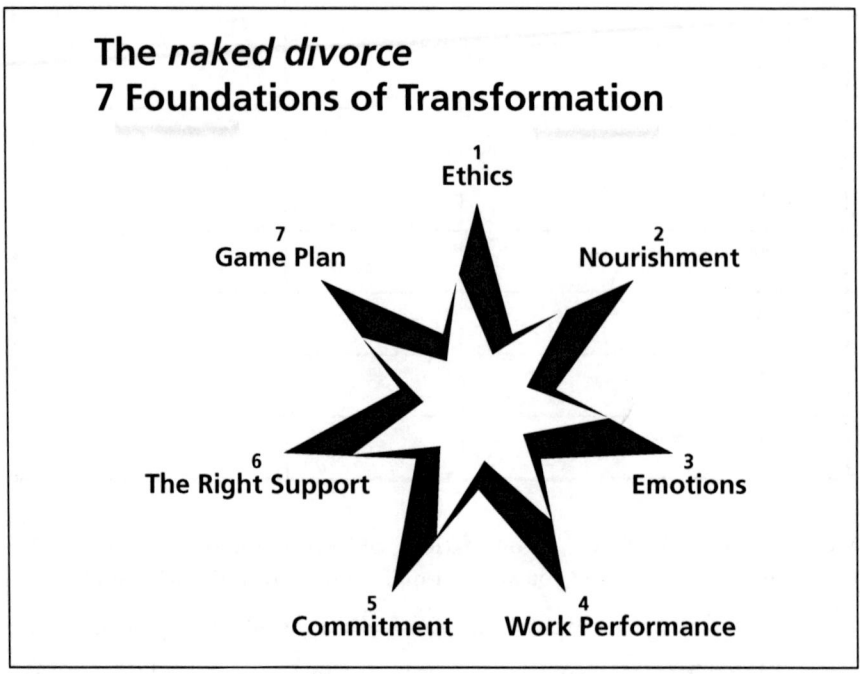

The *naked divorce* 7 Foundations of Transformation

Test

Call your *Divorce Angel* and discuss the work you have done in the past four days.

ONLY IF your *Divorce Angel* agrees that you are ready to move into *Metamorphosis*, will you be ready to move into *Metamorphosis*.

Ensure YOU feel ready to move too!

Metamorphosis

Metamorphosis begins once the *Divorce Cocoon* is in place. This phase lasts for 10 days.

TIP FOR THE DAY: *Whilst working on your relationship story if you notice that you've been living in a dream world, be calm. This is very common among women. Keep in mind that living in a romantic dream world is the thinking of the little girl within you. But inhabiting that world is problematic. It keeps you stuck in a childlike way of being. Girls become women through the pain of facing reality.*

Theme: Your relationship story

Date: Tuesday, _____

🕐 **Estimated time to complete the exercise: 90 minutes**

Remember to go through the daily checklist

Tick when done

Read through the thought for the day:

Today is all about your relationship story. Writing a chronicle of your love life and marriage is very important to your healing. Tomorrow, you'll read the story to your *Divorce Angel*, so schedule time with him/ her for Wednesday.

My story:

In my relationship story I noticed that I was like a princess living with my prince in our castle. Life was perfect. I was one half of the perfect couple and life was a dream. The story went on and on for pages and pages about how we were destined to be together and how we were cruelly ripped apart by my friends who cheated with him.

It was only when I read the story back to myself the third time that I realized that in reality, things were not so good between us. I told myself and the outside world that we were the perfect couple. I felt an inner drive to maintain the illusion because I couldn't handle the thought of failure in my life. My romantic needs weren't being met within my relationship so I became addicted to romantic comedies. I spent hours daydreaming about Prince

Charming and how he would rescue me from my marriage. I cried hopelessly during movies that showed love-torn, passionate couples.

It was only when I read the relationship story I had written back to myself that I noticed that I didn't pay attention to these obvious signs that my marriage was in trouble. I was living in my fantasy world of dinner parties, playing house and being the perfect wife. The break-up of my marriage was accompanied by complete denial and shock within me as I refused to acknowledge that we had split up.

It was only when I committed my story to paper that I realized how my life with him had been unreal and that things were broken almost from the very beginning.

Your relationship story is the key to unlocking how your relationship began but also how your relationship got to this point.

Strive to be brutally honest with yourself.

Read through the exercise you'll be doing later today. Allow yourself to think about it during the day.

Exercise:

Write down your entire relationship story. Write down the whole thing: how you met, all the romance, events, drama, and hurt. Ensure you distinguish the exact moment you 'died' a little in your self-expression or happiness. Those moments are key to working out where things started going wrong. Make sure it's as long as possible and write it like you would a best seller. Don't skip any key details.

- When done, read it to yourself five times. Make sure you re-read it until you know it intimately.

- Make a note in your journal of what happens each time you read your story. How does it feel?

- Remember to schedule time with your *Divorce Angel* tomorrow to read them the story.

day
06
METAMORPHOSIS

*TIP FOR THE DAY: You are making great progress. Now, notice any **Short Term Emotional Avoidance Tactics** that may be creeping in to sabotage you. Anything you're considering doing that could side-track your healing will only slow down your progress. Because your mind is afraid of change, it will plot to take you out of the game. Remain vigilant and guard against S. T.E.A. T.s.*

Theme: Lessons from your relationship story

Date: Wednesday, _____

🕒 **Estimated time to complete the exercise: 60 minutes**

Remember to go through the daily checklist

Tick when done

Read through the thought for the day:

☐

Today is all about completing the writing of the story and reading your story to your *Divorce Angel*, looking for the signs that pointed to your divorce. Focus on what you can be responsible for. Responsibility is not about assigning blame, it's about looking at what you contributed to the break up, what you learnt from it, and what you can take into your next relationship. This is learning for the future.

Read through the exercise you'll be doing later today. Allow yourself to think about it during the day.

Exercise:

- How did it feel reading the story to your ***Divorce Angel*?**

- Read the story to yourself again.

- How does your story feel now?

- Work on writing down ten good things you have learnt from your relationship.

- Work on writing down ten things you will do better in your next relationship.

day
07
METAMORPHOSIS

TIP FOR THE DAY: We all have a little critic in our heads telling us bad and unhelpful things about ourselves. Whenever this critic has anything to say about how you should or shouldn't be handling your divorce, I would like you to practice saying this, "Critic, thank you for sharing. Now SIT DOWN AND BE QUIET."

Theme: Considering your relationship from different points of view

Date: Thursday, _____

🕐 **Estimated time to complete the exercise: 60-90 minutes**

Remember to go through the daily checklist

Tick when done

Read through the thought for the day:

☐

It's very common during divorce to become stuck in rigid thoughts about your ex or about your relationship. It's also normal to make glib generalizations about the relationship, for example, "He is a bad man and never lifted a finger during our entire marriage," "He never loved me and I was never good enough for him" or, "We were happy for years and then suddenly everything fell apart."

When we make sweeping generalizations and then become really fixed and certain about those generalizations, we can get stuck and unable to move forward. We can also become very angry if anyone challenges the validity of those fixed thoughts and emotions we hold so close.

I'm particularly talking to those who have been holding a grudge against their ex (or even their new partner) for some time. If a little voice in your head is vehemently denying this, you probably don't even realize you're holding a grudge.

If you do have a grudge and are feeling very angry or upset about the end of your relationship, it's okay. It's normal to be upset.

But to heal, it helps to take a step back and to be open to considering different points of view. Did he never lift a finger to help? Was he really all bad? Changing perceptions is difficult. It takes great humility and courage to fight through your resistance.

When you hold a grudge you see only one side of the coin, and that's the message you deliver to your brain. That becomes your reality. If you change your frame of reference by looking at the same situation from a different point of view, you can change the way you respond to situations in life. You can change your representation or perception about anything. In the same way, you can change your states and behaviors.

We tend to see a situation in one frame. A frame can refer to a belief, which might limit our view of the world. If we let this limiting belief go, new ideas, interpretations and possibilities can develop.

Being open to healing

- Be open to the possibility of forgiving your ex and all those involved. This doesn't mean you have to do it. Just begin to be open to the fact that someday soon, you will forgive them. Forgiving does not condone what someone else did; it simply releases YOU from the pain of their actions.

- Consider making a place for the event in your life and then put it in its place. It's important to remember that it did happen and it did affect you. At the same time, its place is in the past, much like a chapter in a book you have read and choose not to read again.

Read through the exercise you'll be doing later today. Allow yourself to think about it during the day.

PART I of Rebalancing your view of your ex

In the space below, describe a central problem you're experiencing in your divorce with regards to your ex-spouse and then complete the table below.

Example: I am angry at him for parading his new girlfriend around in front of our children.

1. Reframing the contact of your ex's behavior

#	Write down ten things that describe how this problem is a stumbling block to you (here are five):	What is another context for this behavior where the meaning may be different?
1	I feel embarrassed and want to hide away.	Him moving on so quickly shows how much he hates to be alone. I am a stronger person emotionally than he is and willing to heal vulnerably and authentically.
2	I feel our children will get upset because it's too soon to introduce her to them.	I have shielded and protected our children all their lives. Maybe it is a good thing that they fend for themselves now.
3	I feel lonely and alone.	This is probably a good opportunity to get out there and start playing tennis again. I have actually been feeling lonely for a decade.
4	I cannot believe she is only nineteen! I feel so embarrassed that I am being replaced by someone so young.	Him dating a 19-year-old demonstrates my feeling that we were never really on the same wavelength. Maybe it is time to find a more mature man who will appreciate all my qualities.
5	I will never find anyone again. I will die alone.	Ok, ok, I know this is slightly dramatic. Someone at work already asked me out for a drink. My friend Sam literally just met someone new so if it's possible for her, it's possible for me!

Now, it's your turn!

In the space below, describe a central problem you're experiencing in your divorce with regards to your ex-spouse:

....

....

....

....

....

#	Write down ten things that describe how this problem is a stumbling block to you:	What is another context for this behavior where the meaning will be different?
1		
2		
3		
4		
5		
6		
7		
8		
9		
10		

2. Think about your divorce from different angles

- What are the generalizations you've made about your ex?
- Now imagine an alien lands on our planet and they watch a movie of your life. Watch the movie through their eyes. What point of view might this alien have about your situation?
- Notice the differences. What are they?
- Why is your point of view different to the alien's perspective?

3. The critic in our heads

We all have a little critic in our heads BUT it is key to challenge the validity of what your little voice tells you. This exercise will help you to find other meanings in what is happening in your life which can be more empowering than the disempowering meanings you may have in place today.

The little critic in your head is not you.

You are the one who notices the little critic.

The little critic is just your worst thoughts, worst meanings and worst nightmares voicing their negative commentary. To help me with my little critic in my head, I gave it a name.

My little critic's name is Fred. Whenever I hear it say, "Adèle, you are ugly, you are unattractive and you are going to wind up alone" I just say, "thanks Fred, but your opinion is not valid, so shut it."

Sometimes I have amusing moments where I notice *my Fred* going off on one, but since separating my 'Fred' from me, my ability to control the negative chatter in my head has improved.

TIP FOR THE DAY: *"Whatever you do, you do to yourself.*
To judge others only compounds your own faults."
~ Buddha

"A pedestal is as much a prison as any small, confined space."
~ Gloria Steinem

Theme: Perception VS projection and *Pedestal Shift*

Date: Friday, _____

🕑 **Estimated time to complete the exercise: 120 minutes**

Remember to go through the daily checklist

Tick when done

Read through the thought for the day:

☐

It is dangerous to put anyone on a pedestal but equally damaging to hate or loathe them.

All people possess both positive and negative traits, even your ex-husband. It's normal to be feeling very strong negative emotions about your ex. You may be feeling he's the most hated person in your life or perhaps you are completely indifferent to him. Alternatively, it's also completely normal to be pining for him and you may be experiencing very strong, positive feelings towards him. You may have placed him on a pedestal and are struggling to get over him.

Today's exercise is about rebalancing any highs and lows you're experiencing in this regard. Returning to a neutral space where you can see that both the positive and negative traits are critical to your healing. There are two parts to this exercise: one part is if you are feeling strong negative emotions and the other is if you are feeling strong positive emotions. Pay attention to which part you are doing.

Undertake this exercise, even if you feel you're just fine. It's natural to want to avoid confronting these issues. Keep focused on the end game and keep moving forward.

Read through the exercise you will be doing later today. Allow yourself to think about it during the day.

PART II of rebalancing your view of your ex

*If you are feeling very strong **negative** emotions about your ex, balance out those strong emotions by doing this exercise.*

1. Perception is Projection

Perception is projection is a concept coined by Richard Bandler (the founder of Neuro-linguistic programming). Essentially there are millions of bits of information per second that our unconscious minds are aware of but our conscious minds can only process 134 bits of this data at a time. How we choose what information to delete comes from our beliefs and perceptions about life. Essentially, you cannot see anything outside of you, unless it exists within you. Your ability to see and acknowledge a character trait in another is only possible because on some level, you possess this character trait within yourself.

Have there been times in your life when you reacted very strongly when you met someone and thought, "they are so bitter" or, "they are so superior".

To actually SEE or recognize bitterness, superiority or any other character trait, you must possess this trait to some extent. Either way, I want you to acknowledge that it is unjust to label people according to your own perception.

In terms of healing from your divorce, do this exercise:

Think of a situation in which your ex is pressing your buttons	Describe their behavior	Do you ever do the same thing? Be honest.	How would you prefer them to behave in that moment?	How can you behave better when you display the same behavior?
Example... He spends hours on his laptop.	Engrossed in his laptop and totally oblivious to me.	Sometimes I can become engrossed and not want to be interrupted. I get that.	Turn around when I talk to him and listen intently to what I have to say.	I can listen more to others. I notice that I tend to think more about what I will say VS truly listening to others when they speak.

It all comes down to removing the log from your own eye before you run around taking splinters out of other people's eyes.

If you focus on being a better person in your own life, then you will no longer attract these negative traits towards you.

Sometimes our biggest button presser might be a mirror for our own personal issues. It's good to remember that challenging people and situations serve as our master teachers. Without them we would not grow.

It's also important to remember that when you have an emotional charge with someone, you become a victim to that person. You're giving them rent-free space in your head. By owning your projection you disarm and remove the intensity of the emotional charge. Owning your projection means that you have control over it, rather than it having control over you.

2. Pedestal Shift

If you are feeling very strong positive emotions about your ex (you've allowed him to stay on his pedestal), balance out those strong emotions by doing this exercise.

If you are struggling to get over your ex, it may be because you have banished all negative thoughts of him and can only remember and see positive things about him.

If that is the case, it's time for a little reality check because if your relationship was so wonderful, you would still be in it. There HAD to be things that did not work about the relationship and about your ex that it's time to be honest about. It is time that you move your ex off the pedestal.

Note: if you struggle to do this exercise alone, contact your **Divorce Angel** and request to do the exercise together.

Answer these questions:

- Was I truly happy in my relationship? And if so, why? Was the happiness real or was it simply what I told myself was real?
- Did I feel like the BEST version of myself when I was with him?
- Was he definitely feeling like the BEST version of himself with me?
- What about him was irritating that I have glanced over?
- Describe 10 events in detail that hurt me in the relationship.
- What characteristics came out in him which were undesirable traits that I am willing to acknowledge (close your eyes and replay each of those events in

your mind. Turn up the brightness of each event in your mind's eye as you replay it.)

After replaying each event, journal how you feel about him now.

For the rest of day, question if you were in reality about your relationship and whether he truly deserves his pedestal upon which you have placed him

day
09
METAMORPHOSIS

TIP FOR THE DAY: According to countless research studies mentioned within the Bibliography of this book, a leading cause of depression is suppression of emotions over a long period.

Let go, surrender to all your emotions and feel them fully. When you do actually feel your emotions fully, none of them last more than 30 minutes. It's the resistance to feeling emotions that leads to depression.

Theme: Releasing strong emotions

Date: Saturday, _____

🕐 **Estimated time to complete the exercise: 4-6 hours**

Remember to go through the daily checklist

Tick when done

Read through the thought for the day:

Today is about exorcising your negative angry or sad emotions and fully expressing any major emotions that are locked within you. Even if you think you have healed or can consciously rationalize why your marriage ended, the thoughts in your subconscious mind are the ones that actually decide on your future. Relationship baggage, insecurities, doubts, jealousy and all disempowering thoughts arise unconsciously within your subconscious mind. Your subconscious mind is ruled by your emotions. To truly heal on an unconscious level, you need to pay attention to what your emotions are telling you. Emotions are there as warning signs that something is not quite right. Most of us ignore our emotions or rationalize them away. This is the time to feel them fully.

Day 9 was the most important day in my healing. Here's why…

My story:

This was the day I truly let go. I was sitting on the edge of my bed and the rage began building up like a volcano about to erupt. I felt it trapped in my stomach. I wanted to scream.

My body started shaking. I was so mad with anger that I stood up with one clear thought, "I am going to wreak havoc on our house." I looked around my bedroom. First, I grabbed the picture frame with our wedding picture in it and smashed that on the floor. Next was the vase he'd bought me for our anniversary. As I worked my way from the bedroom into the kitchen, I broke anything and everything I could get my hands on. I was like a hurricane but with each item I destroyed, my anger subsided. I broke nearly everything I could find in the kitchen, thinking that I'd want to buy new crockery anyway. After an hour of mayhem, I was standing in the kitchen, surrounded by broken glass and feeling alive. I wanted to destroy more. Releasing this anger, rage and fury was a new experience.

I opened the freezer and took out a bag of ice. I went in search of my baseball bat. I couldn't find it. I grabbed my squash racket, put a photograph of our wedding day on the ice and then beat it, screaming until the ice had shattered. Exhausted, I collapsed on the floor and cried. My anger transformed into a sadness I had never known before. I surrendered to despair completely until I felt it would swallow me. It was unbearable, but I stuck with it, knowing that in time it would pass. The sense of failure was overwhelming and I cried out, "How could I have been so foolish?", "Why did I marry him?", "How could he do this?" At the core of everything was my absolute terror of being alone, unloved and unwanted. I knew that this was the final emotion I had to exorcise. I was so afraid. I hugged my legs, sobbing like a little girl.

The emotion changed again and moved into grief. I spent 20 minutes crying and lying on the floor. The grief soon changed into despair, followed by panic and then shaking fear. The pain of each layer was almost unbearable but I kept drawing it towards me and felt every layer of it. All the way through, I kept my heart open. I did not shut down. I felt every part of it knowing that my emotions would not kill me – they simply needed to be expressed.

After six hours or so, I felt nothing. There were no strong emotions left. There were no more tears to cry. I was spent.

There was this eerie space all around me. I sat in silence in a pool of shattered glass, ice and debris.

I walked to the lounge door and opened it. It felt like everything was moving in slow motion. I stood outside and took in a deep breath of fresh air. I sat on the grass outside and noticed birds, noticed the wind caressing the shrubs in my garden. I watched ants making their way along the grass. I sat like this for what must have been a few hours. No thoughts went through my mind, I was simply present to nothing.

My first thought was that I was thirsty. I walked through the garden and tiptoed through the glass on the floor of the house to a cupboard in my kitchen. I managed to locate one lone mug that had not been destroyed and made myself a fruit smoothie with whatever I could find of the crushed ice in the bag I had decimated. I even found a little tropical umbrella in the drawer left over from a party years ago and stuck it into a piece of pineapple on the side of the mug. As I made the fruit smoothie, each piece of fruit I sliced was cut in slow motion. I was astounded at how present I felt. When done, I carried my mug with me and slowly walked over to the sofa in the lounge. As I sat there I was present to silence. Emptiness. There was no more anger, no more sadness, no more despair, and no more depression - just nothing.

I felt like I was standing at the beginning of something. Almost like I was standing in an empty white room ready to be created. It was a life transforming moment and life has never been the same since then.

Over those hours I'd not only destroyed everything breakable in my home, I'd killed the old married-Adèle. Like a phoenix rising from the ashes, a new Adèle emerged from the broken glass. The emotions I had unleashed every day in the preceding nine days culminating in today's final outburst of emotion was a purifying hurricane. Previously hidden from me, a new door opened. Letting out those emotions on the ninth day was the key.

Sure, that evening there was some mess to clean up. I do remember wondering what the hell I had done to my house, but it was an amazing moment of clarity and peace.

I encourage you to let out your strong emotions today. Sitting with your anger, resentments, sadness and not expressing it can eventually lead to resistance, resignation and depression. Holding on to those emotions will eventually kill all aliveness in your life because your ability to allow your anger to be expressed is linked to your ability to be vulnerable and connected with others. Let your anger go and your intimacy with everyone else will be improved because your ability to love and experience peace will expand.

This is the day for courage as you must walk this path alone. If you surrender to all your emotions, experiencing them fully, you'll find that inside the core of your anger is sadness, despair and regret and inside the sadness is fear. Fear is at the core of many negative emotions. Be comforted by the fact that few emotions last longer than 30 minutes when fully experienced and embraced.

WARNING:

I don't advocate releasing emotions 'at' anyone. This is called ranting and is not a responsible action of someone living at the cause of their life. Be responsible for the timing in terms of releasing your emotions.

Complete your daily homework – start this in the morning.

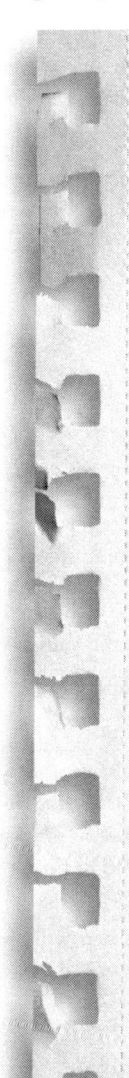

Exercise:

Release your strong emotions like anger/upset and despair

This exercise is designed as a catalyst to help you trigger your emotions into action. Even if you are not feeling angry, you can tap into your anger with this exercise. It is healthy to feel your anger. There is no judgment and this exercise is not about being enlightened or positive, just be angry.

You need:

1 baseball bat/squash racket/cricket bat or sturdy stick.

Five large bags of ice, gloves and goggles.

A large, open space that is easy to clean afterwards and where you can smash the ice and not be heard or disturbed.

Wear loose clothing and shoes.

Make cards for all the things that make you angry in your life.

Steps:

- Clench your fists and teeth and breathe angrily to get into the mood
- Lay out the bag of ice on the ground and look at it. Lay the cards, photographs or symbols of your anger on the bag of ice.
- Think about all the things you're angry or upset about, everything that should have happened in your marriage, in your life, in your divorce. Allow yourself to embrace these emotions and then allow yourself to feel them, express them through shouting or swearing or screaming.
- There is no need to think, just feel and express.
- When you're ready, beat the living daylights out of that bag of ice!
- Roar, yell, scream, and cry. Don't stop until the ice has been destroyed.
- Feel and release any other emotions that arise. Allow them to be. They will not last for more than 30 minutes to a few hours if you surrender to them (then they are done.)
- You will know you are done feeling your emotions when you can feel no more and are simply present to nothingness and the feeling of 'space'.

When done:

- Ensure you drink water or juice. Releasing emotions is thirsty work!
- Clean up any mess.
- Rest. You'll probably feel very tired.

SPECIAL NOTE: If you did not complete Day 9's exercise, then delay progressing with Day 10 of the *naked divorce* until you have completed the exercise from Day 9.

day
10
METAMORPHOSIS

TIP FOR THE DAY: There is a temptation to think that the reason your relationship failed was because of your ex and who he is. Be careful of falling into this trap. The common person in all of your relationships is you.

If you have the courage to find out where you can be responsible for your relationships not working out, then you have the power.

Theme: Completing your past relationships

Date: Sunday, _____

🕐 **Estimated time to complete the exercise: 3-5 hours**

Remember to go through the daily checklist

Tick when done

Do the reading and exercise for the day in one go:

[ ]

The first step is to complete Day 9 and think of everything you learnt from your past relationship. Your emotions now released, will leave you with some things you have learnt from your past relationship.

Completing Day 9

- Underneath your anger are needs you had within your marriage that you never communicated. What did you need in your marriage that you never received? Write down those needs. Remember to have compassion for yourself. Whatever you expressed yesterday, back in your past you did not have the insights you have today.

- List the things you have learnt from the relationship and that you will never repeat or do again.

- Keep going until you have a list of 50 things you have learnt.

Completing your past relationships

When done working on everything you learnt from your marriage, it's important to look into the source or reason your relationship ended BUT the key is to look at this from the place of *what you can be responsible for.*

In this exercise, it's important to view your marriage in the context of all your relationships in the past as this helps you remain impartial. It may be tempting to say, "Yes, but what about him and him taking responsibility?" Unfortunately this kind of thinking will not help you. He is on his own healing path. The common thread in all your relationships is you, so look within yourself for the things you know contributed to the demise of the marriage.

Why? Because if you can be responsible for the source of your part in the marital breakdown, you are in control of changing this pattern in the future. You are not in control of his thinking or relationship patterns. What goes around comes around, so focus only on yourself and your own happiness and he will learn the lessons he needs to learn in his time.

My story:

It would have been easy to blame Bruce for the failure of our relationship. He did have so many affairs that it would clearly appear to an external observer that the failure of our relationship was his fault. This thinking gave me no power.

When I did this exercise, I realized that I was responsible for marrying him knowing we didn't have real chemistry together. Even though I was crazy about him, I knew he wasn't crazy about me and I stepped over knowing that he was lying to me about his affairs. I was responsible for emasculating him on many occasions because I earned more money than he did and rubbed it in his face. I was responsible for being unfaithful, a coward and for putting up with an unworkable situation in my marriage. My lack of standing up for myself and what I deserved in a relationship contributed to the relationship carrying on much longer than it needed to.

My need to be claimed and walk up the aisle superseded my feelings that something was not quite right. I did that. I was responsible. Taking responsibility not only set me free, it gave me back my power.

When I did the exercise for Day 10, I realized that my pattern with my ex was not an isolated event. My previous relationships ended in a similar way. I had a pattern of attracting men who would leave me emotionally and then I would either dump them or be left with him cheating. I unconsciously sought out men who would leave.

Harville Hendrix, author of 'Getting the Love you want' believes that we all have a **core issue** (for want of a more accurate term) that emerged in our lives as a result of growing up as a human being.

If you look back at all your previous relationships, you'll probably notice a pattern. Often the relationships end in the same way or for similar reasons. Once you see your pattern in relationships, you'll see those patterns everywhere in your life. Your patterns are driven by your core issue. The good news is that this pattern is your mind's unconscious desire to help bring your core issue to the surface of your awareness so you can heal it once and for all and create the life you want. The problem is that most of us have no idea what our core issue is and how to resolve it.

Below is an example pattern discovered by one of my clients in reading back the stories of her past romantic relationships:

1. *Most of my relationships have ended with my partner leaving me.*

2. *Most of my relationships have ended because I became attached to the relationship not ending. I didn't want to feel abandoned, so the minute I felt like my partner was withdrawing from me, I would take my focus off my own life and put it on saving the relationship. Often, the relationship didn't actually need saving because nothing was wrong, I'd just interpreted it that way e.g. when my partner would withhold communication or go quiet or show an interest in other women, I'd perceive that they were going to leave, so I'd go straight into, "save the relationship" mode. This change of focus would make my partner feel that something was wrong, and instead of communicating my fear to him, I'd become needy and go into pleasing him to try to make him stay. Neediness is never attractive and it repels people and so I would unconsciously drive my partner away and eventually my partner would leave...*

3. *Whenever this pattern has played out in my life, I have ALWAYS (as in every time) felt abandoned (my core issue and biggest fear).*

4. *I seem to always attract people who abandon me and who are not actually suited to me.*

What my client acknowledged after completing this exercise was that she was unconsciously attracting people who would abandon her because how the world occurred for her was that people abandoned her.

It's a bit like buying a red car and all you can see are red cars.

She could therefore ONLY attract what she could perceive which, were men who would abandon her.

Consider that if she widened her perception to include people who would love and cherish her, she would be able to see them when they came along.

Discover your own unconscious patterns in relationships and your core issue

The important part in discovering your core issue is to identify what you feel whenever you play out your pattern. Your feelings will point in the direction of your core issue. Take a moment now and do this exercise:

1. Write down a brief story of all your past relationships using the table below. Every one you can remember. Write down what happened to end the relationship and the feelings you felt when it ended. (be more honest with yourself than you've ever been before):

Name of the person?	How did you meet them?	How long you were together?	How it ended?	Who ended it?	What do you believe ended it?	What did you decide about yourself at the end of this relationship?

2. Now, read all your stories back and if you haven't already, find the common threads in what you wrote. Perhaps you have abandonment issues, perhaps you consistently attract cheaters or abusive men. Perhaps it always ends with an argument. Maybe you can't commit because you feel like committing is a sure path to feeling hurt if your partner leaves. Maybe you don't speak up because you're scared that you'll get into trouble.

3. Look over what you wrote in the previous step and identify the common feelings you felt in most of your relationships. Usually these feelings surface as fears, particularly when you perceive that you are somehow under threat. These fears will point you to your issue that you keep on inviting into your life.

My pattern in relationships is .,..(describe your repeating pattern).

When complete, journal what you noticed…

Can you find any patterns within your past relationships?

If so, list all the patterns you have found.

Keeping those patterns in mind, what choices do you now make for your future?

Drink at least six glasses of water during the day.

day

11

METAMORPHOSIS

KEEP THIS IN MIND FOR THE DAY: To get complete emotional release from your marriage, you might need to hear your ex say sorry. Realistically, very few of us will ever get the 'sorry' we need to help us heal.

The exercise is all about how you can be in the driver's seat when it comes to hearing the perfect apology.

Theme: Hear the 'sorry' you have always wanted to hear

Date: Monday, _____

🕐 **Estimated time to complete the exercise: 90 minutes**

Remember to go through the daily checklist

Tick when done

Read through the thought for the day:

☐

My story:

I got to a point in my healing, where I needed to hear Bruce say sorry. Unfortunately at that point I knew I would not hear it from him in the way I needed to hear it. Consequently, I designed this exercise with the help of my friend Olwen Renowden and her experience in resolving a past relationship.

Try it. It really works!

It began with writing a letter from Bruce to me, titled: **What I really always wanted to hear from Bruce**. I didn't hold back and wrote the most elaborate apology letter I could create. In the letter, I literally had him apologize for everything I ever wanted him to apologize for. In short, it was a fantastic process. I designed this exercise to be dramatic and over the top. The idea is not to be responsible or enlightened in this letter. Just let go, be self-indulgent. Have fun with it. Before you write yours, here is an excerpt from mine to inspire you:

My dearest lost love Adèle (the most perfect woman on the planet ever.)

You are beautiful, gorgeous and I completely desired you and if I ever said otherwise I was lying to you and to myself. I married you because I loved you completely and you were my soul mate. And whatever happens in the future, that was really why I married you and whatever I did or said later, that was the truth. For some reason I was a complete idiot and I cheated on you. I cheated on the woman I loved the most in the world. I am so sorry for talking about how beautiful other women were instead of pulling you closer and telling you that you were beautiful or gorgeous. You really were the perfect wife – you really took care of me and I never took care of you or honored you in our relationship.

I never wanted to hurt you. You are the closest, dearest person in my life and what saddens me is that I will probably never have anyone again who will get as close as you did.

Etc. etc. (I went on for 22 pages. It was great fun.)

....

I hope you forgive me, Adèle.

Love

Bruce

Spend today thinking about your letter. If you want to start writing it during your lunch break, do so but you'll have the opportunity to write it later on.

Read through the exercise you will be doing later today. Allow yourself to think about it during the day.

Exercise:

Write a letter from your ex to you.
In the letter, write:

1. Everything you ever wanted him to apologize for: ([Your name], I am so sorry I ever did xxxx or made you feel xxxx, or didn't love you like you deserved to be loved...) Make sure it is a long letter and do not leave anything out.

2. When done, read the letter out loud to yourself.

3. Journal how you feel.

4. When you are done, rewrite each point of the letter in your own words to yourself. (For example, I forgive myself for being with a man who I knew didn't love me in the way I deserved to be loved, xxxx.)

5. When done, read the letter out loud to yourself.

6. Journal how you feel.

day
12
METAMORPHOSIS

KEEP THIS IN MIND FOR THE DAY: "I never regretted the relationships I had, they always made me better for the next one..."
~ David Beckham

Spend today thinking about what you learnt from your old relationship and how it has made you more aware and better prepared for your next one.

Theme: Framework for my future relationships

Date: Tuesday, _____

🕐 **Estimated time to complete the exercise: 90 minutes**

Remember to go through the daily checklist

Tick when done

Read through the thought for the day:

☐

Now that you have written the letter from your ex to you, the next step is to forgive yourself for anything that you feel you did which contributed to the demise of the relationship as well as acknowledging your successes. My divorce left me with a huge sense of failure. I had planned to spend the rest of my life with Bruce, so the relationship ending felt like an insult to myself and what I was meant to accomplish on every level. I worried about what other people thought about me and wanted to hide.

Today's exercise is about starting the process of getting those feelings of failure complete, so you can have a more balanced view of the relationship.

Read through the exercise you'll be doing later today. Allow yourself to think about it during the day.

Exercise:

Go through the letter you wrote from your ex to you.

1. Read the letter from your-ex-to-yourself out loud.
2. Read the letter from yourself-to-yourself out loud.
3. Write down what you are acknowledging yourself for in the relationship (in present tense; this is very important).
4. Write down what you are unwilling to tolerate in a relationship. Journal how you feel about it and write down what you notice.
5. Optional: When done, burn the letters.

Here is an example of what I wrote:

What I acknowledge myself for is...

- *I am supportive and caring.*
- *I am the wind beneath my man's wings and I am elemental in his success.*
- *I am courageous, adventurous and up for adventure.*
- *I am responsible and aware.*
- *I am sexy and fun to be with.*

What I am unwilling to tolerate in a relationship is:

- *Cheating.*
- *Stealing.*
- *Lying or whimpish behavior.*
- *Hypocrisy.*
- *No ambition (endlessly sitting with a Play Station or taking drugs.)*
- *Uncommitted behavior.*
- *Unwillingness to grow or look at himself.*

day 13

METAMORPHOSIS

KEEP THIS IN MIND FOR THE DAY: There is a temptation to become obsessed with how your ex is doing, replaying the tape in your head of what he said and what it could have meant, and what should or shouldn't have happened in the relationship.

Instead of focusing on those thoughts, become fascinated with learning everything you can about the background dynamics of your relationship and the lessons you have learnt. Become keenly aware of yourself as a science project, where you use this event as a catalyst or experiment to learn everything you can about yourself and how you operate in a relationship. Learn those lessons now, so that you can put these to work successfully in your next relationship.

Theme: Learning from past patterns in your relationship

Date: Wednesday, _____

🕒 **Estimated time to complete the reading/ exercise: 90 minutes**

Remember to go through the daily checklist

Tick when done

Read through the thought for the day:

☐

Today is all about learning about some of the patterns that we commonly experience in a relationship. There are three in particular that I will cover today and they're truly fascinating. Put on your science experiment hat and let's see whether you identify with any of these patterns in your old relationship.

Antony Robbin's five R's of romantic relationship communication

Far from running from the idea of relationships during my divorce, I found myself fascinated by the dynamics of successful relationships. I wanted to learn everything I could about relationships and what makes them successful. This model from world-renowned life coach and self-help author Antony Robbins made an enormous difference to my life. Essentially, he moves through the cycles of how we communicate with each other in a romantic relationship and how, if we're not vigilant, intimacy and love can break down. The five R's are:

⇨ Resistance

➡️ Resentment

➡️ Rejection

➡️ Resignation

➡️ Repression

 VIDEO: There is a video on my YouTube channel that talks about the 5 R's of relationships. Watch it here: **www.youtube.com/nakeddivorce**

Initially, you start out your married life with some kind of hope for a prosperous relationship. You're in love, your partner is amazing and everything is perfect. One day, something happens. He says something unkind or does something that elicits **resistance** in you. You get that, "Whoa! Hold on, that was not okay!" feeling. This initial **resistance** is a completely normal reaction to learning new things about your partner and also normal for any behavior he displays that is not okay with you. As women, we often assume that men will know when they've done or said something wrong. So we wait for them to acknowledge this by sulking or withdrawing into silence.

Some men are very perceptive and will know something's up, others won't have a clue that their behavior has made their partner unhappy. When we keep quiet about our **resistance**, the feeling can shift into **resentment**. Many people in unhealthy relationships simply avoid facing reality. Sometimes this can be because the people involved may be trying to make themselves appear superior. Or perhaps they don't want to face the fact that their mates really aren't who they say they are, or that they've fallen from the perfect mate perch.

For example, Anne B covers up and makes excuses for her mate, Ben B, who is always late from work and almost always misses family functions. She might be trying to avoid the truth: that he's a workaholic, or having an affair. She does so because she doesn't want to destroy their perfect couple image in everyone's eyes – and perhaps even in her own eyes.

It's like ignoring that broken handle on a door in your home or not replacing that light bulb. If you don't address the **resentment**, other resistances and other resentments will begin to build up. Once there is some momentum with your **resentment**, then you or your partner may begin to experience **rejection** within the relationship.

Once **rejection** creeps into a relationship, it becomes overwhelming and makes it difficult to create or sustain an intimate sexual relationship. Those of us who have been married a long time know that once the relationship feels strained, the regularity of sex is affected, and things can spiral downhill very quickly. The bed becomes divided into his and hers zones and intimacy suffers. Even the smallest things he says or does are irritating and more **resistance**, **resentment** and **rejection** builds up. If you don't discuss your feelings of rejection, then your relationship can shift into the place of **resignation**.

This is when you can so easily slip into co-habitation; operating as housemates or mere friends. Passion, love and chemistry, and all the elements needed to maintain the spark and fire within the relationship, exit through the window. You can end up with an amicable friendship.

This is dangerous! Contentment and harmony are wonderful hallmarks of a marriage, but be sure they're not camouflaging deep **resignation** in a relationship. When left too long, **resignation** can lead to **repression**. We've all been out to dinner and watched the married couple opposite sitting in complete silence. They're courteous to one another and exchange pleasantries, but perhaps they have succumbed to **resignation** or **repression** and no longer actively discuss their relationship.

Repression completely kills the passion and chemistry in a relationship. At this point you may begin to question your commitment to the relationship. You may wonder if your partner was ever right for you. You may begin to spend hours day-dreaming about escaping from the relationship. When we're not claimed as women by our men in a relationship, we can become obsessed with romance and escapism, daydreaming about being rescued from the disappointing reality of life and marriage.

When you're removed from the reality of your relationship and your life and escape into a fantasy world, then you're in real danger of seeking fulfillment outside your relationship and marriage. This is fertile ground for cheating. This is when the midlife crisis happens. This is when we start eating for comfort.

Because we didn't communicate openly, vulnerably and humanly about all the little resentments, in the moment, they built up and killed the relationship.

Spend time today thinking about your communication in your previous relationships and what you can learn from the patterns established. In the exercise later today, you can look at your discoveries.

Karpman's Drama Triangle

The Drama Triangle is a psychological model of human interaction first described by world-renowned psychologist Stephen Karpman. According to various texts from Karpman, Lynne Forrest who wrote 'The three faces of Victim' and Lynne Namka 'The Drama Triangle', many of us fall into this triangle at some point in our romantic relationships. See if you can identify with this pattern in your previous relationship.

Think of a situation in your relationship where you felt stuck in a rut or disempowered.

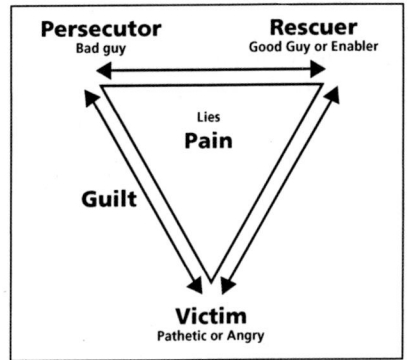

Typically, there will be three roles at play in those relationships:

- The person who is treated as, or accepts the role of Victim or Damsel in Distress. This person needs to be rescued to feel validated as a person.

- The person who pressurizes, coerces or persecutes the victim (the Villain, Bully or 'Angry' victim). This person needs to feel power over others to feel validated as a person.

- The Rescuer, Martyr or False Hero, who intervenes out of an ostensible wish to help the situation or the underdog. This person is not an honest rescuer in an emergency and needs to rescue to feel validated as a person.

Whenever we operate within these roles, we act upon our own selfish needs, rather than acting in a genuinely responsible or altruistic manner.

The Victim or Damsel in Distress

This person needs rescuing or feels victimized, somehow repressed or in need of help. Victims love the drama and will sometimes unconsciously create situations high in drama where they are cast as the leading actress. Victims will always attract rescuers to rescue them from their situation but at the same time, by being rescued, it perpetuates their negative feelings. They will receive a great deal of attention and will simultaneously love being saved by the rescuer.

The trouble is, whenever you allow someone to rescue you, you hand over the reigns of your life and block yourself from solving your own problems and having the pleasure of being independent. When dealing with Bruce's infidelities during my divorce, I was dying to play the victim. I wanted him to be the perpetrator and the bad guy, so I could feel absolved of all responsibility for the failure of my marriage.

I soon realized that being the victim sucked and I urgently looked for ways to move out of that disempowering space. If you're operating as a victim, you're going to get stuck there.

Common phrases the victim uses:

"Why don't you", "If it weren't for you", "Why does this always happen to me?" "I can't cope", "Please help me and tell me what to do. "

How to stop being a victim:

Start taking charge of your life and being responsible for your life. Learn to set boundaries (see Day 19) and make your own decisions. Victims need to learn to stand on their own two feet without a rescuer. Stop being concerned about making the wrong decisions, just practice making your own decisions and being responsible for the outcomes, no matter what happens.

The Persecutor, Bully or Villain

This person blames, criticizes and keeps the victim oppressed. Like the bad guy in the movie, they enjoy the feeling of authority and control.

Common phrases the villain uses:

"It's all your fault", "See what you made me do", "You got me into this."

How to stop being a villain:

Focus on your own problems. Realize that you get your kicks out of controlling others and that this makes you a bully. Give people the freedom to communicate and live their lives as they see fit.

The Rescuer, Martyr or False Hero

This person rescues even when they really don't want to. They have strong feelings of guilt if they don't rescue the victim. This person usually sighs a great deal and feels the burden of the world on their shoulders because there's so much rescuing to be done!

The relationship between the victim and the rescuer can be one of co-dependency. The rescuer keeps the victim dependent on them by playing into their victimhood. The victim has their needs met by having the rescuer take care of them.

Common phrases rescuers use include:

"Let me help you", "Look how hard I've tried", "I'm only trying to help you", "I will sort this out, you're not capable of doing it on your own".

How to stop being a rescuer:

By rescuing, you become an enabler of victim-like behavior all around you. Realize that you have an unhealthy NEED to be NEEDED. Focus on your own life and your own problems. You may provide guidance, but your job is not to help the person, your job is to empower them to help themselves. Instead of giving them the fish, teach them to fish for themselves. Stop getting your kicks out of being needed by other people.

Harville Hendrix's Fuser-Isolator model

You end a relationship and a few months or years later, you meet a new partner. You fall in love again and everything feels rosy for the first few months. Then, before long you realize that you are basically in the same relationship as you were in before, just with a different person.

The same issues surface again. You have the same arguments and often, the relationship ends in the same way as your last one. Sound familiar?

Dr. Harville Hendrix has an interesting perspective on this phenomenon which he talks about in his book, 'Getting the Love you Want'.

In his years of research helping couples resolve their relationship challenges, Harville discovered that he could divide his clients into two broad categories, **Isolators** and **Fusers**.

Isolators seek independence and autonomy in life and unconsciously push others away. As such, they need a lot of space around them and the freedom to come and go as they please.

On the other hand, **Fusers** have an insatiable need for closeness and reassurance and often need to stay in constant verbal contact with their partners. Fusers want to do things together and often are prone to feeling abandoned.

Here's the breakthrough phenomenon that Harville discovered...

Isolators and **Fusers** almost always end up in relationships together. They are attracted to each other like opposite side of a magnet, and so begins an infuriating game of push and pull that leaves neither partner satisfied. **Isolators** often report that their **Fuser** partners engulf them in their neediness and they just want to run away.

"I am feeling so trapped"

"I need to get away"

"I need some space"

Fusers in contrast often feel unloved or abandoned.

"Is he going to leave?"

"Is he unhappy?"

"Does he still love me?"

The more independence the **Isolater** craves, the more connection the **Fuser** craves.

When a **Fuser-Isolator** couple come together, they initially feel the magnetism of falling in love, but soon realize that they are not getting their need for connection or independence met. At this point, most couples end up in conflict and more often than not, either separate or only survive in the relationship (often for the sake of their children).

The reason these relationships fail is because the couple is totally unaware of the unconscious dynamics they are playing out.

Like most things in life, the solution is AWARENESS.

SO, if you can recognize that you are a **Fuser,** then your job is to give your **Isolator** partner space and independence. Slowly you will learn that your world does not come crashing down around you, and your partner does not leave.

Conversely, if you can recognize yourself as an **Isolator,** your job is to stretch yourself to reassure your partner and learn that your independence is not threatened and you can still be a separate Self while being connected to another.

Read through the exercise you will be doing later today. Allow yourself to think about it during the day.

Exercise:

In examining the reading for today, journal about any patterns you can identify within your previous relationship. Look at which role you played and where you can be responsible for any negative patterns in your relationship.

1. Think about the five R's of relationships. Where didn't you communicate your resistances and resentments?

....

....

2. What can you be responsible for in not managing the five R's of your relationship?

....

....

3. What actions can you take to remedy this in the future?

....

....

4. Think about Karpman's Drama Triangle. Were you stuck in one of these roles?

....

....

5. What can you be 1% responsible for being stuck in a disempowering role in your marriage?

....

....

6. What actions can you take to remedy this in the future?

....

....

7. Are you a **Fuser** or an **Isolator** in relationships?

....

....

8. In the next few weeks, practice the steps explained above. If you are a **Fuser**, grant **Isolators** around you space and independence. If you are an **Isolator**, Gift the **Fusers** around you closeness and reassurance.

....

....

day
14
METAMORPHOSIS

KEEP THIS IN MIND FOR THE DAY: It takes great courage to find the root cause of your divorce, but if you can be responsible for what happened in your relationship, you will free yourself of it. Responsibility does not mean blame. It means acknowledging that you were part of what didn't work so that you learn from the situation.

You will carry this sense of empowerment within yourself and into any new relationship. Think of it as an investment in change. If you leave your marriage with nothing but blame and the feeling that you were a victim of a bad situation, you'll remain disempowered and stuck.

Theme: Finding the source of your divorce

Date: Thursday, _____

🕐 **Estimated time to complete the reading/ exercise: 120 minutes**

Remember to go through the daily checklist

Tick when done

Read through the thought for the day:

☐

When things aren't working between couples, it's often because neither is taking responsibility for the relationship.

There is a misunderstanding in life that partnership means that each person is responsible for 50% of the relationship. It takes two people to be in the relationship so what is powerful if you were being *cause in life* is to feel like 100% of the relationship is owned by each party. In your failed marriage, owning your part of the demise of that partnership is courageous and freeing. Although you accept your ex did whatever he did, stepping up to own your part in the breakdown of your marriage leaves you free to be in your next relationship with ease and without blaming your ex.

Today I'd like you to spend some time thinking about the root cause of your divorce. Take a look at what you can be responsible for, irrespective of whatever your ex did or didn't do. What you learn from this exercise will be critical to the success of your next relationship. So this is about you and your new life and not about the final tally of the scoreboard of your previous relationship. Read through the list below and see how many of the root causes of the divorce you're big enough to own.

Finding the source of your divorce is about finding the origins of where the relationship stopped working so you can release the negative emotions from your body, shift your paradigm and make you think differently about your life. You may find that you identify with more than one source and if that is the case, learn everything there is to learn for your next relationship.

When you started this book, I promised to accompany you on this journey, particularly when things get tough. I also promised I'd kick your butt if you shied away from tough stuff. This is a heads up: this is a tough exercise. This is the kick-your-butt part. You may find yourself getting reactivated by some of these sources. That is a good sign so step up to the plate, even if you're cursing me under your breath. I'm okay with that. As I mentioned above, finding the root of your divorce is absolutely essential to your next relationship. This exercise requires self-knowledge and honesty. You deserve that.

> NOTE: Ironically, if there is one you feel particularly strongly about, consider that this is probably the cause of your divorce.

While this isn't an exhaustive list, it will give you some food for thought:

1. Not managing the five R's

Refer to Day 13. Not managing your daily resistances and resentments in your marriage can lead to its death. When one half of the partnership habitually shuns or ignores the other, it's a sure sign of an unhealthy relationship.

The reality

Confront the fact that you didn't communicate openly about resentments in each moment they arose during your marriage. What was the impact of not doing so?

What to do if this was the source of your divorce

Go back to the relationship story you wrote. Underline trigger points in your story so you can identify when things changed between you. If necessary, make amends with your ex and make a commitment to be aware of communication in your future relationship and to manage the five R's responsibly. Communicating vulnerably and openly in each moment takes commitment and courage. This is what a healthy relationship demands of you.

Question to ask yourself

Think about the five R's of relationships. Can you think of instances in the past when you didn't communicate your resistances and resentments?

2. You didn't let him win at loving you

Perhaps you were an ice queen or perhaps you never stopped testing his commitment in the relationship. Either way, nothing he ever said or did seemed good enough for you. You kept dishing out criticisms, comments and suggestions. He felt invalidated and probably ended up thinking or even saying: "I just can't win."

The reality:

> To stay in love, a man must feel that he can succeed in loving you. He should feel that you need him in some way and that he makes a difference to your life.
>
> **What to do if this was the source of your divorce:**

NOTE:

A man must feel he can win at loving you.

> If your man feels he never satisfies you, he will feel he's failed at loving you and will eventually withdraw his love and attention.
>
> Follow the steps in the section entitled *Principles on Keeping Love Alive* in the final section of this book to keep the love fires burning. Ensure that in your next relationship, you stop being a know-it-all, dragging a sack-full of criticism around with you, and waiting to dish it out to the hapless man in your life. Relationships are fragile and if they're taken for granted and not nurtured, they will die.

Question to ask yourself:

Where did you not allow him to win at loving you in your relationship?

3. The checklist

No one is perfect but you handle your partners as if they should be. You have a checklist against which you grade them and if they don't make the grade, you punish them, make their lives hell, dump them, become indifferent to them or discard them. The sad thing is if you run your relationship according to a checklist of attributes, you'll never get to know your partner. You cannot be present to the person you are with because you are so busy comparing them to an unrealistic set of expectations that they cannot live up to.

> **The reality:**

Those who can't respect their partner's right to their own space, opinions and ways of doing things can expect to see their future relationships nose-dive. Relationships fed on criticism and resentment soon become like wilted flowers.

What to do if this was the source of your divorce:

Consider letting go of the controls, and letting go of how things ought to be.

Suspend your rules for how the house needs to be organized, what kind of work he should be doing, chores he should be performing or ties he should not be wearing. Consider that if you have a checklist, you hold the masculine energy within the relationship. There will be no space for anyone else to step up and live anywhere else but in your shadow. Count the costs of your checklist for partners. If you're not aware of the costs, complete the *Real Impact of my Divorce* exercise earlier in the book. You're living in a dream world if you believe that any man can measure up against your high expectations. You'll never be happy in a relationship. You'll move from partner to partner. Much like a dinosaur crashing through a forest with its tail swinging backwards and forwards, flattening everything in sight, you're oblivious to the destruction you leave in your wake. You'll also make your partner miserable because being with you will be hell.

This is your wake-up call. Bin the checklist and have a shot at an amazing relationship with someone who is not on tenterhooks all the time he's with you.

Question to ask yourself:

Think about your relationship. Did you hold him up against your checklist of perfection?

4. Living in a dream world

Many people in relationships simply avoid facing reality. There are many reasons for this. Perhaps they can't cope with the fact that their partners and lives aren't picture-perfect. Or perhaps they don't want to face the fact that their mates aren't who they say they are. Or perhaps they can't be bothered quitting a bad relationship.

The reality:

Simulated relationships or those living under the illusion of a happy, healthy relationship are destined for failure. Wake up and smell the coffee. The disguise you've put in place won't last. If you can't see it as a façade, the people in your life probably can.

Often people who are resigned to living in a dream world are often conflict-averse, pretending everything was okay to keep the peace.

What to do if this was the source of your divorce:

Realize that you were a little dead in your marriage. Whenever we are not truthful with ourselves and others, we kill our self expression and a piece of ourselves. Consider the impact of pretence on your life.

Start telling the truth to those around you. Start with a small group of people and then move onto your family. Tell the truth and blow the lid off the facade in your life.

Question to ask yourself:

Were you avoiding the truth about your relationship?

5. No perseverance or commitment, gets bored easily

A sign of a great relationship is not how you cope when things are going well, it's about the toolkit you've assembled and built up for when things go pear-shaped. Commitment is what keeps you in the relationship during those for worse times within your for better or worse vow. If one person begins to feel disillusioned with the marriage, or trapped, tired, helpless, depressed or let down and turns to alternatives like drugs, elicit relationships, gambling, etc., the relationship will suffer. Caring only about having your own needs met and neglecting what's healthy for the relationship is a death-knell.

The reality:

The honeymoon period does end in every relationship. Those who are able to work at fuelling the love fires during marriage, have a better chance of survival. Couples need to face issues together; add some new goals to the relationship, list some activities both enjoy, talk more, etc. This can happen only when each person has both feet in the relationship, and is committed to ensuring the relationship is regularly spiced with fun, adventure, and romance. Selfishness is the prime cause of marriage breakdown. Growing couples need maturity to develop together as they face adult issues in life and marriage.

What to do if this was the source of your divorce:

Firstly, acknowledge that you weren't committed to the relationship. Ask yourself why. Do you run when things don't feel good or the relationship requires some adjustment or retuning? Wanting to run in the face of testing will impact all facets of your life. Nothing meaningful is ever accomplished without commitment. If you have a problem with commitment, set yourself a challenge and draw up some boundaries. What will it take to see the project through? What makes you lose commitment? Lack of a common end goal? Lack of success markers? Stick with it through to the end and make a note of what you learnt about yourself.

Secondly, acknowledge that you're a bit self-centered. List the things you did at the expense of your partner and your relationship. If it's my way or no way, you'll probably accomplish a great deal, but it will be at the expense of your relationships. And if you're the kind who upsets the apple cart when you don't get your own way, you'll leave a trail of destruction in your wake. If you know that selfishness is your problem, commit yourself to finding that breakthrough. Practice being aware of your partner's needs.

Question to ask yourself:

Was your relationship characterized by a lack of commitment or selfishness on your part? Acknowledge the lessons you've learnt.

6. Stuck in the Drama Triangle/co-dependent relationship

See the reading on Day 13 for more on the Drama Triangle.

The reality:

If your relationship was modeled on the Drama Triangle, where neither party is willing to acknowledge the characteristic problems, or the need to shift to a healthier model of communication, then severing that relationship was possibly the best solution.

What to do if this was the source of your divorce:

Follow the recommendations listed in Day 13 in future relationships.

How to avoid victim mode:

Start taking charge of your life. Learn to set boundaries (see Day 19), make your own decisions (even if they're wrong) and accept responsibility for the outcome. Avoid rescuers.

How to avoid being a persecutor/perpetrator:

Focus on your own life and your own problems. Leave other people to tend to their lives. Stop nit-picking and bullying people to do what you believe is right.

How to prevent being a rescuer:

Stop getting your kicks from being needed by other people. If you want to help someone, teach him/ her to take care of themselves. As they like to point fingers at others, it's very important that victims take responsibility for their own lives. Focus on your life and your problems. Provide guidance by all means, but remember, your job is not to help the victim. Your job is to empower them. Read 'Codependent No More' written by Melodie Beattie.

Question to ask yourself:

Were you stuck in any one of these roles within your relationship?

7. Being his mummy VS being his woman

You mothered him, took care of him, supported him, packed his suitcases, pressed his clothes, fed and clothed him.

The reality:

Although you win top marks for taking care of him, he did not marry you to be his mummy. Acting as his mummy probably killed your sex life. The sad thing is for many of us, our only role models as wives and mothers were our own mothers who were often very nurturing and caring so you cannot be blamed for believing that this role extended to your husband. Someone should have told you that this was one sure fire way to kill intimacy in a relationship.

By doing everything for everyone, there's no room for anyone else to step up. This makes you an enabler of laziness and victim-type behavior around you. This ensures that you never have anyone taking care of you because they have no opportunities to do so. You're communicating that you don't believe that others can be responsible. Do you struggle to delegate? Do you struggle to trust others to get on with things? If the answer is yes, your life will become exhausting and you will never be taken care of.

This happens at work, too. Someone indispensable leaves the company and for a few days' chaos reigns as people find their feet. And then someone steps up to take charge and things begin to run smoothly. But you need a gap for that to happen. Someone had to step down and someone had to step into the breach.

What to do if this was the source of your divorce:

Stop caretaking. Leave the man in your relationship to take care of himself. Follow the steps in the section entitled *Principles on Keeping Love Alive* in the final section of this book to keep the love fires burning. If you're prone to mothering, be aware of this in your next relationship. If you begin to feel responsible for your man, stop and take a step back. Sometimes it's important to have the house a little messy, to wash his white shirts with your red underwear so the color runs, to eat frozen fish fingers for dinner or to forget to do the shopping. Sometimes it's important to take yourself out on an outing mid-week and leave your partner with no food in the refrigerator. All these little activities remind the man in your life that he too needs to step up and sort things out within the household and that all his caretaking needs are not your responsibility.

Note: To keep sexual chemistry alive in your relationship, remain feminine in your relationship and true to your feminine essence. Allow your man to be the man in your life.

Question to ask yourself:

Did you mother your ex-husband?

8. Using the relationship as a dumping ground

An occasional outbreak during a stressful moment, such as swearing at your partner in moment of high tension, while not admirable, can be considered normal.

However, harmful, violent physical responses, actions or verbal abuse is not. The latter have no place in healthy relationships.

The reality:

Verbal abuse or a violation of your partner, their personal property, friends, etc., is a red flag for an unhealthy relationship.

What to do if this was the source of your divorce:

If you have problems expressing your anger in a healthy way, Day 9 has a recommended exercise for releasing anger in a way that doesn't affect anyone. You should also examine the way you deal with stress. If you're harming others when you express anger, you need help. Sign up for an anger management seminar or stress coaching. Refer to www.nakeddivorce.com/resources/

Question to ask yourself:

Are you responsible for using your relationship as a dumping ground for your anger and issues?

9. Physical appearance

Disregarding your physical appearance is also a sign of an unhealthy relationship. It could signal substance abuse, depression or loss of interest in your partner.

The reality:

We all want to be with a partner we're attracted to. If you've let yourself go, either in the way you dress, your weight or physical attractiveness, it's time to do something about it.

What to do if this was the source of your divorce:

Consider the impact your physical appearance has on your life. If you put up with your partner's deteriorating physical appearance, practice the exercises listed on Day 19.

Questions to ask yourself:

Did you let yourself go during your relationship?

What will you do about that now?

10. Worrying that you love your partner more than he loves you

If you were always worried about your partner leaving you or doubting his commitment to you, you may just have gotten what you were most afraid of. Constantly fretting will only make you unhappy and precipitate all kinds of problems in your relationship.

The reality:

You're the one who's decided that you're not good enough for him, which means that you're the one who has to turn things around. Work on improving your self-image. Days 18-21 will help you.

What to do if this was the source of your divorce:

It's a matter of learning what creates attraction within a relationship. At the end of the book, there are some *Principles on Keeping Love Alive* which cover some core concepts on how to keep a man in love with you. Maintaining separateness, moving to your own rhythm, understanding that longing is often equated with love and focusing on making yourself happy whenever your partner disappears on you are some of the lessons from that section. Ultimately, love is a risk. Love cannot be controlled and nor can relationships. Sometimes they end. Control is an illusion and when we live our lives completely focused on controlling everyone and everything around us, we kill the joy and spontaneity. Living without loving is not living at all.

> **❝** *Worrying is praying for what you don't want.* **❞**

No longer succumbing to worry is easier said than done. I was a prize-winning worrier, so follow the steps on beating worry in the *Worry Buster* exercise on

Day 17 and practice your Daily Declarations to improve your self-image as well as combating worry in the moment whenever it arises.

Question to ask yourself:

Did you suffocate him with your love and did you worry constantly that something would go wrong?

11. Being a control-freak or Miss bossy boots

Did you boss your man around? Did you emasculate him to the point where he lost his identity and manliness?

The reality:

If you were a complete bossy boots in your relationship then I can tell you for sure, your man was suppressed and depressed being with you. No one likes being controlled or told what to do every minute of the day. The reality is when you boss your man around, the polarity of your relationship has reversed. You are holding more masculine energy in the relationship and he holds more creative/feminine energy. For there to be strong passionate sexual chemistry in a relationship the woman must hold the feminine energy and the man the masculine energy. These kind of relationships (where the woman is the one bossing the man around and controlling everything) can work provided that the man gets to be the man in your life in other ways.

1) Did you make all the decisions?
2) Were you the more forceful one?
3) How does he handle you exploding/ throwing a tantrum? Did he retreat/ do anything to keep the peace? Did he withdraw?
4) Who dealt with all the finances?
5) Who took the sexual initiative? Did you have an active sex life?
6) Did your marriage end with him having an affair?

What to do if this was the source of your divorce:

Follow the steps in the section entitled *Principles on Keeping Love Alive* in the final section of this book to keep the love fires burning. No matter how successful you are compared to your man or powerful you are in comparison to him, when you get home, allow your man to be your man in your life. Empower his leadership. If you are constantly telling him he's doing something wrong or controlling or bossing your man around, pretty soon he will not enjoy how he feels about himself when he is around you. He may seek to feel different about himself and there are many ways that a man can fulfill on this desire. Focus on your man feeling like the best version of himself with you.

Many women in long happy marriages have found this secret and manage it every day. Even if u know exactly what u are doing, play the dumb fox to let him feel like your man.

Forgive yourself for being a Miss Bossy Boots – you didn't have the insights about life back then that you have today.

Questions to ask yourself:

Are you willing to step back from how you think things must get done in life? Can you allow your man to lead you?

12. Being a doormat or a poodle

Sherry Argov coined this phrase of 'behaving like a poodle' in a relationship. A poodle was usually at the receiving end of a control freak. If you can recognize that you spent most of your marriage jumping through hoops for him and being willing to do anything for him. Perhaps you were always rushing in to take responsibility for everything. Perhaps you take care of everything and clean up after everyone so that you can be at peace. But by the end of the day you're exhausted and resentful. You probably do this elsewhere in your life.

The reality:

You're the one who decided to be a doormat. It's time to work on your self-image.

What to do if this was the source of your divorce:

Follow the steps in the section entitled *Principles on Keeping Love Alive* in the final section of this book to keep the love fires burning. Follow the tips on Day 19 and practice the Daily Declarations to improve your self-image.

Question to ask yourself:

Were you a doormat in your relationship?

13. Incompatibility

This can be an easy one to hide behind. Everyone can cite instances of incompatibility in their marriage. But in this instance we're talking about the odd couple; the super manager and the super sloth; the ugly guy and the beauty queen, the older man and the young woman.

The reality:

The old adage tells us that opposites attract. But do they? You knew he wasn't your type, but somehow you fell into a relationship with him. There was that strange attraction… Opposites may attract, but ensuring you have some basic things in common is important for a lasting relationship. Some of these odd relationships do work, but it's not commonplace.

What to do if this was the source of your divorce:

Examine how you got into the relationship. Did you fall into it? Next time, be clear about what you're looking for in a mate and be more conscious about your compatibilities. Having common pursuits, activities and interests will feed your relationship and keep the fun alive.

Question to ask yourself:

Were you in an incompatible relationship? If so, what actions can you take now to prevent a repetition of this in the future?

14. Not making the relationship #1

You, your partner and your relationship must be ring-fenced. This triangle is paramount. Other obligations and commitments come second. Not being able to draw boundaries or sustain limits is a death knell to many marriages. And while it is fine for your marriage to take a back seat once in a while, in healthy relationships both parties need to feel and share the value of being number one in their partner's eyes.

The reality:

Relationships have a life and they need to be fed and nurtured.

What to do if this was the source of your divorce:

Make your relationship the centerpiece of your life. Spiritual considerations aside, in marriage there is nothing and no one else that should take precedence.

Questions to ask yourself:

Am I responsible for not making my relationship number 1? Am I hiding behind other activities?

15. The end of an exchange of benefits

Every relationship is based on an exchange of benefits, such as companionship, love, caring, friendship, and so on. When the exchange of benefits ends and neither of you is gaining anything from the relationship, it will naturally fizzle out.

The reality:

You must identify the source of the problem that got you to this point. When did you stop being friends, companions, lovers? This is usually not the root cause of divorce but a flag alerting you to the fact that your relationship is in danger.

What to do if this was the source of your divorce:

Look for the true source of your divorce that led to the exchange of benefits ending.

Questions to ask yourself:

Why do you think you stopped exchanging benefits in your relationship? What can you do to ensure this doesn't happen in the future?

Read through the exercise you'll be doing later today. Allow yourself to think about what you read during the day.

Exercise:

After examining the reading for today, find the source(s) of your divorce. If the source is not on this list, describe it in your own words.

The primary objective of this exercise is to take responsibility for what the source of the divorce is.

Note: The more honest you are with yourself now, the better chance you have at a successful relationship in the future.

Release

You are now on the home stretch.

Statistically, most road accidents happen just outside cities. When people begin their journeys, they are alert, focused and have a high level of concentration. They take breaks and drive cautiously. They stop for lunch and let their co-driver take the wheel.

But close to the destination, they beginning to relax and become complacent. They let their mind wander with arbitrary questions like, "How is the dog doing?" "Has the garden been watered?" OR they may think it's a good idea to take a detour.

Be vigilant in the final five days – they are very important to your healing.

day
15
RELEASE

KEEP THIS IN MIND FOR THE DAY: Holding a grudge is like drinking poison, hoping the other person will die. Forgiveness doesn't mean you're condoning what the other person did. Forgiveness is about setting you free...

Theme: Stepping into forgiveness

Date: Friday, _____

🕐 **Estimated time to complete the exercise: 120 minutes**

Remember to go through the daily checklist

Tick when done

Read through the thought for the day:

> **❝** *The pathway to love is forgiveness and forgiveness is the tablet that dissolves resentment and resignation* **❞**

When someone you care about causes hurt, you can hold on to anger, resentment and thoughts of revenge and remain stuck, or you can embrace forgiveness and move forward.

How you forgive is very important. There are two distinctive types of forgiveness:

1. Shallow or 'cheap' forgiveness

Shallow or cheap forgiveness is when we forgive quickly and without thought, perhaps to look good, avoid conflict, or convince ourselves that we're fine and aren't holding a grudge. This type of forgiveness is a quick and easy pardon that doesn't get to grips with your emotions or how you come to terms with the injury to yourself.

When you refuse to forgive, you hold on to your anger. When you forgive cheaply, you simply let your anger go. If you forgive too easily, you fall prey to what Dr. Robert Emmons (a renowned U.S. professor at the University of California) calls calls a, "chronic concern to be in benevolent, harmonious relationships with others." This can lead to people seeking ways to numb their emotions through substance abuse.

Often, when people have moved through the **naked divorce grieving cycle**, they mistake the stage of acceptance for forgiveness. Acceptance means that you have come to terms with the reality of the situation and you accept the situation for what it is and for what it isn't. Authentic forgiveness goes hand-in-hand with responsibility. When you're ready to be responsible, when you reach a point of being grateful for everything that has happened and for everything you've learnt from your marriage and subsequent divorce, then you're ready to authentically forgive your ex.

The **naked divorce grieving cycle**

1. Denial

2. Anger and betrayal

3. Panic and negotiation

4. Humiliation, fear of failure or looking bad

5. Despair

6. Loss, grief and depression

7. Space and nothingness

8. Acceptance   **◄ Acceptance ≠ Forgiveness**

9. Responsibility and forgiveness

10. Gratitude

2. Authentic forgiveness

When you hold on to pain, old grudges, bitterness and even hatred, many areas of your life suffer. Your health suffers. When you're unforgiving, it's you who pays the price, over and over. You can bring your anger and bitterness into every relationship and new experience. Your life can become so wrapped up in the wrongs of the past that you can't enjoy the good things in the present.

Forgiveness is a choice to let go of resentments, hurt, anger and thoughts of revenge. Forgiveness is the act of untying yourself from thoughts and feelings that bind you to the offence committed against you. This can reduce the power these feelings exert over you, so that you can live a freer and happier life in the present. Forgiveness can even lead to feelings of understanding, empathy and compassion towards the person who hurt you. It is easier to get to this place if you're willing to look at what you can be responsible for in the breakdown of your marriage.

Forgiving isn't the same as forgetting or condoning what happened to you. Forgiveness doesn't mean that you deny the other person's responsibility for hurting you, and it doesn't minimize or justify the wrong. Forgiveness, however, can lessen its grip on you and help you focus on other more positive parts of your life.

You can forgive the person without excusing their actions.

My story:

> I forgave Bruce when I completely accepted him, both for what he was and what he couldn't be, combined with taking personal responsibility for the failure of our marriage. This was the key. I acknowledged that he is who he is and me suffering because of it was pointless. He just wasn't that into me and wasn't that into monogamy either and there was nothing else to say about that. For most of our marriage I'd tried to change him into someone who embraced monogamy and traditional family values or into someone who would truly desire me. I secretly hoped that once we signed the marriage certificate he would change his ways and no longer need to be a wild child, or need to be around beautiful women. This was the lie I lived.

> The day I accepted him completely and took responsibility for my inability to acknowledge the truth in our relationship, I sat on the couch and laughed. I laughed at the absurdity of how I suffered in anger over someone I could not control. Once I let go that he is who he is and I am who I am, I forgave him completely.

Forgiveness is a function of acceptance. What makes acceptance easier is that you're not condoning the behavior, you're simply accepting the person for who they are to release yourself from unnecessary suffering. If the person you need to forgive is yourself, then this is no different. Accept that who you are today is different from the person who made mistakes in the past. Learn what you need to learn from the past and record those lessons in the exercise below. You don't need to continue suffering or punishing yourself. Just choose to let go.

Forgiveness is also a commitment to let go of suffering.

What if I'm the one who needs forgiveness?

My story:

> When I found out about Bruce's betrayal, I began to feel guilty about cheating on him. I also cheated on an ex-boyfriend when I was at university. The thought

went around and around in my head that because of my own betrayals, Bruce had betrayed me in our marriage and I'd deserved it. Not only did I need to forgive Bruce, I needed to forgive myself, too. I also felt angry with myself for all the times I confronted Bruce and whenever he denied any wrongdoing, I believed I was paranoid and stopped trusting my judgment. I was also angry with myself for cheating and for ignoring all the signs that my marriage was doomed.

It took two hours but when I completed the exercise below and focused on my healing, I realized that harboring resentment against myself could be just as toxic as holding on to resentment against someone else. I recognized that poor behavior or mistakes didn't make me worthless or bad. I came to a place of acceptance that I, like everyone else, am not perfect. I accepted myself, warts and all. I admitted my mistakes and chose to contact my ex-boyfriend from university again to apologize for being a jerk all those years ago. It was great doing that. I released myself from guilt. I felt compassion for my imperfect self and I also felt compassion for imperfect Bruce. I committed myself to treating others with compassion, empathy and respect.

Forgiving yourself or someone else, though not easy, can transform your life. Instead of dwelling on the injustice and revenge, instead of being angry and bitter, you can move toward a living in peace, and with compassion, mercy, joy and kindness.

Steps to forgiveness:

⇨ Recognize the value of forgiveness and its importance in your life at a given time.

⇨ Reflect on the facts of the situation: how you've reacted, and how this combination has affected your life, your health and your well being.

⇨ Choose to forgive. Move away from the role of a victim and free yourself from the control and power the person or situation has exerted on your life.

⇨ If you are the person who needs forgiveness, take responsibility and make amends with anyone you have hurt in the process. You will feel so much better.

⇨ Read through the exercise you will be doing later today. Allow yourself to think about it during the day.

Exercise: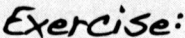

Forgiving my ex:

1. What do you not accept about your ex that you are still holding on to?

2. What expectations of your ex and your marriage were not fulfilled and how did this make you angry?

3. What impact does holding this grudge have on your life?

4. Does holding onto this resentment change the situation in any way?

5. Make a list of the things you'd like to forgive your ex for being or doing. Write each point like this...

I forgive [your ex's name] for XXX because YYY

For example: I forgive Bruce being with other women. Taking the poison of resentment, hoping he will die, is only hurting me. I release myself from this pain, knowing I cannot change what is and what isn't true about the past.

6. Read the list out loud to yourself in the mirror until you genuinely 'feel' different about the situation and your ex.

7. When you genuinely feel differently about the situation and your ex: Make a list of everything you have learnt from the marriage.

8. When you genuinely feel differently about the situation and your ex: Make a list of everything you are grateful for from having been married.

9. When you genuinely feel differently about the situation and your ex: Make a list of everything you are grateful for in getting divorced.

Forgiving myself

1. What don't you accept about yourself that you are holding onto?

2. What expectations of yourself didn't you fulfill? Why does this make you angry?

3. What impact does holding onto this suffering have on your life?

4. Does holding onto this resentment change the situation in any way?

5. Make a list of what you would like to forgive yourself for. Write each point like this...

I forgive myself for XXX because YYY

For example: I forgive myself for cheating on my ex-boyfriend at university because it happened so many years ago and the person I was then is not the person I am today. I learnt many lessons from that betrayal. I learnt about the pain and impact my actions had on him and on my own life. I learnt how important it is to apologize for the wrongs I committed. I learnt the valuable lesson of trusting myself and my fidelity in relationships.

6. Read the list out loud to yourself in the mirror until you genuinely 'feel' different about the situation and your ex.

7. When you genuinely feel differently about the situation and about yourself: Make a list of everything you have learnt about yourself from the marriage.

8. When you genuinely feel differently about the situation and about yourself: Make a list of anything you are grateful for from your marriage.

9. When you genuinely feel differently about the situation and about yourself: Make a list of anything you are grateful for following your divorce.

Note: If you're still holding onto guilt, complete the *Real Impact of my Divorce* exercise, using "I am holding onto suffering and refuse to forgive myself or my ex," as the problem and then work through the negative impacts and juicy benefits of remaining in this place.

TIP FOR THE DAY: This is the final stage of washing the bitterness, resentment and anger of your divorce out of your hair. Today is about the Vow Break.

Theme: The *Vow Break*

Date: Saturday, _____

🕐 **Estimated time to complete the exercise: 2–3 hours**

Remember to go through the daily checklist

Tick when done

Read through the thought for the day:

When two people get married, there is usually a beautiful ceremony and celebration in the company of friends, family and community.

Everyone is willing you on to succeed. Sadly, when two people get divorced there's is no ceremonial breaking of the sacred vow you made. You're on your own.

Today is about completing the *Vow Break*, an exercise to help sever the ties with your ex in a healthy, ethical and supportive way.

> VIDEO: I created a YouTube video on the topic of the *Vow Break*. To watch me explaining the steps in more detail, go to **www.youtube.com/nakeddivorce**

Complete your daily homework – start this in the morning.

Exercise:

The *Vow Break*

Begin by journaling the following about your ex
(do this as if you were talking to him):

• What can I acknowledge you for in our relationship?

• What was awesome about our relationship?

• What hurt me and what did I need to hear from you
while we were married?

• What parts of you did I not see, acknowledge or accept
while we were married?

• What are all the things I learnt from our marriage?

• What are all the things I learnt from our divorce?

• What do I need to hear from you now? (Do this after
your letter from him to you.)

• What I wish for you now?

• What promises and commitments do I make to you for
the future (if applicable)?

• What promises and commitments do I make with regards to our children and your relationship with them (if
applicable)?

Separately:

• Review your marriage vows and look at the promises
you made. Acknowledge which promises you did and
didn't keep.

• Forgive yourself for any promises you broke and acknowledge yourself for all the promises you kept.

When complete, here is a bonus opportunity for you.

Bonus opportunity:

Write a completion letter to your ex saying everything you want to say from the *Vow Break* above.

If you feel really brave, approach your ex to do the Vow Break together or send him your letter. What I can say is that doing the exercise WITH your ex is a truly remarkable experience full of forgiveness and completion.

day

17

RELEASE

THINK ABOUT THIS FOR TODAY: "Our lives improve only when we take chances and the first and most difficult risk we can take is to be honest with ourselves." ~ Walter Anderson

Everyone has some form of baggage from a relationship, a nasty break up or divorce. Without being insensitive, if you're really committed to making your next relationship work, you need to purge that baggage, or manage it. Many people I have worked with have unresolved baggage spanning more than a decade. This baggage ruined any chance of happiness in their lives. Dealing with your baggage today could add years to your life. It could even save your life.

Theme: Unpacking your relationship baggage

Date: Sunday, _____

🕐 **Estimated time to complete the exercise: 3-4 hours**

Remember to go through the daily checklist

Tick when done

Read through the thought for the day:

☐

You know that question they ask at the airport: Did you pack your own bags? Well, we all pack our own bags, but the good news is that you can unpack them, too.

Don't expect to be healed by the end of the day. The goal is to become aware of what your baggage is and to focus on releasing it completely over the coming weeks. Some baggage takes a few minutes to be released whereas some baggage may take some practice over a few days or weeks because you need to catch it and manage it within each passing moment. There are many texts I researched on relationship baggage, all of which are cited in the Bibliography.

Let's start by looking into the different types of relationship baggage and then look into what to do about it.

The 'waiting to be hurt' baggage

What is it?

You desperately WANT to be in a relationship but you have incredible fear inside of you. One minute you are happy, but the next minute you run or explode in a hurricane. You have a belief that you are bound to get hurt and unconsciously, you may even attract men who will hurt you to reinforce this pattern in your life.

What are the facts?

It was Henry Ford who said, "Whether you think you can or whether you think you can't, you're right"

So, if you feel you don't deserve to win, achieve success or to be happy in your new relationship, you'll tend to manifest your worst fears. If this baggage is running the show, when things finally go right and happen the way you want them to, it will feel too good to be true and somehow disappear.

Love is a risk. Love demands courage because it makes you vulnerable. Relationships end. If you constantly think about the end of your relationship, you may unwittingly be working to that end. Love can't be controlled and neither can relationships. Control is an illusion and when you live life completely focused on controlling everyone and everything, you smother the sense of joy and spontaneity in your life. You can avoid love, hoping you'll never be hurt again, or you can surrender to the experience of love, with all its benefits. You don't want to end up like old Miss Haversham, the bitter spinster in Charles Dickens's 'Great Expectations.' So, let go. You may get hurt; you're human after all. But you'll be living life and not avoiding it.

No longer succumbing to worry is easier said than done. I was a prize-winning worrier, so let me go through what I did to put worry in its place.

What can you do to put this baggage in its place?

Here is the technique I use to put my worry in its place. If you are a prize-winning worrier, too, then let me tell you it's something you will always need to manage.

However, the better you get at managing it when it arises, the less worry you'll experience over time. You can train your mind to stop seeing worrying as a viable option.

This Neuro-linguistic programming-based technique may seem like a game at first but let me assure you: visual imagination has a very powerful effect on feelings.

Exercise: The Worry Buster

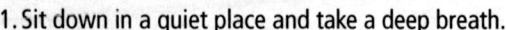

Feeling the angst of worry?

1. Sit down in a quiet place and take a deep breath.

2. Notice where you are feeling the worry in your body.

3. Imagine that it has a shape and a color. Think about its shape, texture, size and color until you are clear about what it looks like.

4. Then imagine moving it outside of your body, almost as if it's on a table in front of you so you can look at it.

5. Imagine wrapping it in a tight ball of putty.

6. Then, imagine throwing this putty-ball away with great force. If you can include arm movements in throwing it away, even better. If you can say out loud 'I banish you from my body!' while throwing the putty ball away, it will be even more effective.

7. Now, notice how you feel.

8. If there is any part of that 'old' feeling left, keep repeating this exercise until you cannot remember what you were thinking about.

The 'ex' baggage

What is it?

Rich Santos who wrote 'Do you have Emotional Baggage' defined this type of baggage whereby you just can't get over your ex-husband and you nurse the idea that your ex may come back into your life or you compare everyone new to your ex. This will be horrible for your new partner who will hate feeling compared and may even leave you if you don't resolve your feelings.

What are the facts?

Your relationship ended and you need to confront that perhaps the relationship was not so great to begin with. Maybe you were living in a dream world, fantasizing about the relationship, rather than being real about what it was truly like. The fact that you're no longer together with your ex should be sufficient indication that you were not meant to be together forever.

What can you do to put this baggage in its place?

Having completed days 7 and 8, you should be feeling much better about your ex and you should be able to see both sides of the relationship. If you're still struggling, repeat the exercises from days 7 and 8 until you can see the relationship in its true light.

The 'angry woman' baggage

What is it?

This is the most damaging kind of relationship baggage because you're just extremely angry at men. I have seen this happen when women label all men as bastards because of what one man did.

What are the facts?

One bad situation from your past does not mean that all men are bastards and deserve your anger. Anger makes us tired. You have a choice:

✓ either you waste your life by being angry at life and men and remaining a bitter, twisted angry person, or

✓ you let go of the anger in a healthy way.

What can you do to put this baggage in its place?

Day 9 has a great exercise for dealing with extreme anger. If you still feel angry towards men, then it may be necessary for you to repeat the anger releasing exercise three to six times until you feel no more animosity. There is also the *Real Impact of my Divorce* Exercise. Substitute the problem statement with, "I refuse to let go of the anger I feel towards my old relationship" to realize the impact holding onto this anger will have on your life.

The 'I'm not attractive enough' baggage

What is it?

You just never feel good enough. Perhaps this issue came about because your ex used to stare at other women or cheated on you. Perhaps you have some issues from childhood.

What are the facts?

If you are constantly dependent on the affirmation of those around you to feel attractive then those around you have a great deal of control of you. This is not a particularly powerful way to live.

What can you do to put this baggage in its place?

Simply act like a fantasy woman for yourself. There is a strong connection between the body and the mind, so fake it, until it feels real.

The Daily Declarations are also very useful here. Repeat them daily, the repetition will be healing in a few days or weeks.

The 'he's going to cheat on me' baggage
What is it?

If you have previously been cheated on or cheated on a partner before, you may be suspicious of people cheating on you. If you've been cheated on in the past, you might not be able to trust your instincts.

What are the facts?

This baggage creates paranoia. You may become that woman who checks his phone, email, computer and anything else for evidence of affairs. If you assume he will cheat on you and you are always looking for problems; you'll eventually manifest it.

Case study: Mickey

Mickey worried that her husband would cheat on her. She always asked where he was going and who he was going with. Whenever he assured her that nothing was going on, she'd cry and apologize for mistrusting him. But she continued asking. Eventually he got fed up and had an affair. Later, he said he'd felt pushed into the arms of another woman. He was happy in their marriage but Mickey's suspicions had sowed the seed in his mind. They divorced a year later. Mickey realized that she'd contributed to his unfaithfulness by believing he would cheat on her.

Note:
Whatever you believe to be true, you will make true – so be careful about what you believe.

What can you do to put this baggage in its place?

Ask questions but a tip is to tell your new man that you trust him completely and then trust him. Walking around wondering if you will get hurt again is bound to cause pain and anguish. Love is a risk, so surrender to your new relationship and practice chilling.

The 'I am terrible in bed' baggage

What is it?

This baggage is usually linked to previous relationship history. This baggage can make you very insecure during sex and can turn you off trying anything new and exciting.

What are the facts?

Great sex has absolutely nothing to do with how many acrobatic antics you can perform. It also has nothing to do with how beautiful your body is. Great sex is about feeling sexy, enjoying yourself and losing yourself in the pleasure and moment of it. Sex is also a form of self-expression and an opportunity to express to your partner how you feel about him.

What can you do to put this baggage in its place?

I'm suggesting something controversial... Have sex for you and not to make your partner happy. Have a go at losing yourself during sex. If you struggle with this, pretend you're someone else. Buy some sexy underwear, buy a book on burlesque dancing, imagine asking your new man to come up and change the light bulb in the bedroom and seduce him. Start a little project focused on having sex for the sake of simply having sex. Go on. I noticed that I became completely sexy when I stopped trying so damn hard.

Complete your daily homework – start this in the morning.

Exercise:

Spend some time today diagnosing your baggage type and complete the remedial work. You may have more than one baggage type running the show. If this is the case, do the remedial work indicated for all these baggage types.

There is some work you will need to do consciously whenever this baggage comes up over the next few weeks or months. It may come up from time to time but whenever it does, knock it on the head immediately. Focus on what you want to have happen in your life rather than indulging in the negative thoughts of your baggage.

But make a choice today to dump the relationship baggage.

My story:

The biggest compliment I received after my divorce came from my partner Simon. A few days into our relationship he said to me, "You know, Adèle, you have never felt like a divorced woman to me. You just don't have that brittle wounded thing that so many divorced women have. You are strong, confident and clear about who you are and what you want."

I burst into tears. I was determined to truly heal from my divorce, take responsibility and come out fresh, clean and pure. This statement was testament that I had achieved that goal. I felt immense pride in myself over what he said that day.

An even bigger compliment was the day that a client of mine received exactly the same compliment from her new partner. She was SO excited at not feeling like a divorced woman.

day 18

18

RELEASE

KEEP THIS IN MIND FOR THE DAY: "Our deepest fear is not that we are inadequate. Our deepest fear is that we are powerful beyond measure. It is our light not our darkness that frightens us. Actually, who are you not to be? You are a child of God. Your playing small doesn't serve the world. There's nothing enlightened about shrinking so that other people won't feel insecure around you. We were born to make manifest the glory of God that is within us." ~ Nelson Mandela, inaugural address, written by Marianne Williamson

Theme: Your values and what you want out of your next relationship

Date: Monday, _____

🕐 **Estimated time to complete the exercise: 90-120 minutes**

Remember to go through the daily checklist

Tick when done

Read through the thought for the day: ☐

One of the common phrases I hear after women experience a divorce is, "I don't know who I am now that I'm not married…"

There is a great deal of fear associated with being suddenly single when your identity has been bound up with someone else for several years or decades.

It's vitally important that you distinguish where the centre of your life is after your divorce. And if you don't know, this is a great opportunity to do so!

If the centre of your life is no longer healthy or supportive to you, make a choice to change it to something you feel will be worthy.

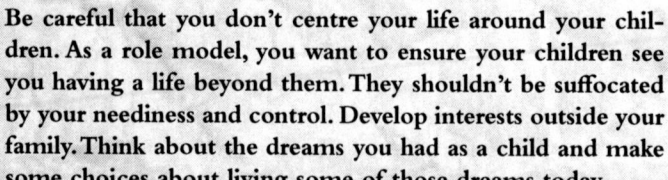

WARNING:

Be careful that you don't centre your life around your children. As a role model, you want to ensure your children see you having a life beyond them. They shouldn't be suffocated by your neediness and control. Develop interests outside your family. Think about the dreams you had as a child and make some choices about living some of those dreams today.

1. What do you value in your life?

It's great to re-evaluate your values now that you have a new life ahead of you. You may notice that in the past, your values were intimately tied to whatever your husband valued. Now it's your opportunity to choose your values for yourself.

2. What do you want in a relationship?

Begin to think about what is important to you in a relationship. Even if you don't want to have one for the foreseeable future, it's key to think about what you want so when that lucky guy comes bounding into your life, he's someone you have chosen rather than just someone who chose you.

Once you have articulated what you want, be responsible for getting it. Many women fall into a trap of believing that it's up to their man to make them happy and give them what they want and deserve.

This is not a very powerful way to approach a new relationship. Your job in a relationship is to make yourself happy and ensure you are fulfilled.

Your man's job is simply to top up or add that extra sweetener or sugar to your life. The exercise below shows you how to be responsible for giving yourself what you deserve in a relationship.

Tip—

A woman who feels fulfilled as a woman has great charisma. This charisma acts like a magnetic force and is very attractive to a man.

Read through the exercise you'll be doing later today. Allow yourself to think about it during the day.

3. What is at the center of your life?

Take a minute and list the people or things that your life revolves around. It may be one thing or a combination.

Here are some examples:

- *Romantic relationship*
- *Job*
- *Children*
- *Hobbies*
- *Financial resources*
- *Favorite activities*
- *House, car and possessions*
- *Friends*
- *Health*

What would you like the center of your life to be?

Now, rewrite the list above in the order you'd love your life to reflect.

4. When done, look at what are the things you value in your life?

Look at the list below and put these values in the order of what you value most in your life.

1. Acknowledgement
2. Security and stability
3. Family
4. Wealth/abundance/excess
5. Relationships
6. Having fun
7. Travel
8. Material things
9. Looking good
10. Relaxing (reading/ watching movies/massage)
11. Confidence
12. Learning new things
13. Mastering something
14. Having children

5. Being responsible for getting what you want out of a relationship

Complete this table below in your journal. The first example is from my own relationship journal:

What I need to feel nourished, honored and secure in a relationship	At least 3 actions I can take to provide this for myself
To know that I am beautiful and desirable as I am and that I have a healthy self-esteem about my body and looks.	• To look in the mirror every day and tell myself how gorgeous I am. • To have a special bath at least twice a week where I pamper myself and take care of my body. • Go to the gym 4 to 5 times a week and train for and complete a triathlon. • Eat healthily (lots of healthy salads, no snacking in -between meals, no junk food, drink 10 glasses of water daily).

You need to know how to achieve each of those objectives yourself or you will be no help in educating your new man in how to fulfill on those objectives. How else will you tell your man HOW to help you feel beautiful and desirable.

Now it's your turn!

What I need to feel nourished, honored and secure in a relationship	At least 3 actions I can take to provide this for myself

My story:

I was born physically disabled and spent the first two years of my life in and out of hospital having operations to build hip sockets. My early years were pretty non-physical. I didn't do much sport as I was growing up and devoted myself to academic pursuits. When I reached my thirties, I watched some of my friends participate in marathons or triathlons and I was a bit jealous thinking it would be so great to accomplish that goal. I had always wanted to do a triathlon. When I was going through my divorce and created this exercise for myself, I decided it was time to begin training and do something I had always dreamed of and could never imagine myself doing. I hired a personal trainer and worked hard at it. It was a grueling experience building up my fitness but I loved feeling strong and athletic. I completed my first triathlon eight months after starting the training. I cannot even describe how amazing it felt to cross the finishing line. At my second triathlon my parents came to watch and my mum even cried as I received my medal. She said that she remembered those early days in and out of hospital learning to walk and that she had never dreamt that I would ever do something so athletic in my thirties. They were so proud. Now I have a goal to do at least four major events each year, whether it be a cycling event only or a duathlon or triathlon. It's a great way to keep me in shape and I feel great about feeling strong and training.

6. What is your dream?

What have you always wanted to do, but never believed you were capable of accomplishing? Your divorce is such a great catalyst for life-changing transformation. Go on, give your dreams a go!

day

19

KEEP THIS IN MIND FOR THE DAY: Today is also an opportunity to learn about and define your boundaries in life. A strong sense of self-esteem is a function of your boundaries. A person with weak boundaries will have low self-esteem.

Theme: Loving yourself is often a function of setting boundaries in your life

Date: Tuesday, _____

🕐 **Estimated time to complete the reading/ exercise: 90 minutes**

Remember to go through the daily checklist

Tick when done

Read through the thought for the day: ☐

Today is about learning to set boundaries with others. If you struggle to love and honor yourself, this is a wonderful exercise. People who have healthy boundaries naturally have a healthy self-esteem and love themselves compared to those who do not.

Go back to Day 12 and reacquaint yourself with what you said you wouldn't be prepared to tolerate in a relationship.

Have this with you as you complete this exercise.

In terms of this section on boundaries, I want to provide some background context and explore the concept of archetypes which is essentially a model of a type of behavior.

Psychologist Carl Gustav Jung described several archetypes in his many bodies of work. Certain energies, personalities and behaviors are encapsulated within those archetypes and are very useful in exploring different ways of being.

Many of us experience some difficulty in setting boundaries in our lives. This is largely because we are unconsciously stuck in a particular paradigm or archetype which is undistinguished for us. We set boundaries using those paradigms without even being aware of them.

I am describing these archetypes in a way that is only relevant in exploring boundaries in a particular way.

Arche-type	Boundary Personality	How I set Boundaries	Energy
Queen	You are a careful and respected leader in your life. You are confident, powerful and knowledge-able. You have no problem setting boundaries with people in your life and you do so gracefully and with ease. You know who you are, know what you want and do not allow anyone to take unfair advantage of you.	Powerful, regal, cen-tered and graceful	Spiritual and inte-grative
Magician	You are the performer and will come up with an elaborate clever excuse rather than admit the truth as to why you are setting the boundary. You don't enjoy conflict, so think of wily ways to set boundaries so that you achieve your objec-tive without causing any discomfort.	Manipulative, sly, strategic and can be slimy	Mental and intellec-tual
Lover	You are a hopeless romantic. You have no boundaries and everyone is allowed to come into your space. You allow anyone close to you, allow people to walk over you and are often un-able to say the word 'No'.	Doormat, poodle, de-pendant, coward, easily manipulated or cajoled	Emotional
Warrior	You are full of action and direction, you know what you are doing. You have no problem with conflict or in setting boundaries but sometimes your approach in setting boundaries leaves a trail of destruction in your wake.	Curt, abrasive, bully, can cause offence	Physical

It's important to acknowledge what your default is in setting boundaries in the past. Perhaps you struggled to say no or perhaps you developed an elaborate story to squirm out of unpleasant situations. Study the table above and identify which arche-type you generally stepped into when it came time to set a boundary.

Learning to set boundaries is a vital part of learning to communicate in a direct and honest manner. It's impossible to have a healthy relationship with someone who has no boundaries or with someone who cannot communicate directly, and honestly.

Learning how to set boundaries is also a necessary step in learning to be a friend to yourself. It is your responsibility to take care of yourself and protect yourself when necessary. It is impossible to learn to love yourself without owning yourself and owning your rights and responsibilities as co-creators of your life.

The most effective archetypal approach in setting boundaries is that of the Queen. The Queen can say no, but with power, grace and peace with no side agenda or abrasiveness. The Queen is taken seriously by those around her and has a healthy relationship with herself. Setting personal boundaries is key to truly loving, respecting and honoring yourself. Boundaries let other people know that you deserve and command respect.

Setting boundaries

Any woman who has become powerful, went through the journey of learning to assert herself. Setting a boundary is not making a threat or behaving in a warrior-way, it is communicating clearly what the consequences will be if the other person continues to treat you in an unacceptable manner.

Setting a boundary is also not an attempt to control the other person in a magician-way by adopting a sophisticated way of manipulation.

The difference between setting a boundary in a healthy way and manipulating is that when you set a boundary you let go of the outcome.

Whenever you set a boundary, adopt the approach of HIGH INTENTION of what you want and LOW ATTACHMENT to the outcome.

> **❝** *With boundaries, as in every area of the healing process, change starts with awareness.* **❞**

Codependency Therapist, Robert Burney, defines the formula for emotionally honest communication as follows:

Your sentences begin with phrases such as:

    "When you…"

    "I feel…"

    "I want…"

The key to Robert's formula is in being incredibly specific and questioning the assumptions you have made before accusing the person you are talking to.

An example of this is covered on the next page:

"When you..."

The "When you... " statement describes their exact behavior in detail so that it's not subject to personal interpretation or assumptions.

Examples include:

"When your face gets red and your voice gets louder and your hands clench into fists"

"I feel..."

This is the part where you express your emotions.

Examples include:

"When your voice gets louder and your face gets red and you clench your fists, I feel scared, intimidated and like running away. I feel as if you're going to hit me."

"I want... "

"I want" is a clear description of what you are looking for from this person to alter the situation. Again, be completely specific. Saying "you want to feel more love" is too general.

Examples include:

"I want you to tell me directly and clearly what you are angry about, so if you are just angry about your favorite team losing, tell me, rather than me wondering if you are angry with me"

I have found that in setting boundaries that what works is finding your own self expression in it. I often use humor. I am direct and straight but not overly heavy or significant about it.

I say things very firmly and loudly but with a broad smile on my face. Examples include:-

- *"I am not very happy about that. If you continue that, I am outta here!"*
- *"Look, this happened, but if it happens again, I won't be as understanding. I deserve more than that so please don't do it again."*

Dealing with your children's strong emotional outbursts

You may become an expert in dealing with your own emotions but there may be situations whereby you need to handle someone else's strong emotions and setting boundaries at these points is very useful. Whether this be your ex's outbursts or your children, having an effective way of handling other people's outbursts will be helpful in life. But first, let me share an example.

Case study: Rosie

I had a client Rosie, whose daughter Sophie was very angry that her parents were going through divorce. She would have angry outbursts at her mother on regular occasions. This left her mother completely distraught and at the effect of her daughter's mood swings. She kept asking me, "how could Sophie be so insensitive to my feelings? It's not my fault that her father left but she keeps saying it is."

After some coaching, Rosie realized that even though Sophie was 18, the divorce was hitting her much harder than her younger sister who was reveling in all the attention she was suddenly receiving from her father now that her parents had split up. Sophie felt incredible rage that there were no custody battles over her and felt that her sister who was 9 was being favorited.

Sophie would say the vilest things to her mother. It included statements like, "It's your fault dad left, you are the worst wife in the world and you pushed him away with all your nagging." "I hope you die, because you are worthless now that dad has left us" and my personal favorite, "you are a worthless horrible mother, I hate you and wish my sister was never born because I hate her too."

These outbursts upset Rosie incredibly and all outbursts would descend into an argument, followed by slamming of doors and many tears. When things had calmed down, the guilt would set in and Sophie would apologize but Rosie was beginning to feel like she was walking around on eggshells in her house.

Additionally, whenever she had an open mediation session with her soon-to-be ex-husband, he would shout, scream and perform, telling her it was her fault he left and that she was a horrible woman.

Rosie needed a mechanism to not get riled by her ex or Sophie's outbursts. She followed a particular process I taught her and within a few weeks, her relationship with Sophie improved so remarkably that she received a card from her saying that she was the best mummy in the world. Sophie also felt validated and heard, so consequently became calmer and more pleasant to be around. Rosie realized that whereas her younger daughter was coping quite well, her elder daughter's model of relationship and family was shattered. Most children believe in the fairy tale aspect of marriage, i.e. that you get married and live happily ever after, forever. Sophie's model of marriage and paradigm for relationships was broken so she was trying to reconcile if marriages ever worked and trying to work out why this fairy tale did not have a happy ending. It HAD to be someone's fault and unfortunately she decided it had to be her mother so she focused all her anger on her. Once Sophie had calmed down, Rosie and her had long discussions about marriage and through counseling sessions, Sophie healed. She still had the occasional outburst but Rosie knew how to handle it and the anger would die down quite quickly.

Rosie also noticed that her mediation sessions and contact with her soon-to-be ex-husband became much more relaxed as she became more powerful. She stopped resisting and fighting against him, which diffused his anger. She is now well on her way to achieving a settlement.

This is the process she learnt:

Being powerful in the face of your children's strong emotional outbursts

STEP 1: Understand that the angry or emotional outburst is not personal to you. It's about the wounded little boy or wounded little girl inside your child who is shouting or screaming.

Stand tall and BE THE PARENT. In other words, this is the time to step up and be powerful, stable and reassuring. Getting angry and upset will not help the situation.

STEP 2: Look intently at your children, to assure them that you are listening. Stop doing what you are doing. Do not fidget and switch off the television. Often what riles people the most is the feeling that they are not being listened to. Eliminate this possibility by giving them the assurance that you are listening to them.

STEP 3: Do not react. Allow whatever they are saying to wash over you, like it is simply words that have no meaning. Even if they say that they wish you were dead or that they hate you. Often, these words are not meant when things have calmed down. When they are done ranting or having their say, simply do the following:

Take a deep breath and say, "I understand that you are feeling angry [or upset, or disappointed, etc.] and I understand that because of this situation, you feel this emotion very strongly."

Be calm and speak with an even tone. Visualize a positive outcome. Apologize that this divorce has had this impact on their life. Say you are sorry that they feel this strong emotion and simply continue to reassure him or her that no matter what they say, you still love them and are here for them. When your child has calmed down, ask him or her how they are doing and how they are feeling. Talk about the divorce and talk about it from their perspective. There is no need to react. This is the moment to be stable and reassuring. Sometimes children will test you to see if you will stop loving them. It's therefore important to be loving and BE the parent.

STEP 4: Once done with the discussion, give a reassuring hug and ensure you let them know that they are loved as they are and that they have a right to their anger or emotions. This ensures that they know they can always come to you with any discussion they wish to have and that you will listen to them and respect their emotions. Try to do something together, like drinking a cup of tea or going for a walk. Often these kind of outbursts are cries for attention.

STEP 5: Write regular reassuring letters to your children so that they always know that this divorce is not their fault and that they are precious and perfect as they are. Invite them to discuss with you how they feel at any time.

Dealing with your ex-husband's strong emotional outbursts

The vast majority of boundaries are in fact a negotiation rather than a rigid line in the sand. Adults need to negotiate boundaries between themselves. This is the standard for all relationships and is particularly true for romantic relationships.

If you don't risk sharing how you feel and don't speak up, you'll blow up and/or become passive aggressive and damage the relationship.

Being powerful in the face of your ex-husband's strong emotional outbursts

STEP 1: Understand that the angry or emotional outburst is not personal to you. It's about the wounded little boy or wounded little girl inside the person who is shouting or screaming.

If seated, stand up and stand tall with your shoulders back and hands at your sides. As the person is saying whatever they are saying, tell yourself that whatever they are saying is about them feeling hurt and wanting to hurt someone else. It has nothing to do with you.

STEP 2: Look intently at your ex-spouse, to assure them that you are listening. Stop doing what you are doing. Do not fidget and switch off the television. Often what riles people the most is the feeling that they are not being listened to. Eliminate this possibility by giving them the assurance that you are listening to them.

STEP 3: Do not react. Allow whatever they are saying to wash over you, like it is simply words that have no meaning.

When they are done ranting or having their say, simply do the following:

Take a deep breath and say, "I understand that you are feeling angry (or upset, or disappointed, etc.) and I understand that because of this situation, you feel this emotion very strongly." Do not respond to the specific points of what they said. Simply say that you are, "willing to talk when things are calmer."

STEP 4: Simply walk out of the room and leave. Have a cup of tea and be still. Try not to raise your voice to match them, just refuse to play the game.

STEP 5: If you feel that discussions are impossible, write a letter adopting a very factual matter-of-fact tone.

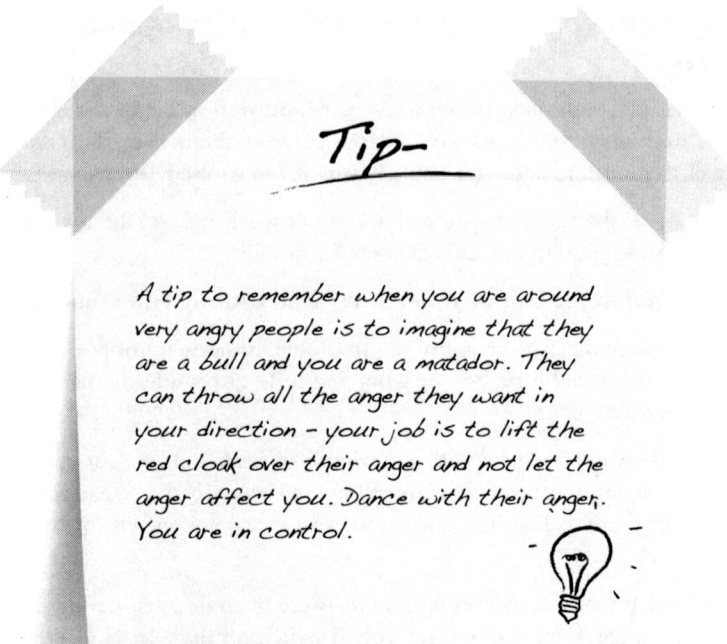

Tip-

A tip to remember when you are around very angry people is to imagine that they are a bull and you are a matador. They can throw all the anger they want in your direction - your job is to lift the red cloak over their anger and not let the anger affect you. Dance with their anger. You are in control.

You always have a choice

You always have a choice. The choices may seem to be awful, but in reality, allowing yourself to buy into the illusion that you are trapped will have worse consequences in the long run. Owning your choices, no matter how outrageous, is a step in owning responsibility for your life. If you are blaming and being the victim, you will never be happy. Personal boundaries exist to teach us to be discerning in our choices, to teach us to ask for what we need, and to teach us to be assertive and loving in meeting our needs.

Read through the exercise you will be doing later today. Allow yourself to think about it during the day.

Exercise:

Make a list of all the relationships in your life in which you experience a loss of power. Plan the emotionally honest conversations you want to have with these people, or the boundaries you will set with them. Schedule times over the next few weeks to have those conversations. If possible, have one of those conversations in the next 48 hours.

Getting really good at emotionally honest conversations and setting boundaries, needs practice. The good news is that the more you practice, the better you will become, so your job for the next thirty days is to practice, practice, and practice!

day

20

RELEASE

KEEP THIS IN MIND FOR THE DAY: "*Life is too short to wake up in the morning with regrets. So love the people who treat you right, forget about the ones who don't and believe that everything happens for a reason. If you get a chance, take it. If it changes your life, let it. Nobody said that it'd be easy, they just promised it would be worth it.*" ~ *Author unknown*

Theme: What is your new life going to look like?

Date: Wednesday, _____

🕐 **Estimated time to complete the exercise: 90–120 minutes**

Remember to go through the daily checklist

Tick when done

Read through the thought for the day:

☐

Today is all about your future and what you want to do with your life.

1. Firstly, today you will have an opportunity to assess how you feel about the various areas of your life using the Wheel of Life.

2. Next, you will sit back and think of all you dreamed for your life when you were a child. You will have the opportunity to create a list of things you'd like to do before you die.

3. You'll be asking yourself, "What do I want to change about my life?" and "How can I use this divorce as a catalyst to live my dream life?"

4. You will also develop a *Personal Manifesto* whereby you will define who you are from today onwards. What will your life be about?

5. You will choose a *Personal Anthem*. This is a song that lifts you up and is the theme tune for your new life. You may already have your song in mind but if you don't, there are some suggestions in the exercise list below.

Today is the day you reconnect with the dreams you had for your life. You have one life, so live it!

Read through the exercise you'll be doing later today. Allow yourself to think about it during the day.

Exercise:

1. Below is an image called the Wheel of Life. Firstly, assess the various areas of your life by putting a score between 0 and 10 in each area, 0 being the score that requires the most work and 10 requiring no additional work at all.

2. Next, decide on three actions you can take in each area to bring the scores in all areas of your life up to 10.

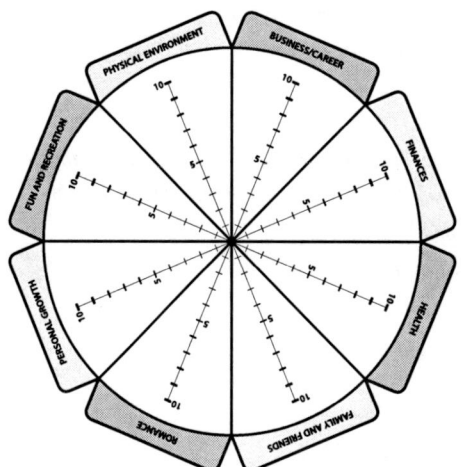

Ask yourself: What do I want to change about my life? How can I use this divorce as a catalyst to live my dream life?

3. Take a moment to think of the dreams you had as a child for your life. Create a comprehensive list of things you'd like to do before you die. Here are some examples from my list. I've crossed off quite a few off since articulating my list, so you never know where your life will take you! Whether you have five or 200 things on your list, allow yourself to dream big!

    1.   1.   *Fly into space.*

    2.   *Climb Mount Kilimanjaro.*

    3.   *Scuba dive the Great Barrier Reef in Australia.*

    4.   *Raft the Colorado river.*

    5.   *Ride the 10 biggest, baddest rollercoaster's.*

    6.   *Dog sled in Norway.*

    7.   *Boat trip through the fjords in Finland/Norway.*

    8.   *Fly a MIG jet to the edge of space.*

    9.   *Go on safari in north Africa.*

10.   *Ride a motorcycle from Cape Town to Cairo.*

11.   *Ride a motorcycle from LA to Buenos Aires.*

4. Develop a *Personal Manifesto* where you define who you are from today onwards. What will your life be about?

5. Choose your own *Personal Anthem*. This is a song that lifts you up and is the theme tune for your new life. You can listen to it whenever you want to feel pumped up, moved or excited about your life. If you don't have something in mind, here are a few suggestions:

- *Let Go - Frou Frou (this is my anthem for why I do what I do) then there's If you're Gonna - Natasha Bedingfield (this is my anthem for getting pumped up)*
- *I'm a Bitch – Tracy Bonham*
- *I'm a Survivor – Destiny's Child*
- *Video – India Arie*
- *Strength, Courage and Wisdom – India Arie*

Think of your anthem now…

The first naked pic – destiny awaited!

Me in hospital at the age of 2 getting my hip sockets built

Happier times with Bruce

My many cousins and beloved Ouma

Many adventures we had together. This was taken in the Himalayas

Our wedding day

An absolute mess after Bruce left

Clothing purge after divorce

My amazing parents

The day I got my divorce, celebrating with my family

My amazingly supportive friends

With my ex-stepmother in law post-divorce. I was a bridesmaid at Bruce's cousin Roz's wedding.

Getting back on track, I had a little makeover!

With my wonderful partner, Simon

My corporate self

My 2nd triathlon

*Some participants from a change management
workshop I lead in Zurich, Switzerland*

Speaking about naked divorce

part five

your future

What's next?

Well done! You've completed the 21-day program.

Does this mean your transformation is complete? To put it briefly, no.

But don't be discouraged. This is good news. You are only just beginning your new chapter and learning how to handle the challenges along the way is part of living a full life, the life you've been working towards realizing by completing the *naked divorce*.

Imagine how mundane your existence would be without challenge, upsets or emotions to deal with?

Here are some tips to deal with some of the longer-term challenges that are certain to come your way.

The first year after your divorce

⇨ Keep working with the ETHICS and **7 Foundations of Transformation** for a minimum of three weeks after completing the program. Whenever I have a tough time of anything, I go back to it and make it a part of my life so that I'm contained. In those down moments, I feel strong no matter what comes my way.

⇨ Review your exercise and diet regime and audit how you feel physically.

⇨ Review your finances and ensure you have finalized things with your ex.

⇨ Put into action some of the activities you came up with from Day 20. Get stuck into the creative endeavors that inspire you.

⇨ Plan activities throughout the year so that you have events to look forward to, especially on anniversary dates, as discussed below.

⇨ Take up some new hobbies. Have you always wanted to belly dance or do karate? Now's the time to do it. And find some new avenues to make new friends.

Dealing with down days

Whatever comes up in the next 12 months, be kind to yourself. Accept that there will be reminders and times when you feel sad, or have a flash back to the past. When negative emotions surface, feel them and BE with them. If you surrender to them, they will pass. There's no reason you can't keep practicing many of the exercises you've done over the 21 days of the **naked divorce** for years to come. Here are some suggestions:

✔ **What to do when you feel you've lost the love of your life:** Repeat the *Pedestal Shift* exercise from Day 8. You can never do this exercise too many times.

✔ **What to do if you put your ex back on a pedestal:** Repeat the homework exercises for Days 7 and 8 (Different Points of View, and Perception is Projection).

✔ **When you're feeling overly emotional:** Re-read the sections on emotions, ensuring you follow the tips to understand your emotions and where they're coming from.

✔ **When you're angry or upset:** Repeat the exercise from Day 9. I make a point of doing this exercise every few months. It's very cathartic!

✔ **When things are a bit haphazard in a new relationship:** Re-read and practice all the tips from Days 13 and 17.

✔ **When you're worried or stressed:** Repeat the *Worry Buster* exercise from Day 17. It really works.

✔ **When you're feeling like a doormat and need to set some boundaries:** Re-read Day 19 and practice the suggested exercises.

✔ **When feeling extreme emotions at work:** Practice the exercise for handling emotions whilst at work, or practice the Emotional Freedom Technique of tapping (described below).

When you're very weepy and emotional, do this five times using both index fingers:

Tap above eyebrow X10

Tap under eye X10

Tap under armpit X10

Tap under collarbone X10

Tap on index finger X10

Tap under pinky finger on back of hand X10

ASK YOURSELF: How am I feeling now?

Keep repeating the exercise until you're no longer present to your weepiness.

Anniversaries

Certain times of the year are loaded with memories and if you can anticipate these occasions and prepare for them, they'll be easier to get through. Those old important dates will gradually lose their significance as you fill your life with new memories, events and people. Nicci Talbot who wrote 'Get over your Break-up' shared some ideas on how to handle these different days.

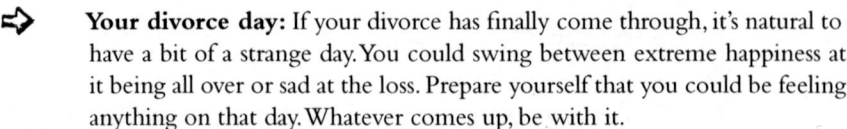

Tip-

Buy a new calendar and mark only those dates that are meaningful to your new life. Plan ahead for days marking old anniversaries, etc, so that you're busy doing something special when that date rolls around. Plan an activity or an outing with family or friends. Make sure you have a great day.

➡ **Your divorce day:** If your divorce has finally come through, it's natural to have a bit of a strange day. You could swing between extreme happiness at it being all over or sad at the loss. Prepare yourself that you could be feeling anything on that day. Whatever comes up, be with it.

➡ **Your wedding anniversary:** The first wedding anniversary after a divorce can be difficult if you were in a long-term partnership. I always take myself out on a date or purchase something special to commemorate my achievement. Sometimes my ex-husband and I will have a chat to acknowledge how far we have both come. My aunt Helen buys plants to celebrate her milestones and now has a flourishing patio garden that attracts birds.

➡️ **Your birthday:** Do something you have always wanted to do, but never gave yourself permission to do when you were married.

➡️ **Your ex's birthday:** It's up to you how you handle this one, but plan ahead so that you're not caught out. I have a good relationship with my ex, so I usually call or text him (as he lives in a different time zone). Do whatever feels comfortable for you.

➡️ **Your children's birthdays:** Prepare for the day well ahead of time. Ensure that the day is about your child. Agree ahead of time on who does what, particularly when it comes to gifts and a party. You shouldn't be trying to outdo each other.

KEEP THIS IN MIND FOR THE DAY: Discuss presents in advance so that you and your ex don't duplicate gifts or try to compete against each other.

Changing your name

For information on changing your name in different countries, visit the **naked divorce** blog – I wrote an article all about it which can be found under www.nakeddivorce.com/blog/.

Managing finances in the future

➡️ How are your finances now? Have you finalized things with your ex and are there any further loose ends to be tied up?

➡️ Even if the split was amicable, you need to agree on what will happen to joint accounts, the house and shared assets.

➡️ Consider that if you haven't drawn up a financial clean-break order to resolve your finances legally, your ex could lay claim to any money you inherit. If you need to, get things in writing and seek financial advice.

➡️ If your ex is paying you maintenance and you decide to remarry, that may stop. Are you prepared for that financially? Have you discussed this with your new partner and is he willing to support you and your children?

➡️ Are you entitled to any other benefits that you aren't claiming?

➡️ Do you have a long-term financial plan? Do you have savings, investments, a pension plan and a will in place?

➡️ Review your finances every three months and take independent advice if you're unsure of anything.

Ex-Factor Etiquette where there are no children involved

Being friends with your ex

Good for you if you can make the transition from divorced to friends, especially if you don't have children and have no real reason to stay in touch. I recommend ensuring that you've established your new, separate life before you make this transition. If you become best buddies too soon, your relationship with him could become a social crutch, or something you hide behind in place of creating a life for yourself.

The important point about being friends with your ex is that the relationship should evolve naturally. Don't force it.

Also, it will not happen immediately – it cannot. You will need some time to ensure the relationship evolves into something clear where you can be friends.

In the beginning I recommend going cold turkey and not seeing your ex at all. Break all contact, delete him off Facebook and stop stalking him at the supermarket. Use the exercise on setting boundaries to set crucial boundaries with your ex.

When you have a new relationship you must honor your divorce. That means putting your new partner first. Any new relationship takes time to develop and you don't want an ex hanging about in the wings to jeopardize things.

You judge whether a natural friendship with your ex is healthy or not. If it interferes in your new life or your new relationship, end it.

Sex with your ex

Sometimes partners continue their sexual relationship after a break up. It may be that you're less familiar with each other after your divorce so the sex can feel more passionate. Some couples will use each other for sex although this prolongs the hurt. I know of women who continue to sleep with their ex-partners long after they've remarried and had children. One such woman was Sue.

 Case study: Sue

Sue continued to sleep with her ex-husband Ed on and off for three years even after Sue had remarried. It was very detrimental to both of them moving on or committing to their new relationships. When Sue's new husband found out about her affair with her ex-husband, he ended their relationship immediately. Sue's life became turmoil as she went through her second divorce within the space of a year.

This is not moving on. You need a clean break. You need closure. Don't waste your life clinging to old relationships.

Women are particularly susceptible to sleeping with their ex during the Panic/nego-tiation phase of the **naked divorce grieving cycle** as a way of getting back together. For a woman, sex might mean intimacy. But it might not mean anything to the man.

Understand the phases you'll go through after your divorce. Understand your hormones and those angst-ridden feelings and where they come from. The next time you feel compelled to contact your ex, ask yourself:

⇨ Do I miss being with him or do I simply miss being in a couple?

⇨ What if he says, "Let's give it another go." Will you be able to change what didn't work the first time?

⇨ If you're leaving the outcome of your relationship in his hands, ask yourself, "What do I want? Is he the man I want to be with for the rest of my life, even if nothing changed?"

If you are still harboring resentment and anger towards your ex

If you have completed the 21-day program, and still feel strong anger or bitterness, contact the **naked divorce** team immediately as this is not a common response.

If you can't be friends

Be civil and friendly. When you bump into your ex, greet him, shake hands or hug him if you're both comfortable with this, in same way you would greet a business associate. Keep your interactions brief and then move on.

Ex-Factor Etiquette where there are children involved

Don't expose your children to marital conflict

When children are involved in divorce it's very important for parents to behave civilly. I accept that this can be hard. It might always be hard. But there will be times you have to see your ex, particularly at school events or if you need to discuss something related to their parenting. In these cases, the rules are easy:

⇨ **Don't speak badly of your ex in front of your children ever.** Respect your child's right to have a relationship with their father and do not use your children as a go-between or carrier of nasty messages. KEEP your children out of any marital conflicts.

⇨ **Do not volunteer unsavory information about your ex in front of your children.**

⇨ **Do not argue in front of your children.** Be polite and set a good example for your children

⇨ **Prioritize having an amicable relationship with your ex.** It is important that your children feel you are still presenting a united front.

⇨ **Make sure your marital settlement or divorce agreement is clear on ALL the details.** This ensures that there are no misunderstandings in the future.

⇨ **Don't give your children false hopes of their parents reuniting.** It's important that they do not receive confusing messages.

⇨ **If your ex does push your buttons, think ahead before you see him and ask yourself:**

- What are the triggers?
- How will you keep the peace and stay calm?
- What do you want to achieve in your interactions with him?

Helping your children through your divorce

I don't have children. I'm not an expert and can't speak from experience about children and divorce, but I have successfully coached many men and women with children.

Using my experience with my clients who are parents, and having consulted the best parenting-after-divorce experts in the field, I have included this section to help you support your children through the trauma of divorce and its aftermath. What you read below is a distillation of what these experts' advice and recommend and what I have learnt from coaching people. All books, interviews and recommended reading is listed in the bibliography at the back of this book.

In my reading, one of the most useful resources (I highly recommend it) I came across is from 'Don't Divorce Your Children', written by pediatricians Jennifer Lewis and William Sammons (Contemporary, 1999), the website www.helpguide.org as well as in my interview with Sherlyn Luedtke, founder of Present Parent Training.

What do children believe during divorce

Many children believe that they had something to do with the divorce. They may remember times when they argued with their parents, got poor grades, or got into trouble. They may associate that conflict with their parents' conflict and blame themselves. Also, some children may worry that their parents will stop loving them, or that they will never see the estranged parent again. Sometimes young children don't understand the meaning and permanence of divorce. Sometimes they believe that it's one parent's fault or that someone else is to blame.

Reassurance and consistency is important in the early days of divorce.

Sherlyn Luedtke says, "tell your children that although the love between mom and dad has changed, that this kind of love is different than love between mother and child. This love is forever and special." Sherlyn also believes in telling your children the same things over and over again to prove that there is consistency.

Tip-

Treat your child's confusion or misunderstandings with patience. Reassure your children that both parents will continue to love them and that they're not responsible for the divorce.

Gently clarify any misunderstandings about the custody arrangements.

What do children want from their parents

This list is taken from a study done at the University of Missouri where children of divorce were asked what they needed from their mom and dad. The list is written by children themselves:

➡ "I need both of you to stay involved in my life. Please write letters, make phone calls, and ask me lots of questions. When you don't stay involved, I feel like I'm not important and that you don't really love me."

➡ "Please stop fighting and work hard to get along with each other. Try to agree on matters related to me. When you fight about me, I think that I did something wrong and I feel guilty."

➡ "I want to love you both and enjoy the time that I spend with each of you. Please support me and the time that I spend with each of you. If you act jealous or upset, I feel like I need to take sides and love one parent more than the other."

➡ "Please communicate directly with my other parent so that I don't have to send messages back and forth."

⇨ "When talking about my other parent, please say only nice things, or don't say anything at all. When you say mean, unkind things about my other parent, I feel like you are expecting me to take your side."

⇨ "Please remember that I want both of you to be a part of my life. I count on my mom and dad to raise me, to teach me what is important, and to help me when I have problems."

How you communicate with your children is key

Difficult as it may be to do, try to strike an empathetic tone and address the most important points, right up front. Give your children the benefit of an honest, but child-friendly, explanation.

If you go to www.helpguide.org and read the texts I have recommended, they indicate there is a specific way to speak to your children so that you have told them enough but not too much. Sherlyn Luedtke said in her interview that:

⇨ **Provide continuity.** Children need the sense of continuity provided by a certain amount of structure such as dependable meal and bed times, leisure and work times.

⇨ **Be consistent in routines and explanations of what happened.** Children have very keen attention to detail when stressed. Repeat the same reason for your divorce several times if necessary. Sometimes they need to hear the same message 100 times.

⇨ **80% of communication is related to tone and body language.** Ensure you are calm and grounded before engaging in communication.

Normal reactions to separation and divorce

The resources www.childrenanddivorce.com, www.parentcoordinationcentral.com and www.helpguide.org/mental/children_divorce.htm state that although strong feelings can be tough on children, it is normal for them to experience some anger, anxiety and mild depression BUT if things get worse rather than better after several months, it may be a sign that your child is stuck in depression, anxiety or anger and could use some additional support. www.helpguide.org/mental/children_divorce.htm states you must watch for these warning signs of divorce-related depression or anxiety:

⇨ Sleep problems, nightmares or bedwetting.

⇨ Poor concentration.

⇨ Trouble at school.

⇨ Drug or alcohol abuse.

➡️ Self-injury, cutting.

➡️ Frequent angry or violent outbursts.

➡️ Withdrawal from loved ones.

➡️ Avoiding favorite activities.

Steps to reduce traumatic effects of a divorce on your children

There are several steps to follow to reduce the traumatic effects of divorce on children and now that you have taken care of yourself, study the resources, books and texts I have provided in this chapter to ensure you provide stability, structure and continuity for your children. Support them by helping them express emotions, and commit to truly listening to these feelings, without getting defensive. Listen and help them find words for their feelings, acknowledging their right to their feelings. Also let your children know that even though the physical circumstances of the family unit will change, they can continue to have healthy, loving relationships with both of their parents.

Tip-

Sherlyn Luedtke says a great idea is to help children process their feelings by helping them make a hand-drawn book of the family and of how they feel.

Develop a parenting plan

Pediatricians and authors Jennifer Lewis and William Sammons recommend that divorced parents develop a parenting plan for their children.

Most divorcing parents are understandably concerned about the custody status of their children because it defines how the major decision-making responsibilities will be allocated, and may influence where the children live. However, what primarily impacts the children's lives is not their custody status but the schedule of time that they spend with each parent and the nuts and bolts of how that schedule is implemented.

This blueprint for the children's care, Lewis and Samons call the parenting plan, should be a much more comprehensive document than the typical visitation agreement. A successful parenting plan needs to incorporate sufficient details to ensure children will not experience ongoing arguments and conflicts between their parents about the arrangements they are putting in place. A parenting plan could contain the amount of time that the children will spend with each parent, the time(s) and place(s) of handover, guidelines to holidays and vacations, calendar of joint schedule, joint-parenting rules and guidelines so that there is consistency in parenting (including bed times, diet, watching television, homework etc.) It has also been advised to include details such as what to do in the event of last minute delays or cancellations.

Tip-

Share your parenting plan and divorce agreement with your children. This inclusion helps children look to the future with a sense of certainty and decreases the fear that parents are hiding something even direr than the divorce.

Letting your children read the settlement agreement lets them know there are rules that govern your actions post-divorce, which you have agreed you are legally bound to obey. Even for the young child who wants the document read to them - and that usually lasts for about 2 paragraphs since most kids think it's very boring - just hearing it and seeing it are reassuring.

Letters to your children

In my weekly newsletter, you will find LOADS of tips, techniques and letter templates for helping your children comes to terms with the divorce. The templates include letters to young children, older children and letters to the school. Sign up at www.nakeddivorce.com today.

Falling in love again

Ensure you are fulfilled as a woman first

Relax. Focus first on healing and being happy within yourself before you start focusing on finding THE ONE.

Take the trip you always wanted to take. Develop your own interests and pursuits. You have just spent the past however many years focused on being in a relationship. This is now YOUR time to live your life. Enjoy it. Savor it.

NOTE: It's often when you stop worrying about finding a new partner that serendipity steps in and things start falling into place. If you're enjoying life again and looking after yourself - mind, body and soul - you're bound to make an impact and attract attention. But remember, no one wants to be around someone who has lost their sense of humor or who is depressed and uncommunicative.

Be aware of attracting rescuers while you're healing

As you discovered in Day 13 with the Drama Triangle, be wary of attracting rescuers during your time of healing. The men you meet while you're in a compromised state may well be attracted to your vulnerability and that part of you that is needy and wanting to be comforted and cared for.

Don't attach yourself to any new acquaintances or friends who see you as less than you are.

Create your dream relationship blueprint

Answer these questions below in your journal:

➡️ Do you have a certain type of partner you attract and where did this come from? Is this type healthy for you? What type of man do you believe is the type who will be the best for you in your life?

⇨ How was your life when you met your ex? Were you happy and confident or feeling needy and desperate?

⇨ What were your ex's positive traits that attracted you to him and what good aspects or attributes of that relationship would you like to create in your next relationship?

⇨ What are your expectations now? What are you looking for in your dream relationship?

⇨ Think of your dream relationship. Close your eyes and create a little movie scene in your mind of you with your dream partner. How do you know it's your dream partner? What's happening in this scene? Write down everything you see, feel, hear, touch and experience. Ensure it's a vivid scene.

Attract your dream relationship in 21 days

When it comes to attracting the partner of your dreams, your unconscious beliefs are more powerful than your everyday thoughts. You cannot reprogram your conscious mind. Your subconscious mind, however, is like a giant computer hard drive that can be programmed with mental software (i.e. thought patterns and belief systems) to control your thinking.

For example, if you currently have a mental program installed in your subconscious mind that says, "I can't have a beautifully loving relationship with my dream man" or "I never get what I want and I'm not good enough", your subconscious mind will make sure that you don't have any opportunities to attract that amazing man into your life. And even if you consciously want nothing more than to be in an amazing relationship, your subconscious mind can ensure that you sabotage your success.

Until you reprogram your mind to support you attracting your dream partner, your limiting belief systems (or programs) in your subconscious mind will make you think thoughts that limit what you can attract into your life.

The *naked divorce* Dream Relationship audio program is an effortless way to attract your dream partner into your life. Listen to this recording daily for 21 days and see the opportunities that will begin to manifest in your life. This really worked for me and it can work for you too.

Find out more about this program at www.nakeddivorce.com/products/mydream-relationship/

Principles of keeping love alive

I am sometimes really frustrated that the education system today does not prepare us for what it TRULY takes to make a romantic relationship work in the long-term. I wish that I had known some of these principles before I got married. Unfortunately I had to make all the mistakes before I learnt all of these lessons for the future.

I had to develop some compassion for myself because I really didn't have the insights I have today back when I actually needed them. I am therefore committed to keep mastering the principles of keeping love alive, not only to ensure that my clients benefit from all this wisdom but that I ensure my own future happiness in my relationship.

In your next relationship, keep some principles in mind to assist you in keeping love alive. These are tips I have put together after reading 27 books on the topic, interviewing experts and from my own personal experience in working with couples.

Keeping love alive principle #1: Let him win at loving you

This is a lesson I learnt the hard way. I had to own up to the fact that I never let my ex-husband win at loving me. I spent most of the time playing hard to get, difficult, dramatic or testing him.

 **NOTE:**

For a man to feel love for a woman, he must feel he can win or be successful at loving her.

Your man needs to feel that by simply being around you, he can make you happy and that you're at peace and fully satisfied in his company.

This is why an overly-critical woman can make her man feel he's failed at loving her. He'll withdraw his affection and love in return. He may even say things like, "I can't win".

Facing up to how critical I was of Bruce was brutal. I was forced to admit that I might have precipitated his infidelity. So, if you're resisting this one, I get it! Ask yourself, "Have I let him feel he can always win at loving me?" This is a crucial lesson for keeping love alive.

When you come home and you're feeling grumpy, ensure your man knows he is amazing and that he makes you very happy and that your moods have nothing to do with him.

Keeping love alive principle #2: Maintain the polarity of your relationship

The feminine essence is: Loving, caring, spontaneous, crazy, unpredictable, free, fun, mental, dramatic, turbulent, shrieking at the sight of a mouse/spider/creature with more legs than yourself, outspoken, honest, vulnerable, raw, carefree, real, weepy, emotional, a hurricane, self-expressed, creative, chatty, babbling and making no sense, cooking, loud, noisy, peaceful, sexy, goddess-like, mysterious, a dancing nymph, wanting to be comforted, nurtured, supported and loved.

The feminine essence is not: controlling, overly organized, bossy, nagging, changing light bulbs (even if she is perfectly capable of doing so), killing snakes, doing manly chores that require power tools, silent, talking about her emotions instead of feeling them, too intellectual, so damn independent that a man will sense she doesn't need him (sadly, he will be right).

 NOTE: To keep sexual chemistry alive in your relationship, remain feminine in your relationship and true to your feminine essence. Allow your man to be the man in your life.

Focus on remembering these points whenever you feel your man slipping away from you. Step back into your feminine essence and he will come straight back to you.

Keeping love alive principle #3: Maintain separateness and move to your own rhythm

It was Sherry Argov who distinguished that 'men equate longing with love.' If you do everything together, there will be no opportunity for your man to experience any longing for you. So, don't jump through hoops for him. Don't suffocate him by always wanting to be where he is or checking up on him. If he texts you, don't respond immediately if you are busy with something else. Wait a little while until you have completed what you were doing before texting him back. If you get home and see there is a message from him, wait until you've settled in, made a cup of tea, had a bath or dinner, or anything else you want to do before checking the message.

Keep your own interests and activities alive. Every few nights, ensure you have a gym class, dinner, a movie or a book club with a girlfriend or something that ensures he doesn't always have your movements pinned down. You'll see when you get home afterwards that he's missed you…

Keeping love alive principle #4: When he disappears on you, focus on making yourself happy

Men disappear from time to time and as author John Gray stated in 'Men are from Mars, Women are from Venus.' They do go into their caves from time to time. It's a basic need and one that too many women don't understand.

When he disappears, he's usually still physically present, but emotionally distant and distracted. At these times, dig deep, practice *the Worry Buster* exercise on Day 17 and reassure yourself that this is a test. He is testing your reactions.

Our natural instinct is to want to know why. We'll want to know if there's something wrong.

No! No! No! This will drive him further into the cave. You have to focus on making yourself happy. Organize a dinner with your girlfriends. Play tennis. Go to the gym. Have a luxurious bath and pamper session. Whistle while you're cooking dinner. Leave him be. Don't question or enquire. Smile at him and give his hand a squeeze, then walk away and go and be happy.

This will surprise him because men are used to women acting very clingy whenever they retreat into their caves. He will be concerned that your life does not revolve around him and that you seem happy without him doing anything. The hunter within him will return from his cave very fast to reclaim his woman, you'll see!

Keeping love alive principle #5: Communication strategies

You have learnt some valuable communication strategies in this book like the five R's from Day 13 and Setting boundaries on Day 19.

If you want your man to do something for you, avoid giving a command. Try this communication approach:

- ⇨ Acknowledgement… "Thank you darling for…"
- ⇨ I need…
- ⇨ I feel…
- ⇨ Would you provide [solution]…

VIDEO: Watch me explain this communication
method on the *naked divorce* YouTube
channel on **www.youtube.com/nakeddi-
vorce**

NOTE:

Help your man by giving him a clear roadmap
of what you would like him to provide.

Here's an example of an approach you can use to get him to pay attention to you
(and not while he's watching television!):

> "Darling, I get it that you're driven to do well in your work and I love it that
> you're so committed. You know I'm learning to express my needs. What stands
> out is that I really need to feel connected with you, which means I need to
> feel a deep connection to you every day. It might be five minutes, but when
> you stop what you're doing, touch my face, grab me around the waist, kiss me
> passionately, I feel incredibly loved and our relationship seems magical to me..."

Keeping love alive principle #6: Don't lecture him...

Sometimes men can be real bad-tempered grumplestiltskins. Perhaps their football
team lost, maybe they had a bad day at work or they bit your head off about something menial. Maybe they went out late and got drunk with the boys or gambled
some money away.

He is not dating his mother, so this is not an opportunity to lecture him. Men do
not respond well to being lectured or bossed about. They respond much better to
action.

He knows he behaved badly and the best way to handle his bad behavior is to get
up, get dressed and go out. Your silence or absence will tell him that you will not
tolerate being around him if he is like this. If you show him that you are not affected by his bad behavior, you are just busy, by the time you arrive home, the
house will be cleaned, he would have sorted himself out and there will be flowers
waiting in a vase for you.

Keeping love alive principle #7: Maintain the mystery

One of the biggest mistakes women make when they get married is they become boring. They tell their husbands every mundane detail of their day, like the coupons they got at the supermarket and how they found a carwash which does a wash and dry on your car for 9.99. They get their nails done but then they tell their husbands all about it. They go to the toilet in front of them, they wear their sweats or tracksuits all the time, they relax with their appearance or stop making a special effort to look great.

It's important to remember that it was back when you were the sexy girlfriend that he fell in love with you. This was the time you had an allure of mystery about you and put in the work with cooking, doing your nails, shaving your legs and maintaining your figure. You also didn't tell him everything. You left details out because you wanted to appear sexy or cool.

This is a secret I have learnt from my mother (who has been married to my dad for 36 years), namely: Maintain some mystery. There is no need to over-communicate with men. Here is what this looks like:-

⇨ Get your nails done but don't tell him. Let him notice. You looking amazing must appear effortless, like it simply happens with ease. He doesn't need to know how excruciating your last bikini wax was or how long it took to get your hair done. You do all these things with a smile on your face.

⇨ If he asks you what you did today, sometimes just say, "you know, stuff" and then give him a wink. If he probes for more details, try saying, "well what do you think a hot woman like me gets up to ALL day" then walk out the door giving up a little wiggle of your bum. Sometimes it's healthy to not tell him what you got up to (particularly if you had a very boring day). All these little moments are perfect recipes for fun later on but it is in maintaining some mystery that you reignite the spark in a long-term relationship.

⇨ Pamper yourself. Men like it when their woman disappears for the day of pampering and luxuriating. He will conclude that you will arrive home relaxed and ready for a night of passion.

⇨ Don't tell him you bought lingerie, just show him.

⇨ If you have found the secret to unlocking his desire for you – don't give your game away. Never tell him so he feels like a pawn in your game.

⇨ Wherever possible, don't go to the toilet in front of your man, let him clean up your vomit or see you with your hair or body unwashed or makeup smeared all over your face. You immediately go from being his sexy goddess to someone entirely ordinary. He will conclude you do not respect yourself and don't care what you look like around him and something dies in that moment. I know this may sound ridiculous and not very feminist of me but I say this with a caveat: you can be a feminist and in your fight for equality, carry more of the masculine energy in the relationship than your man (thereby emasculating him) OR you can have a great sexy relationship. All I know is by being the girl in my relationship, it works and the passion and chemistry does not die or burn out.

Keeping love alive principle #8: Professor cheerleader

I find it really important to allow my man to feel in charge. Even if I know exactly what I am doing and don't need his help, I will still ask for it wherever possible so he has an opportunity to feel like he can make a difference and that his contribution is the reason I am where I am today.

The more I surrender to my man making a difference to me, the better my life and my relationship with him is. He has contributed massively to my success but I had to surrender to allow him to make this difference. In the beginning I felt like a professor (I knew exactly what I was doing and didn't need help) who was dumbing herself down to become a wide-eyed cheerleader but once I saw the closeness that came with allowing someone to contribute, the benefits outweighed my need to control and feel independent. The key is whenever he does rush in and solve an issue, to pause, touch him tenderly and thank him profusely for his help. Men value admiration and acknowledgement above all else as well as the feeling that they can win at loving you.

Keeping love alive principle #9: The five love languages

Gary Chapman is a genius for writing this book 'The Five Love Languages'. I recommend you go and get yourself a copy immediately. I believe that every couple committed to having a happy long-term relationship, needs to read this book and do his *Love Language* test.

Gary's premise is that there are five love languages that are ways that human beings give and express love. The overarching idea is that you give love in the language that you need it expressed to you. If you don't receive love in your love language, you will feel unloved and unfulfilled in your relationship. The five love languages as Gary describes them are:

⇨ Words of affirmation (feeling more connected through talking and telling someone you love them)

⇨ Physical touch (feeling more connected through physical touch and sexual intimacy)

⇨ Gift giving (feeling more connected through the giving and receiving of gifts)

➡️ Acts of service (feeling more connected through doing things for your loved one)

➡️ Quality time (feeling more connected by spending undivided time together)

The idea is that each of has one of these as our primary love language and we will naturally express love in this language. To feel loved, we need to have love expressed in this language. Most often, couples are not matched in their love languages so there will be conflict in the woman who wants to spend time her man but he doesn't understand this need because he had just given her a nice necklace this morning.

What is so great about his book is that it explains why a woman may struggle with her husband's sexual advances unless he has spent some quality time wooing her. In this particular instance, her primary love language may be quality time, whilst his love language is physical touch. By him understanding this, he can ensure he spends some time with her before making his advances, if he wants them to be successful, that is! It also explains why someone may say the words, "I love you" 100 times to her partner but he doesn't think they mean anything because she hasn't helped him around the garden with an act of service for at least five months.

Keeping love alive principle #10: Handle with care

It's important to remember that relationships are vulnerable. You may relax into your new relationship and then think you can get away with some bad behavior from time to time. In reality, there is a limit on how much bad behavior a relationship can handle.

Be cautious of how many tantrums you throw, loud arguments you can have and how many times you can tell him off over not taking out the trash before you will find the love and intimacy between you has died.

Keeping love alive principle #11: Men need to feel...

I surveyed 39 men over a period of 6 years and found there to be certain feelings men need to feel when they are with you. These feelings are:

➡️ **Trust** – he needs to feel that you completely trust him and trust his decisions, choices and approaches to life. He needs to feel that you trust him to be true to you.

➡️ **Acceptance** – he needs to feel that you completely accept him as he is and that his worst qualities are endearing and adorable.

➡ **Appreciation** – he needs to feel that you appreciate him and notice the little things he does for you.

➡ **Admiration** – he needs to feel that you admire him and empower his leadership.

➡ **Approval** – he needs to feel that you approve of him and his decisions.

➡ **Encouragement** – he needs to feel encouraged, even when you are both terrified of something.

So whenever you feel like you want to draw him closer to you, focus on how you can make your man feel these feelings when he is with you.

Keeping Love Alive principle #12: Elicit the correct response in him

Here is a matrix you can use to elicit the desired response in your man:

	YOU	**HIM**
✓	Give yourself freely	He feels masculine
✗	Be resistant at times	He becomes less involved
✓	Express your feelings honestly and calmly	He likes to talk
✗	Show little emotion	He doesn't feel close to you and your intimacy suffers
✗	Wait for his approval with everything	He feels annoyed
✓	Decide yourself that you approve of yourself	He appreciates it
✗	Support his decisions	Feels important
✗	Question everything he decides	Tires of you and feels undermined or bored
✓	Compliment him occasionally and authentically	Engages with you
✗	Notice every imperfection	Feels less chemistry
✓	Accept his natural self	Respects you
✗	Ask him to be better all the time	Feels undermined

Join the *naked divorce* community

Share your story with the world and empower other women like you

I would love to hear your story so you can share it to inspire other women around the world, so email us on mystory@nakeddivorce.com

Community

Go to www.nakeddivorce.com and join the *naked divorce* community, receive loads of free newsletters, information, free tips, insights and friendship by signing up to the weekly Musings of the *naked divorce* Coach: www.nakeddivorce.com/book.

Forum

Share with others who are going through the *naked divorce* either in the forum www.nakeddivorce.com/forum/ or join one of the programs and chat to other participants on the secret Facebook group.

Blog

Subscribe to www.nakeddivorce.com/blog/ to receive weekly updates on a range of musings from the *naked divorce* coach.

The topics include: Divorce VS Separation, Mediation, Children/ friends/ family, Child Maintenance and Custody issues, Letter Templates, Handing your living situation, Handing your finances. Parenting, Domestic violence, Health, Dating, Love and Relationship tips, Anger management and much more!

Twitter

@adele_theron

Facebook

http://on.fb.me/nakeddivorce
http://on.fb.me/Adele_Theron

Youtube

The *naked divorce* YouTube channel is www.youtube.com/nakeddivorce.

Web resources

Searching for information in your country? Find great information on organizations that can assist you in the handling of divorce for your country: www.nakeddivorce.com/resources. Topics include:

- Helping your children cope with divorce
- Dating websites
- Coping with domestic violence and divorce
- Managing my finances through divorce
- Managing my health during my divorce
- Legal aid and divorce
- Parenting resources
- Personal and Professional Development
- Other Divorce resources

A final word

Dear Powerful Courageous One,

I honor you for coming on this journey with me. I honor your strength, courage and wisdom.

I know what it took for you to take the road less travelled. Your courage of spirit and bravery you displayed as you walked through the flames of divorce.

As you look back, do you recognize yourself?

Are you present to the woman you have now become?

You experienced pain and discovered that you are stronger than you ever imagined. You experience purification and the hurricane of change and pain triggered a rebirth within you. I pray that this rebirth freed you from any suffering, from any upset and from focusing on your ex.

I pray that you discovered and remembered who you are. Your dreams, your life and your purpose. Thank you for tumbling down the rabbit hole with me. Thank you for trusting me with your heart and with your healing. It was a privilege to walk this path with you.

Now Go.

Go and have the most wonderful life.

LIVE and suck the marrow from life.

Do everything you have ever wanted to do. Do it now and waste not another moment.

I wish you the brightest, most beautiful and amazing life!

With love

Pages to Print

Pages to print: x1

The *Healing Formula*:

```
Healing Formula = Focused Intensity +
3 Key Breakthroughs + 7 Foundations of Transformation
```

The *naked divorce* Foundations of Transformation

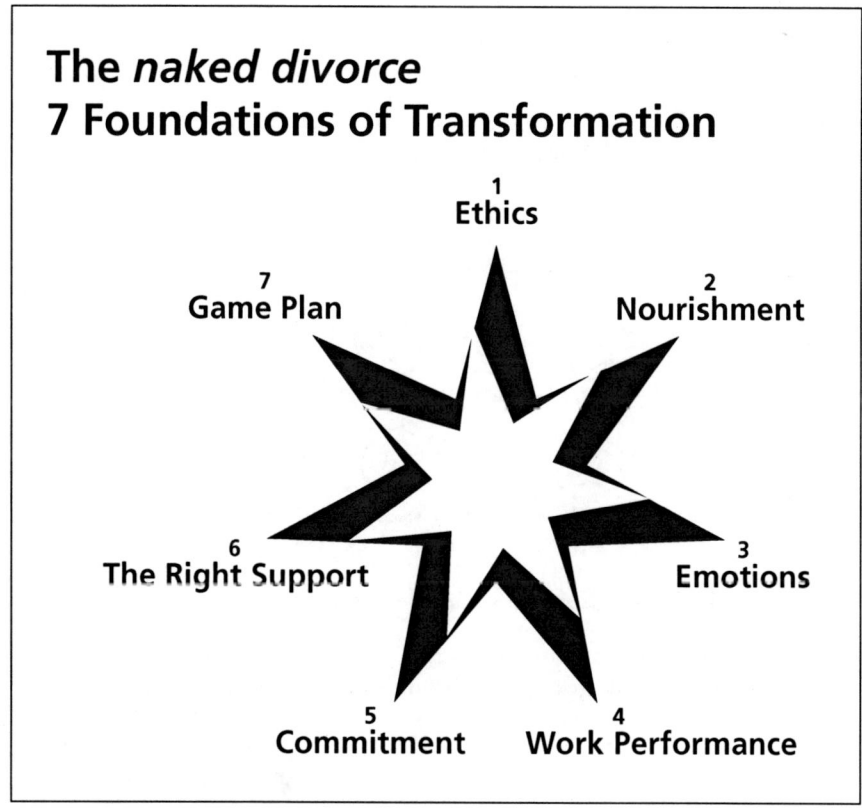

The ***naked divorce***
7 Foundations of Transformation

1
Ethics

7
Game Plan

2
Nourishment

6
The Right Support

3
Emotions

5
Commitment

4
Work Performance

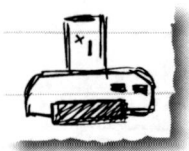

Pages to print: x21

The *naked divorce* Checklist

Day: ....

Date: ....

MORNING

Drink a glass of hot water with a squeeze of lemon,
take your supplements. ☐

Read through the Thought for the Day ☐

Read through the exercise you'll be doing later today.
Allow yourself to think about it during the day. ☐

I feel... ☐
(Circle the emotions that are most appropriate. At the end of the day update the chart
to see what other emotions you experienced.)

Angry   Confident   Confused   Content   Depressed   Flirty   Frustrated   Gloomy

Happy   Insecure   Irritable   Relaxed   Spacey   Stressed   Tired   Weepy

Do your Daily Declarations while in the shower. ☐

Get dressed and put on your make-up;
make an effort to look good, even if you're not going to work. ☐

GOING TO WORK

Optional: Take the *naked divorce* to work with you
You may want to work on it during your break.

☐

Drink at least six glasses of water during the day.
Crying is thirsty work.

☐

Practice the four A's.

☐

When you're feeling overly emotional at work and you feel you need to put your emotions aside to focus on your day, practice the four A's taken from the *naked divorce exercise for handling your emotions whilst at work.* Practice being **A**ware of your emotions as they arise. **A**ccept them. **A**cknowledge your right to have them. And then simply **A**ct Normal. Know that the moment you get home or get to the bathroom at lunchtime, you can let loose!

NOT GOING TO WORK

If a weekend, start on the exercise for the day as soon as you can.

HOME

Prepare dinner.

☐

If you have children, put them in front of a DVD while you prepare dinner. Take time to cook the food with love and care. Cry if you need to. Wail and sob while you're slicing the onions. It's a good cover! Whatever you do, let go completely, surrendering to all your emotions. When done, drink lots of water.

Try to get some exercise today, even if it's a 10 minute walk.

Check in with your *Divorce Angel*
and let them know very briefly how you're doing.

☐

List at least five successes you enjoyed today:

1 ....

2 ....

3 ....

4 ....

5 ....

Did you notice anything you did ☐
**to sabotage your healing or detract from your goal of healing today? If so,
list what happened below:**

....

....

....

ETHICS of the Program (Rate yourself on a scale of one to 10, one being 'needs
work' and 10 being 'I feel absolutely balanced here'):

Ethics	Rate yourself on a scale of 1-10	Actions I will take to move this ETHIC to a level 10 in my life
Full self-expression		• • • •
Avoid STEATs		• • • •
Establish a Grounded Routine		• • • •
Sleep on any drastic changes you wish to make in your life		• • • •
Say no		• • • •
Cause VS effect		• • • •
Focus on you VS him		• • • •

day
21
RELEASE

Theme: Celebration!

Date: Thursday, _____

🕐 **Estimated time to complete the exercise: 30 minutes**

Remember to go through the daily checklist

Tick when done

Read through the thought for the day:

Today, I acknowledge your courage and your immense achievement.

I don't take it lightly that you've accomplished what you have as I've walked this path myself. I know how tough it is and, you did it!

Spend today getting reacquainted with who you are as a woman, how extraordinary you are and how damn fantastic your life will be from today onwards.

I'd like you to walk around with your head held high wearing your invisible crown. You did it. You are a heroine and you are free. Make a list of everything you acknowledge yourself for today. Today there is no homework, only celebration.

Do a little jig around in your shower, put on your new theme song and dance, and indulge in a makeover, a massage or have a drink to celebrate. Throw yourself a *Divorce Party* and invite your closest and dearest friends, or go out on a mission to have fun. You have completed the **naked divorce** program!

I'd love to hear your story so you can inspire other women around the world, so please email us on mystory@nakeddivorce.com

Checklist for the *naked divorce*

Tend to the children. □

If you have children, remember to check in with them and ask them how they're doing. Ensure that you give them the space to communicate their vulnerability, knowing that you will have the time to experience your emotions later.

Complete your daily homework. □

BEFORE BED

Optional: Have a soothing, hot bath, light some candles and allow yourself to feel any emotions bubbling under the surface. Allow yourself to feel them fully. If you want to cry, do it, and then give yourself a big hug in the bath. Drink water while you're bathing, particularly if you're crying. □

Optional: When in bed, listen to the **naked divorce** Break Up Reboot and allow yourself to drift off to sleep. If you fall asleep while listening, that's fine. It also works on your subconscious while you sleep. □

Pages to print: x1

The Daily Declarations

I AM WONDERFULLY CREATED, A BEAUTIFUL AND GORGEOUS

CREATURE WHO DESERVES ALL THAT IS WONDERFUL IN THIS WORLD.

I FORGIVE MYSELF COMPLETELY FOR ANYTHING I HAVE SAID OR DONE TO MYSELF OR OTHERS IN MY LIFE.

I AM A PRECIOUS TREASURE AND HAVE ENORMOUS VALUE TO ADD TO THE LIVES OF THOSE I LOVE, AND PARTICULARLY TO THE MAN I CHOOSE TO SHARE MY LIFE WITH.

I TREASURE MY FEMININITY AND WOMANHOOD AND WILL NEVER COMPROMISE THOSE ATTRIBUTES FOR ANYONE OR ANYTHING.

I AM DESERVING OF LOVE AND HAPPINESS AND THERE ARE MANY PEOPLE IN MY LIFE WHO LOVE AND ADORE ME.

I AM ENOUGH. I AM ATTRACTIVE ENOUGH, GOOD ENOUGH AND ACCOMPLISHED ENOUGH. I AM MORE THAN ENOUGH.

I LOVE WHO I AM AND WILL FOCUS ON DEVELOPING MYSELF AND FULFILLING MY DESTINY.

I AM PERFECTLY MADE TO BE THE WOMAN, GIRLFRIEND, WIFE, MOTHER OR GRAND-MOTHER I AM INTENDED TO BE.

I TAKE CARE OF MY PARTNER AND SUPPORT HIM IN SPECIAL WAYS. I AM ALWAYS THERE FOR HIM.

BUT NOW IS THE TIME IN MY LIFE TO CARE FOR MYSELF AND TO PUT MY NEEDS FIRST.

I SET HEALTHY BOUNDARIES WITH OTHERS IN MY LIFE, GAINING POWER AND RE-SPECT.

I AM SEXY, FANTASTIC IN BED AND GREAT FUN TO BE WITH.

I AM THE AUTHOR OF MY LIFE. I ALONE CAN MAKE THE CHANGES I NEED TO BE FUL-FILLED.

TODAY I WEAR MY INVISIBLE CROWN BECAUSE IT IS MY DAY, THIS IS MY WORLD. AND I LOVE IT.

OVER AND OUT!

Acknowledgements

There are so many people to thank for helping bring this book together. Firstly I wish to thank Mike Harris for that day that he looked me straight in the eye and told me to write this book and take the **naked divorce** concept out to the world. Without that conversation, I am not sure I would have written this book at all. I would also like to thank Daniel Priestley for his support and for believing in my process and what my message is. I would also like to thank S.N. Goenke for developing Vipassana, the 10-day silent retreat that provided such clarity and inner power - without this clarity, I would never have had the foresight to develop anything. Werner Erhardt for being an important mentor throughout my life and for giving me the understanding of how to transform anything in my life.

I would like to thank Ilya Prigogine for coming up with the concept of *Perturbation* and to Marilyn Ferguson for suggesting that it could be used in human transformation too. I wish to thank my publishers, editors, proofreaders and in particular Clem for jumping in at the final hour. I wish to thank Dickie Bielenberg for all his support and guidance throughout the early stages of the **naked divorce** development, many of our conversations resulted in breakthroughs within this book. To my amazing family for their love and support - my mum for being an early victim in reading the book cover-to-cover and to my dad for being the original change management guru. I also wish to thank my ex-husband for our story that gave rise to all of this happening. I wish to thank all of my clients and worthy guinea pigs who ensured that the concepts were tested and for proving that the *Healing Formula* worked.

Last, but by no means least, my amazing partner in life, Simon Williams for being the most empowering person I have ever been with. He is my beacon and my home.

Bibliography

- Abraham, R. (1994). Chaos, Gaia, Eros: A chaos pioneer uncovers the three great streams of history. New York. Harper San Francisco.
- Abrahams Spring, J. (2004). How can I forgive you? Perennial Currents.
- Angrist, S. W. and Hepler, L. G. (1967). Order and chaos: Laws of energy and entropy. New York. Basic Books.
- Argov, S. (2011). Why men marry bitches. Argov and Adams Media.
- Assagiolo, R. (1974). The act of willl. NY. Penguin.
- Atkins, P. W. (1984). The second law. New York. Scientific American.
- Aziz, R. (1990). C. G. Jung's psychology of religion and synchronicity. New York. State University of New York Press.
- Bailey, Kenneth D. (1990). Social Entropy Theory (term: "Prigogine entropy", pg. 72). New York. State University of New York Press.
- Bailey, Kenneth D. (1994). Sociology and the New Systems Theory: Toward a Theoretical Synthesis (term: "Prigogine entropy equation", pg. 123). SUNY Press.
- Balfour, M. (2004). Smart Dating – how to find your man. Mary Balfour Publishing.
- Bandler, R. (2009).Conversations: Freedom Is Everything & Love Is All the Rest. Health Communications.
- Bandler, R. (2008).Get the Life You Want: the secrets to quick and lasting life change with neuro-linguistic programming. Health Communications.
- Baynes, J., Dominiczak, M., Medical Biochemistry. Elsevier Limited; Third Edition (2009). ISBN 978-0-323-05371-6.
- Beattie, M. (1989).Codependent No More: How to Stop Controlling Others and Start Caring for Yourself. Hazelden Information & Educational Services.
- Beattie, M. (1990). Beyond Codependency: And Getting Better All the Time. Hazelden Information & Educational Services.
- Behrendt, G; Tuccillo, L. (2004). He's just not that into you. Harper Element.
- Blackerby, R. F. (1993). Applications of chaos theory to psychological models. Austin, TX. Performance Strategies.
- Bolen, J. S. (1979). The Tao of psychology: Synchronicity and the self. New York. HarperSanFrancisco.
- Briggs, J. and Peat, F. D. (1989). The turbulent mirror: An illustrated guide to chaos theory and the science of wholeness. New York. Harper & Row.
- Brown, S. (1999) Do you Regret your divorce? Daily Mail
- Burney, R. (1995). Codependence: The Dance of the Wounded Souls. Joy to you and Me.
- Butz, M. R. (1997). Chaos and complexity: Implications for psychological theory and practice. Washington, DC. Taylor & Francis.
- Capek, M; Whitrow, J.G. (1974). Time/Time & Measurement: Two essays (18 pages) in the 'Dictionary of the History of Ideas'. Studies of selected pivotal ideas, Volume IV. Scribner's Sons
- Çambel, A. B. (1993). Applied chaos theory: A paradigm for complexity. Boston. Academic Press.
- The Canadian National Statistics Agency. (2000-2011). Divorces across Canada. Each year between 2000-2011. <http://www.statcan.gc.ca>
- Carnegie, D. (1944). How to Stop worrying and start living. Pocket Books.
- The Census Bureau of the United States of America. (2000-2011). Divorces across the United States of America. Each year between 2000-2011. < http://www.census.gov/compendia/statab/brief.html>

- Clark, N. (23 June 2011). Email Interview into Therapy vs. Naked Divorce 21-day program.
- Chapman, G. (1992). The Five Love Languages. Northfield Publishing.
- Chopra, Dr. D. (1992). Quantum Healing. Bantam Books.
- Choquette, S. (2000). Balancing your chakras. Piatkus.
- Christ, C. (1979). Womanspirit Rising: A Feminist Reader in Religion. Harper & Row.
- Moore, R. and Gillette, D. (1990). King Warrior Magician Lover: Rediscovering the Archetypes of the Mature Masculine. Harper Collins.
- Cullington, D. (1988). Breaking up Blues. Routledge.
- Dakin, R. (2009). The Girlfriend Experience. John Blake.
- Davies, (1980). Other worlds: Space, superspace and the quantum universe. NY. Touchstone.
- Deida, D. (1997). It's a Guy Thing. HCI.
- Deida, D. (1995). Intimate Communion. HCI.
- Deida, D. (1996). Dear Lover. HCI.
- Deida, D. (1995). The way of the superior man. HCI.
- Demartini, J. F. (2002). The Breakthrough Experience. Hay house.
- Dickens, C. (1992). Great Expectations. Wordsworth.
- Doherty, William J. (1999) Australian poll conducted asked people if they wished they could have made more effort to make their marriage work: 40%
- Easton, D; Hardy, J. (1997). The Ethical Slut. Celestial Arts.
- Eckel, S. (2002). Unpack your Relationship Baggage. Ladies Home Journal.
- EHOW. (2010). How to create your last will and testament. <www.ehow.com>
- Eleoff, S. (2003). An Exploration of the Ramifications of Divorce on Children and Adolescents. The Pennsylvania State University College of Medicine.
- Ferguson, M. (2005). Aquarius Now. Weiser.
- Ferguson, M. (2003). The Aquarian Conspiracy. Weiser.
- Forest, Lynn. (2004). The Three Faces of Victim. http://lynneforrest.com/articles/fov.html
- Fitzgerald, M. (2009). 6 Signs You're Dating A Woman With Baggage. <Ask Men.com and Marie Claire Magazine>
- Furstenberg FF. Morgan SP. Allison PD. (1987). Paternal Participation and Children's Well-Being After Marital Dissolution. American Sociological Review. 52: 695-701.
- Gallagher, M and Waite, L. The Case for Marriage they Don't want you to hear. (Doubleday)
- Gawain, S. (1978). Creative Visualisation. New World Library.
- Gibran, K. (1991). The Prophet. Pan Books; New edition.
- Gilbert, E. (2006). Eat pray love. Bloomsbury.
- Gladwell, M. (2000). The Tipping Point. Abacus.
- Gladwell, M. (2008). Outliers. Penguin.
- Gleick, J. (1987). Chaos: Making a new science. New York. Penguin Books.
- Glenmullen, J. (2006) Coming Off Antidepressants: Successful Use and Safe Withdrawal. Robinson Publishing.
- Godwin, C. and 14 others (2005-2011). How to understand your emotions. Wikihow.com
- Goleman, D. (1995). Emotional Intelligence. Bantam Books.
- Gottman, J.M. (1993). A theory of marital dissolution and stability. Journal of Family Psychology 7 57-75.
- Gottman, John & DeClaire, Joan. (2001). The Relationship Cure: A 5 Step Guide for Building Better Connections with Family, Friends, and Lovers. Crown Publishers.
- Gottman, John & Gottman, Julie. (2002). Why Marriages Succeed or Fail. Simon & Shuster.

- Gould, S. J. (1987). Time's arrow, time's cycle: Myth and metaphor in the discovery of geological time. Cambridge, MA. Harvard University Press.
- Gray, J. (2010). Venus on Fire. Mars on Ice. Mind Publishing.
- Gray, J. (2008). When Mars and Venus Collide. Harper Collins Element.
- Gray, J. (1992). Men are from Mars, Women are from Venus. Harper Collins Element.
- Gray, J. (1996). Men are from Mars, Women are from Venus in the Bedroom. Vermillion.
- Gribbon, J. (2012).In Search Of Schrodinger's Cat. Black Swan; New edition.
- Groenendijk, C. (2000). My Prozac (Sarafem, Fluctin, fluoxetine) Experience. A Prozac-induced "Brain/Body-Crash" at the age of 29. < www.antidepressantsfacts.com>
- Groenendijk, C. (2001). The Serotonergic System, the Pineal Gland & Side-Effects of Serotonin Acting Anti-Depressants. < www.antidepressantsfacts.com>
- Grof. S. (1985). Beyond the brain: Birth, death and transcendence in psychology. Albany, NY. State University of New York Press.
- Gschwendt, K. (2009). Creative Financial and Creative planning. <http://www.divorceandfinance.org>
- Guagenti-Tax, E. (2003). Integrating Imago Therapy and educational techniques for court ordered men who batter: A preliminary investigation. The Journal of Imago Relationship Therapy, 5 (2), 45-54.
- Haken, H. (1983). Synergetics: An introduction: Nonequilibrium phase transitions and self-organization in physics, chemistry and biology. Belin. Springer-Verlag. First published in 1977.
- Haken, H. (1987). Synergetics. In F. E. Yates (Ed.), Self-organizing systems: The emergence of order. New York. Plenum Press.
- Hall, P. (2007). Help your children cope with your divorce. Relate.
- Hall, P. (2007). How to have a healthy divorce. Relate.
- Hannah, M.T., Case, B.A., Fennell, B.A., Argesta, V., Lisi,K., Zebrowski, L.,Berkery, K. (1996). Dyadic Adjustment and the practice of Imago skills by Imago therapists in their current romantic relationships. The Journal of Imago Relationship Therapy, 1(1). 55-65.
- Hannah, M.T., Luquet, W. & McCormick, J. (1997). COMPASS as a measure of efficacy of couples therapy. American Journal of Family Therapy, 25 (1), 76-90.
- Hannah, Mt., Luquet, W., McCormick, J. Galvin, K., Ketterer, K.,May, K., Hayes, R.,& Kott, L.A. (1997). Brief report: Short-term Imago therapy and changes in personal distress. The Journal of Imago Relationship Therapy 2 (2), 55-67.
- Hannah, M.T., Marrone, J.B., Luquet, W., Gondek, D., Long, J., Squadrito, S.J., Bause, M., Clay, M. (1998). The development and psychometric properties of two measures of Imago theoretical constructs. The Journal of Imago Relationship Therapy 3 (1), 49-62.
- Harvey, S. (2009). Act like a lady, Think like a man. Amistad.
- Hay, L. (1987). You can heal your life. Hay House.
- Hayman, S. (2001). Moving on. Breaking up without breaking down. Relate.
- Heath, S. (2008). The Essence of Womanhood – reawakening the authentic feminine. Ecademy Press.
- Hendrix, H. (1988). Getting the love you want: A guide for couples. New York. Pocket Books.
- Hetherington EM. Furstenberg FF. (1989). Sounding the Alarm. Readings: A Journal of Review and Commentary in Mental Health. 6: 4-8.
- Hogan, T., Hunt, R., Emerson, D., Hayes, R., Ketterer, K. (1996) An evaluation of client Satisfaction with the "Getting the Love You want" weekend workshop. The Journal of Imago Relationship Therapy 1 (2), 57-66.
- Horne, F. (2001). 7 days to a magickal new you. Thorson.
- Houck JC, Sharma VK, Patel YM, Gladner JA. Induction of collagenolytic and proteolytic activities by anti-inflammatoes this by inhibiting collagen formation, decreasing amino acid uptake by muscle, and inhibiting protein synthesis.

- Husband AJ, Brandon MR, Lascelles AK (October 1973). The effect of corticosteroid on absorption and endogenous production of immunoglobulins in calves. Aust J Exp Biol Med Sci 51 (5): 707–10. doi:10.1038/icb.1973.67. PMID 4207041.
- James, T; Woodsmall, W. (1988). Time Line Therapy and the basis of personality. Meta Publications.
- James, J; Friedman, R. (2009). The Grief Recovery Handbook. Harper Collins.
- Jens C. Pruessner, Frances Champagne,Michael J. Meaney,and Alain Dagher. (2000). Dopamine Release in Response to a Psychological Stress in Humans and Its Relationship to Early Life Maternal Care: A Positron Emission Tomography Study Using [11C]Raclopride
- Johnson, R. A. (1991). Owning your own shadow: Understanding the dark side of the psyche. United Kingdom: HarperCollins.
- Jung, C. G. (1965). Memories, dreams, reflections. Jaffé, A. (Ed.). Winston, R. and Winston, C. (Trans.). New York. Vintage. First published in 1961.
- Jung, C.G. (1954). The practice of psychotherapy: Essays on the psychology of the transference and other subjects. CW 16. Princeton, NJ. Princeton University Press.
- Jung, C.G. (1968). Analytical psychology: Its theory and practice, the Tavistock lectures. New York. Vintage Books.
- Jung, C.G. (1968). The Aion: Researches into the Phenomenology of the Self, in the Collected Works of C.G. Jung, Volume IX part II, Carrie Lee Rothgeb (Ed.), Princeton University Press,
- Jung, C.G. (1981). The Archetypes and The Collective Unconscious. Princeton University Press
- Karpman, S. (1968). Fairy tales and script drama analysis. Transactional Analysis Bulletin, 7(26), 39-43.
  Karpman, S. (1971). Options. Transactional Analysis Journal, 1(1), 79-87. * *
  Karpman, S. (1975). The Loser's Loop. Transactional Analysis Journal. 5(1), 74-75.
  Karpman, S. (1976). Feeling rackets: Notes from State of the Art Winter Congress, January 1976. Transactional Analysis Journal, 6(3), 339-346
  Karpman, S. (1979). Five trust contracts for couples. Bulletin of the Eric Berne Seminar. 1(3), 26-27.
- Kast, V. (1992). The dynamics of symbols: Fundamentals of Jungian psychotherapy. Schwarz, S. A. (Trans.). New York. Fromm International.
- Katie, B. (1988.) Loving what is. Rider Books.
- Korem, D. (1997). The Art of Profiling. International Focus Press.
- Kubler-Ross, E; Kessler, D. (2005). On Grief and Grieving. Simon and Schuster.
- Kelso, Scott J. A. (1999). Dynamic patterns: The self-organization of brain and behavior. Cambridge, MA. MIT Press.
- Erhardt, W. (1990). Landmark Education Cost/ Payoff exercise from The Landmark Forum. <www.landmarkeducation.com>
- Lewis, J; Sammons, J. (1999). Don't Divorce Your Children. Contemporary Books.
- Lewis, J; Sammons, J. (2000). Children and divorce. Contemporary Books.
- Lickerman. (2010). How to Forgive Others. Psychology Today.
- Luquet, W., & Hannah, M.T. (1996). The efficacy of short-term Imago therapy: Preliminary findings. The Journal of Imago Relationship Therapy, 1 (1), 67-75.
- Mainzer, K. (1994). Thinking in complexity: The complex dynamics of matter, mind, and mankind. Berlin. Springer-Verlag.
- Maltz, M. (1960). Pycho-Cybernetics. Pocket Books, Simon and Schuster.
- Manchester, K.L., Sites of Hormonal Regulation of Protein Metabolism. p. 229, Mammalian Protein [Munro, H.N., Ed.]. Academic Press, New York. On p273.
- Manfield, E. (3 January 2011) Secret Regrets about divorce. Huffington Post
- Markman, H.J., & Hahleweg, K. (1993). The Prediction and prevention of marital distress: An international perspective. Clinical Psychology Review 13 29-43.

- Maslow, A.H. (1968). Toward a psychology of being (2nd ed.). New York. Van Nostrand Reinhold.
- Maslow, A.H. (1971). The farther reaches of human nature. New York. Penguin.
- Mellody, P. (1989.) Facing Codependency. HarperOne.
- McCarthy, B, E. (2003). Rekindling desire. Brunner-Routledge.
- McMillen, A. (2006). When I loved myself enough. Sidgwick and Jackson.
- McKenna, P; Wilbourn, H. (2003). I can mend your broken heart. Bantam press.
- Mintel Consumer Research Reports(2000-2011). Divorces in England and Wales. Each year between 2000-2011. The British Library.
- Moore, T. (1994). Soul Mates. Harper Perennial.
- Mountain-Dreamer, O. (1999). The Invitation. Harper Collins Element.
- Muzik, B. (2007). Mind-Mastery-101. <www.designer-life.com/mindmastery101>
- Namka, Lynne. (2003). Goodbye Ouchies and Grouchies, Hello Happy Feelings. EFT for Kids of All Ages. Talk, Trust & Feel Therapeutics.
- Namka, Lynne. (2001). The Doormat Syndrome. Talk, Trust and Feel Therapeutics.
- Namka, Lynne. (2001). Violence in Families. www.AngriesOut.com.
- Namka, Lynne. (2001). The Right Man and Right Woman Theory. www.AngriesOut.com.
- Naschie, El M. S., Rossler, O. E. & Prigogine, I. (Eds.) (1995). Quantum mechanics, diffusion and chaotic fractals. Great Britain. BPC Wheatons (Pergamon).
- Neumann, E. (1995). The origins and history of consciousness. Bollingen Series XLII. Princeton, NJ. Princeton University Press. First published in 1954.
- Nicolis G. and Prigogine, I. (1989). Exploring complexity: An introduction. New York. W.H. Freeman.
- O'Connor, J; Lages, A. (2004). Coaching with NLP. Harper Collins Element.
- Office of National Statistics. (2000-2011). Divorces in England and Wales. Each year between 2000-2011. < http://www.statistics.gov.uk>
- Officer, C; Page, J. (1993). Tales of the Earth – Paroxysms and Perturbations of the Blue Planet. Oxford.
- Olfsen, Dr. M. (2010). Antidepressant Use Rising as Psychotherapy Rates Fall. Columbia University/ New York State Psychiatric Institute.
- Pang, S. (2011). Interview about helping children through divorce. <www.presentparenttraining.com>
- Parkin, J; Pollini, G. (2009). The way of F**k it. Hay house.
- Peck, Scott, M. (1979). Blame and Forgiveness: 009 [Audio Cassette]. Simon and Schuster.
- Peele, S. (1991). The Truth about addition and recovery. Fireside Simon and Schuster.
- Pert, Candace B. Ph.D. (1997). Molecules of Emotion. Simon & Schuster.
- Pinkola-Estes, C. (2001). Women who run with wolves. Ryder Books.
- Piroli, G. G.; Grillo, C. A.; Reznikov, L. R.; Adams, S.; McEwen, B. S.; Charron, M. J.; Reagan, L. P. (2007). Corticosterone Impairs Insulin-Stimulated Translocation of GLUT4 in the Rat Hippocampus. Neuroendocrinology 85 (2): 71. doi:10.1159/000101694. PMID 17426391.
- Posey WC, Nelson HS, Branch B, Pearlman DS (December 1978). The effects of acute corticosteroid therapy for asthma on serum immunoglobulin levels. J. Allergy Clin. Immunol. 62 (6): 340–8. doi:10.1016/0091-6749(78)90134-3. PMID 712020.
- Prigogine, Ilya. (1945). Etude Thermodynamics des Phenomenes Irreversibles (Study of the Thermodynamics of Irreversible Phenomenon). Presented to the science faculty at the Free University of Brussels (1945); Paris. Dunod, 1947.
- Prigogine, Ilya. (1955). Introduction to Thermodynamics of Irreversible Processes, (pg. 16). New York. Interscience Publishers.
- Prigogine, I. (1980). From being to becoming: Time and complexity in the physical sciences. San Francisco. W. H. Freeman.

- Prigogine, I. and Stengers, I. (1984). Order out of chaos: Man's new dialogue with nature. Toronto. Bantam.
- Prigogine, I. (1997). The end of certainty: Time, chaos, and the new laws of physics. NY. The Free Press.
- Rand, A. (1957). Atlas Shrugged. Penguin Modern Classics.
- Robertson, R. & Combs, A. (Eds.) (1995). Chaos theory in psychology and the life sciences. Mahwah, NJ. Lawrence Erlbaum.
- Robbins, A. (1996). The power of successful relationships audio CD.
- Robbins, A. (2000). A 7-day program to transform your life audio CD.
- Santos, R. (2009). Should you keep the house in a divorce? <http://articles.moneycentral.msn.com/College-AndFamily/SuddenlySingle/ShouldYouKeepTheHouseInADivorce.aspx?page=2>
- Scott Peck, M. (1987). The Different Drum. Simon and Schuster.
- Seligman, Martin. (1990). Learned Optimism. Pocket Books, 1990.
- Soffer, L.J.; Dorfman, R.I.; Gabrilove, J.L,. The Human Adrenal Gland. Febiger, Phil.
- Spurr, Dr. P. (2001). The Break-up Survival Kit. Robson Books.
- Surhone, L. (20). Target Fixation. Betascript Publishing.
- Talbot, N. (2007). Get over your break-up. Hodder Arnold.
- Tolle, E. (2005). The power of now. Hodger Mobius.
- Underwood, Y. (2010). MA, NCC, LPC. Citation: Setting Boundaries. Red Rock Counselling Services <http://www.redrockcounseling.com>.
- United States: Poll statistics conducted in 1999 in State of Minnesota - 66% of those currently divorced answered "yes" to the question "Do you wish you and your ex-spouse had tried harder to work through your differences?". In 2003 in the State of California, 83% of those currently divorced answered "yes" to the question "Do you wish you and your ex-spouse had tried harder to work through your differences?". In 2004 in State of New Jersey - 46% of those currently divorced answered "yes" to the question "Do you wish you and your ex-spouse had tried harder to work through your differences?"
- Ury, W. (2007). Getting past no. Random House.
- Utain, M & Oliver, B. (Eds.) (1998). Scream Louder. Through Hell and Healing with an Incest Survivor and her Therapist. Columbia University Press. http://www.abebooks.com.
- Vaughn, P. (1989). The Monogamy Myth. Newmarket Press.
- Wallerstein, JS. Corbin SB. (1989). The Child and the Vicissitudes of Divorce.
- Wallerstein, JS. (1989) Children After Divorce: Wounds That Don't Heal. The Psychiatric Times. Medicine and Behavior. 8: 8-11
- Wang, Yingxu. (2008). Novel Approaches in Cognitive Informatics and Natural Intelligence (section: Prigogine entropy, pg. 45). Idea Group Inc.
- Whitfield, Charles L. (1993) Boundaries and Relationships: Knowing, Protecting and Enjoying the Self. Health Communications; illustrated edition.
- Williams, L. (1991). Moving On. Pure Praise Publishing.
- Wolcott, I and Hughes, J Australian Institute of Family Studies (1999). Post-divorce regret versus satisfaction. WOMEN http://www.aifs.org.au/institute/pubs/WP20tables.html#table8 MEN http://www.aifs.org.au/institute/pubs/WP20tables.html#table9

About the author

Adèle Théron has spent twelve years working with individuals within some of the world's largest corporations as a change management specialist, helping people adapt to new situations and experiences created by mergers, acquisitions and large software implementations. The techniques and processes she created have helped companies and individuals adapt to change and have successfully aided thousands of individuals within 18 separate organizations.

Having separated from her husband in March 2009, Adèle researched to find that there was no structured process or program to heal from divorce and that many professional women and men wound up in years of counseling or experience long-term illness and depression as a result of divorce. Adèle was also astounded at the high second and third-marriage divorce rates worldwide and decided that healing from divorce was critical to successful relationships in the future.

She tried therapy and counseling but found the lack of structure and goal-oriented healing didn't work for her. She realized that as a process-expert, she was the one she was waiting for, so she consequently used her change management techniques to develop a revolutionary systemized process and program for healing from divorce within 21 days. She was her own case study and experienced a life-altering transformation resulting in a new life for herself but also a healed relationship with her ex-husband.

The process she used has since evolved into the ***naked divorce***, capable of dealing with the most dramatic of divorce situations.

Adèle has worked with professional men, women and couples as a mediator, *Divorce Angel* and trainer, helping them heal from break ups, separations and divorce. To ensure that people from all over the world can benefit from the program, she is constantly creating online and live seminar programs and products.

Today Adèle spends her time consulting with companies or coaching and supporting professional career people through divorce as a *Divorce Angel*.

She lives in London with her partner Simon.

Lightning Source UK Ltd.
Milton Keynes UK
UKOW050622200313

207894UK00001B/1/P

There really is beauty

in the breakdown…

There really is!

☺

Adèle

Contents

intro to the naked divorce

This book in a few paragraphs

The problem with divorce is not that a third of all first-time marriages fail, but the fact that there doesn't appear to be any learning happening, which as a consequence, leads to a higher second-time marriage divorce-rate of around 57% and an even higher third-time marriage divorce-rate of 73%. Unless the underlying critical factors are addressed, there is not much of a chance to stop the cycle of failed relationships into the future.

It was a Sunday in November that I sat down in a busy coffee shop in Los Angeles. Most of the people were bustling about, but there were some women who were sitting alone, quietly drinking their coffee. There was nothing momentous or strange about this Sunday except for the fact that I decided to slow my mind down enough to observe these women intensely. I observed their postures, their body language, their facial expressions and noticed the feelings I felt whilst looking at them. I was aware of feeling numb but after a few minutes, I was suddenly aware of feeling intense sadness and just when I felt this sadness, I watched one woman jump up, wipe her eyes and run off, busying herself with the next thing. I sat like this for some time, observing three woman who appeared to be drinking their coffee absorbed in a trance of sorts. They paused only long enough for their faces to droop as they became aware of what appeared to be a painful emotion, before they jumped up and had to dash off. It was the most bizarre experience, almost as if these women had touched a hot plate on a stove and instinctively pulled back. I decided to be bold and introduce myself to two of these women, thinking that if there was anywhere in the world where it might be considered 'normal' to approach strangers in a coffee shop, that it had to be Los Angeles! To my surprise, both of them were incredibly vulnerable and open. One woman even shared how much she wished that people would reach out more to those around them. She shared about the pain she experienced when her husband left her and another choked back tears as she relayed her fears of supporting her two children now that she was all on her own. When I asked them what made them jump up almost the moment they tuned into those feelings of despair, the answer was always the same, "*I cannot fall apart and I just don't have the time.*"

That Sunday in the coffee shop changed everything for me. It was in one of those conversations that I began to think about how much human beings don't want to experience their pain and how many misconceptions there are about how much time it takes to heal from a trauma. What I observed was that many people only prioritize healing when it becomes urgent. It's almost as if some kind of 'rock bottom' has to be reached where they finally become aware of the impact of not taking action. The problem is that the negative impact of being at rock bottom is often worse than the trauma itself.

Unfortunately there are many misconceptions about how to heal, the largest myth being that one should rely on time to heal the wound.

I often hear of counselors giving people advice similar to, "you just need some time." It is as if these well-meaning people are saying, "Just sit back and in time you'll no longer have the sadness, anguish, yearning, guilt, anger, and fear you're feeling now. Those emotions will fade away, and you'll be fine." The problem with believing that time heals the wound is that people wind up doing nothing and passively waiting for healing to 'happen to them'. They start believing that being happy is about finding the right person and rationalize to themselves that the only reason their marriage failed, was because they were with the wrong person. Healing then becomes about finding the right person because if you find him, you have filled the void and forgotten those *bad* times. What is not ever discussed is how the cycle of failure perpetuates when there is no discovery of the true source of the relationship breakdown, so moving forward in a way that is most beneficial for the long-term is not always achievable.

In my years in change management, I remember feeling irritated that no one seemed to have done the work to map out the process of healing such that others had a clear pathway to follow. I also began to notice how much our world is set up to *not* feel anything, intellectualize our emotions and be *emotionally intelligent*. Why was it that those women could not stand to think about the pain from their divorce? What made those women tolerate living with pain which they held at arm's length and then pushed away the moment they dipped their toes in it? Was their fear of surrendering to those emotions preventing the feeling of them? Do we, as a society assume that healing takes a long time, so we therefore cannot be bothered to prioritize it, thereby accepting numbness as a worthy price to pay? Has this resultant numbness and resignation just become the norm?

All of these questions and thoughts lead to the development of my theories about healing from divorce and to the development of the **naked divorce**. In short, I believe that taking time to heal, combined with doing nothing leads to numbness, emotional scars and a feeling of resignation. This quicksand of resignation is a silent killer as it tricks people into believing that they are fine when they are not, so they wind up wandering around *a little bit dead* and forget that healing was a priority.

So, now that I have depressed the heck out of you, there is good news. Healing does not need to be a long drawn-out horrendous nightmare. Healing can be a journey of self-discovery. It can also take a shorter period of time than you can even imagine. What I discovered in the early trials I ran was that healing is definitely not a passive process. Real healing requires an active engagement with the subject matter with focused intensity. Without some kind of focused intensity, human beings would not be interested in doing the work to heal as it's easier to take the road most travelled.

The **naked divorce** is not about waiting or wondering what to do. It's an intensive healing journey. It's about taking your healing into your hands and taking action. The program has been created in a way that virtually guarantees your healing, provided you do everything it says to do in the way it says to do it. That is a bold claim, but over the two and a half years of trials, I worked with so many people of different ages, backgrounds and divorce situations that I know the program works.

I fine-tuned, adjusted and tested all the components until I came up with the *Healing Formula*. I then distilled the process into 21 days after researching the maximum length of time human beings can remain focused on something before deciding that they have had enough.

So here is a summary of what this book is about in its five component parts:

- PART 1: The introduction and background to the 21-day program, covering the problems surrounding divorce and why healing is critical to your future happiness.
- PART 2: How the 21-day program works in the context of the *Healing Formula*.
- PART 3: Understanding the **7 Foundations of Transformation**
- PART 4: The **naked divorce** 21-day program itself
- PART 5: The future and what comes next including tips on helping your children handle the divorce as well as principles on keeping love alive.

After working with women who, until they discovered the **naked divorce**, were struggling to heal, move on and live their dream life, there isn't a problem area I haven't seen or a divorce story which shocks me. I am still moved to tears by the desire of the participants in the program to be happy, heal and feel good about their life.

What moved me the first time somebody sat down and cried in my presence and shared their struggles, still moves me today. The single mom who hadn't dated for three years because she still missed her ex who had moved on with another woman. The hard-working doctor who beat herself up relentlessly after her engagement ended. The mother of two children who was bitter and angry with her ex-husband because she financially supported him during their marriage and now has trust issues with men. The angry divorced woman whose husband cheated on her and felt brittle and prickly. The single mom who lost everything in her divorce and is struggling to put back the pieces of her life. The investment banker who lost touch with her femininity when she became a hardened, cold workaholic and now struggles to express herself. The actuary whose twenty-year marriage ended brutally with no explanation or reasoning. I could go on.